Poverty Report 1974

A report of
the Institute of
Community
Studies

TEMPLE SMITH
London

A review of policies and
problems in the last year

POVERTY REPORT 1974

Edited by
MICHAEL YOUNG

To the memory of
HUGH ANDERSON
undergraduate extraordinary

First published in Great Britain 1974
by Maurice Temple Smith Ltd
37 Great Russell Street, London WC1
© 1974 Institute of Community Studies
ISBN 0 8511 7054 4 cased/0 8511 7055 2 paperback
Printed in Great Britain by
Lowe & Brydone (Printers) Ltd,
Haverhill, Suffolk

Contents

1 Introduction

MICHAEL YOUNG

Around about the time of every Budget a number of government White Papers are published which between them present some of the crucial evidence about the principal concern of every government, which is, of course, the state of business. In the light of what official economists think has happened and is going to happen to industry and the balance of payments, the Chancellor, according to the traditional metaphor of the motor-car age, touches either the brake or the accelerator or, with some straining, both at the same time. But nothing is officially published at that period about a subject which seems to the contributors to this book of at least as much importance, the condition of the people who on grounds of sheer need have the foremost claim upon the public treasury. Since no such account is given by the government, the object of this Report is in a small way to fill the gap, and present before the Budget some of the facts which should be taken into account at that time by the Chancellor, by the Secretary of State for Social Services and by their colleagues when they decide how to allot the resources given to them by the taxpayer.

Whitehall follows the earth round the sun, even if with all the little and special budgets of recent fame the rhythm of the financial ritual is not quite so rigidly annual as it used to be in less hectic times. Our purpose being what it is, we must obviously relate our report to the events of a preceding year, and we have chosen the calendar year. This is indeed what the contributors try to do throughout, while of course bringing to witness as much from preceding years as is required to make this one year intelligible.

I must at the start point to a problem which in varying degrees affects every one of the chapters which follows. Pinpointing any events so soon after they have happened is hampered by one pervasive timelag — the lag in the publication of official statistics. While we are journeying through any year, facts and opinion about passing events are rushed

up to us every day as though nothing mattered more than
that every citizen anxiously scanning his newspaper or screen
should be continuously well-informed. Yet on many great
matters of state the date mark is wrongly stamped: information is not rushed, rather trundled up to the traveller, not
about 1973 at all but about 1972 or 1971 or even earlier.
The computers grind exceedingly slow. We shall not know for
some good time yet to come what the detailed composition
of the population of Great Britain was in 1971. It takes that
long for the Census results to appear, and, as later chapters
demonstrate, the story of the Census is to a lesser extent the
story of most of the great series of statistics which almost
alone can measure the order and disorder of the nation.

So how is one to proceed? What happened in 1973 will not
be known till 1975 or after. The historian therefore has all
the aces, except one. He will be better able to reach a more
detached judgement, better able to place 1973 against the
background of the period, better informed with the vital data
which by the time he writes will have been thrown into the
lap of history by the heaving machinery of government. The
only trouble is that his reflections, admirable though they
may be on all these counts, will be without the slightest value
to the policy makers of today. They have to make history
rather than write it, which means they have to act on the
basis of quite inadequate information about what has
happened in the fairly recent past. If that is their fate so is it,
to an even greater extent, that of anyone outside Whitehall
who wishes to take part in the continuous debate about what
the effect of government action has been and what its
policies should be. We have to make do in the present with
what little we can piece together about a past which insists
on refracting itself through the future. To be more precise,
the contributors to this Report have had to manage with what
little evidence they could gather during the year up to the
particular day when the various chapters were completed.

The crucial decision about timing was determined by the
date of publication of the statistics which were in this year
considered critically important. Even in a historian's grip
1973 will never be able to escape the tag of Incomes Policy.
The most vital official figures about earnings are collected in

April of each year; in 1973 they were published on the last day of October. Without that reference point it was not possible to fill out any judgement about the repercussions of Mr Heath's Incomes Policy on the low-paid workers who are naturally one of our chief interests. The first chapters were finished and went to press immediately afterwards in November.

An added impetus was given to the enterprise by the peculiarities of our chosen year. In social policy it has been the most eventful year of any since those just after the war when the foundations of the modern Welfare State were laid. This is partly because to its credit the government did not for a moment pretend there was no problem of poverty, or, as other governments of the same nominal political persuasion did in the 1950s, that the problem would be solved of itself by the natural growth of productivity and affluence. This has been an interventionist government with a far-reaching influence upon how the poor live. Sir Keith Joseph will not, so far at any rate, be remembered like Geddes for his Axe. If that were not reason enough to attempt as much of a balanced judgement as any group of observers filled with their own prejudices are capable of reaching, the inflation which called up the Incomes Policy from the ashes of Selsdon is another. Periods of rapidly rising prices nearly always deal roughly with the poor who cannot manoeuvre away from inflation in the way that richer people may be able to. Has it happened on this occasion? Many may disagree with the answers given in the body of this Report, but if they accept that the poor are as much citizens of the one country as the rich they cannot easily deny the importance of the question. The Queen was voicing a rather general opinion when she said in her Speech opening the new session of Parliament at the end of October 1973 that her government pledged itself 'to secure a prosperous, fair and orderly society . . . with particular regard to the requirements of the old, the sick and the needy'. But sadly the Budget of 18th December did nothing for them.

The subject matter
So much for the period to which the book refers. What about its subject? It is not enough to repeat what is anyway said in

the title, that the subject is poverty, or still more to spin off
the sort of definition contained in dictionaries — of poverty
as 'indigence; want, scarcity, deficiency' — nor of the poor as
'wanting means to procure comforts or necessaries of life'. To
do that does not, except in the most superficial way, pin the
word down, that can only be done by giving it a context, a
forest of other words to grow up in.

With poverty, one way to do this is by recalling some of its
recent history. The word is one of the many whose meanings
are being continuously changed, like coins, having their
milled edges worn away by use, at any rate in the one
context we are particularly interested in, that of social
policy. For a very long time poverty implied that there was
an absolute standard, meaning by absolute a standard which
remained pretty much the same over time. People, it was
thought, needed a certain bitter and constant minimum to
keep body and soul together and if they fell below it they
were in poverty. The word in one sense pointed to a
measurement. Also, more significantly, it suggested with
varying degrees of prescriptive power according to the
conscience of the person who was using the word, or having
it used against him, that anyone who was below the measured
line had some claim upon his fellow human beings to raise
him above it.

The word was (as it remains) both an arithmetical kind of
word and, as well, a belligerent, emotive one, with strong
political implications. The people above the line have seldom
been willing to surrender some of their excess to those below
without a struggle or without inflicting as their price some
humiliation upon those who according to this reasoning
qualified for help. The Victorian attitude to paupers still lives
on in the minds of people below as well as above the line, and
in a somewhat more humane age both givers and receivers are
therefore inclined to avoid the word with all its overtones.
The Supplementary Benefits Commission does not talk of
poverty, nor do the people whom it serves. 'To expect
residents of a given area to declare themselves "poor" is
"both misguided and misleading". It may be less stigmatising,
however, to admit to the status of "claimant", "disabled", or
"unsupported mother". Thus we have seen the emergence, in

recent years, of the Claimants' Union, the Disablement Income Group and Mothers in Action' (Bull 1971).

In so far as it is used — and many are not so reticent — the word has been changing its meaning in the course of the post-Victorian century. In the first stage of moving away from the concept the arithmetic was strengthened. As science began to share the stage with religion, the former in the shape of nutrition was brought to the aid of ethics by making the measurement much more precise. With the help of nutritionists, Seebohm Rowntree, in particular, was able to devise what looked like a scientific minimum level compounded in good part of calories and the other elements of a diet without which health would be impaired, and then proceeded in his first survey of York made in 1900 to discover how many families were below this science-sanctioned minimum. The prescriptive implication, that those below it should be given assistance, was in this way made a good deal stronger. The same basic idea, that there was a minimum standard which could be backed up by high authority, gathered power throughout the first half of the century, motivating dozens of comparative surveys of poverty, and also, more decisively, driving to the very heart of the Beveridge Report from which sprang the main structure which has survived until now in the social services. His central proposition was that no one for any reason whatsoever should be allowed to fall below the doubly sacred minimum.

It was not until well after Beveridge that the notion of the absolute standard began to be questioned, root and branch. It had only been nibbled at before then. Rowntree could see that what was thought a minimum standard of life, when it was broken down into its components of so much food, so much houseroom, so many matches, so many newspapers, was not the same in 1936 or 1950 as it had been in 1900. It is not just that the conventional views change about what basic needs are, but that the rich by getting richer in some ways make the poor poorer — it is more of a deprivation to be without a car when most other people have one and public transport becomes worse, or without a telephone when so many do have one and can corner attention and information for themselves by using it — so that the poor

need more to stop going faster and faster downhill. Rowntree, for such reasons, therefore edged up his minimum to
accommodate 'necessaries' which had not been considered
such when he started off on his pioneering path, but now had
to be. He was following public opinion, although without
following it to the new conclusion which Titmuss, Townsend
and Abel-Smith and other students of the subject drew with
such compelling argument as to change decisively the climate
of debate.

They recognised that, if one held to an absolute standard,
poverty would inevitably be reduced and finally abolished as
incomes rose; and also that this result would fly in the face of
commonsense. People in 1900 or 1936, 1960 or 1973 judge
who is poor not so much by the standards of the past as by
the standards of their own time. Poverty is, in other words,
not an absolute matter but a relative one, relative, that is, to
the prevailing standards of any particular period, which are
therefore changing from year to year. There can be a great
deal of argument about what is the proper cut-off point, but
not that whatever minimum standard is chosen it will have to
go up as the generality of incomes rises: that is what people
at all levels think the only sensible way of looking at the
issue. The widow of 1973 living on a few pounds a week will
be thought poor by contemporary standards because she has
so little compared with other people today. It makes no
difference to the estimation of her situation to be told that
she is richer than the majority of people in the country in
1873.

In the USA, where commonsense on this subject is no
different from what it is in Britain, there is some survey
evidence which makes the point. 'Public opinion surveys
show, for example, that when people are asked how much
money an American family needs to "get by", they typically
name a figure about half what the average American family
actually receives. This has been true for the last three
decades, despite the fact that real incomes (ie incomes
adjusted for inflation) have doubled in the interval.' (Jencks
quoting Rainwater, 1973). The best evidence to the same
effect for Britain is not from surveys but from the practice
on supplementary benefits and retirement pensions of

governments which are in this only responding to popular ideas of what is right. Table 1.1 shows, just to take two examples, the value of each type of benefit for a married couple as a proportion of mean average earnings for those full-time manual wage earners covered by the Department of Employment's annual October enquiry (Field 1971, updated). There have been ups and downs in both indices over the whole period since 1948; but what stands out more than fluctuations is the constancy.

Table 1.1 Value of supplementary benefit and retirement pension as percentages of earnings at different dates

	Retirement pension for married couple %	Supplementary benefit for married couple %
1948	30.5	29.0
1951	30.1	30.1
1954	26.4	28.9
1957	25.8	26.6
1960	27.5	29.2
1963	32.5	31.2
1966	32.0	32.8
1969	29.4	31.6
1970	28.9	30.3
1971	31.4	30.6
1972	30.4	29.7

The fact that supplementary benefit scale rates are raised in this way very roughly in step with average wages has one convenient consequence, if for no one else then for the researcher who wishes to compare the incidence of poverty in one year with that in another, and determines the numbers at each level by reference to the scales. If they were suddenly raised as a proportion of wages, that would bring joy to the poor and their wellwishers; but it would also as suddenly increase the numbers shown by this single criterion, as being

in poverty. The more generous the government, the worse
could seem its record. But the constancy, in proportional
terms, of the scale rates means that comparisons of this sort
can be made of the numbers in poverty between different
years, knowing that these numbers are not being boosted by
a rise in the scale or depressed by a fall.

In view of the fact that, on the arithmetic of it, the
absolute standard has given way to the relative, to a
permanently floating poverty line, there are two different
rules of measurement that can be employed. The one I have
just been describing – a line attached to wages – has the
great advantage when it comes to the other side of the word,
the implications for action, that one can sensibly strive for
the reduction or even abolition of poverty. There is no
necessary reason why *anyone* should be below the scale rates.
The other rule would be to regard the bottom 10% or bottom
20% of the distribution of incomes, or whatever one decided
was the proper cut-off point, as constituting those who were
in poverty. This would have a consequence some people
would find distinctly distressing, that the proportion of
people in poverty would always, by definition, remain the
same as long as there was any inequality at all, and no one
expects that totally to disappear. Who would want to force
acceptance of the antique notion that the poor will always be
with us, and what is more always in exactly the same
inexorable numbers, simply by the power of a definition?
And yet if one leans only on the former rule, running all the
while parallel with the level of wages, it could, as I have said,
mean at any rate in theory that poverty were abolished.
Relativism is now so securely established in people's minds
that even if everyone was above the line the people at the
bottom would still be thought of as poor.

There are some intellectual problems about all this which
need discussion, but not here. If the prologue is too long no
one will wait for the play. Let me only say, before leaving the
subject of the subject, that whichever of the two rules
students of the matter prefer, they are all sufficiently
relativist to see that what matters is not just numbers, nor
even the composition of the people at the bottom (however
defined), but also the multi-faceted relationship between

them and all the rest of the people in society. Poverty at the bottom may or not be more sharply felt if there is a large gap between the bottom and the top than it is if the gap is small. But at least the relationship, and over the whole distribution, not just between the extremes, is a matter of great importance, which is why almost any discussion of poverty, post-Beveridge, or at any rate post-Titmuss, is bound also to be a discussion of inequality. This is why there is so much about the latter in a book which is primarily about poverty.

It would be particularly difficult, even if one wanted, to avoid frequent reference to inequality when it comes to other forms of poverty besides that expressed in lack of income. Another sign of the times, as the debate moves well into the second half of the century, is that poverty has become more decisively plural — the concern is with multiple poverties, not just in income but in housing, in transport, in health, in education, in culture, and all of these across time, from one generation to another. These different forms of poverty are closely related to each other. The person with a very low income is also without a car, etc. etc. But the debate has run a little ahead of the facts, as it so often does, and for the moment not a great deal is known about the connections between the many different forms of poverty, or, to use the word which as I say is almost interchangeable in this wider context, with the many different dimensions of inequality. Some of the main dimensions other than the purely monetary are therefore discussed in Part 2 of the Report without being related in any systematic way to each other. So far each main topic is in purdah. Almost the only place where there is some pulling together, although on a miniature scale, is in Chapter 6 on the little survey tailor-made for the book.

Forward and back

Now that the subject has been described and date-tagged I can come to the main business of this opening chapter, which is to draw together some of the main findings. None of the individual authors can claim to be treating their different aspects of the main subject comprehensively, even within the limits imposed by the dearth of often vital information. Each has to select the facts, or, where the state of a debate as it was proceeding in 1973 is described rather than changes in practice (as Tony Lynes does in Chapter 5) the issues which he or she thinks of special importance. Likewise, I cannot do more, according to my own personal viewpoint, than to pick out the conclusions which seem to me to matter most.

To come to a balanced judgement, when so much needs to be weighed, is not easy. The only thing obvious is that it *is* a question of balance. One of the major objectives of the Incomes Policy was to secure 'an improvement in the relative position of the low paid'; but, as Chris Trinder says in Chapter 2, there is no evidence that low-paid earners did in fact come any nearer the high-paid in 1973. The proviso was that there did appear to be some slight improvement in relative terms for one great group of low-paid workers, women.

This is without taking account of taxation, family allowances or inflation. As each of these is taken into account the picture darkens. More and more poor people have with each year that passes had to pay income tax. The point in the scale of incomes at which people have to pay it — the tax threshold — has not risen in line with rising earnings, so that the Chancellor has each year received out of inflation a bonus for the government from the pockets of the lower paid. Tony Atkinson and Chris Trinder show in Chapter 3 that the tax threshold in April 1973 was only 49% of average earnings; it was 150% in 1938. Most low-paid workers therefore had to pay appreciably larger amounts in income tax, and this while a concession was made in 1973 to those with unearned incomes of £15,000 a year whereby £27 a week was not added on but taken off their taxes. The low paid with children have been the chief sufferers, at any rate where they have not benefited from family income supplement, because family allowances increased not at all in money terms during the year while their value was being every week eaten away. Rent rebates could have helped them substantially, but only, of course, if they knew what they could get and claimed it. Rising prices, especially of food, have hit the low paid harder than others. A special retail price index worked out by Atkinson and Trinder for the low-paid worker demonstrates that prices rose more for him than for others.

As for those not able to work and therefore dependent on public funds, the government certainly deserves credit for having increased national insurance benefits in line with average earnings. Sir Keith Joseph was speaking with the book when he said that these increases were the 'largest ever', even if the shades of the Poor Law are still there in the persisting discrimination against the unemployed after the first 28 weeks out of work. Where they were getting the long-term addition people on supplementary benefit did as well as pensioners and others. As with wage earners, rent rebates helped those receiving benefits but only of course if they claimed them. Tony Lynes in Chapter 5 acknowledges the considerable advance made by the institution of the attendance allowance for the disabled without conditions being attached about national insurance contributions or willingness to work.

Peter Willmott in his chapter on housing underlines more powerfully still one of the conclusions I have already mentioned, that rent rebates and allowances could be of benefit to the poor, especially those in the privately rented accommodation who have in housing terms been the worst off people in the country, but only, only if they are taken up. Some people paid less for their housing. Far fewer actually gained an improvement in its quality. The continued decline in the quantity of council and other building was one of the more depressing features of 1973.

For education the account given by Stella Duncan and her colleagues is very much less gloomy, so much so that if the palm for 1973 is awarded to any Departmental Minister then from the particular point of view of this Report it should go to Mrs Thatcher. It looks from the outside that there has been a rigid adherence to Party animus against comprehensive schools — hardly anything could do more for inner city districts than the creation of small (repeat small) intensively staffed comprehensives which would also be community schools. That apart, there is much to be thankful for. Nursery schools began to be injected into the educational establishment, and furthermore with an initial selective bias in favour of the more deprived districts where the needs are greatest.

Educational Priority Areas received somewhat more support
than in any other year since the Plowden Committee first
proposed it should be given. More was done to help
handicapped children. The school-leaving age has been raised
with less of a juvenile revolution to oppose it than many
expected.

The health service is a very different matter. Phyllis
Willmott draws attention to Hart's inverse care law which
could do as well for education and a good many other things
besides — 'that the availability of good medical care tends to
vary inversely with the needs of the population served'. The
inverse has probably been made even more so by the changes
made by the government when it was nearer Selsdon than it
was in 1973, in the form of the increased charges for
prescriptions, dentistry and welfare milk, all of which are still
bearing down on the poor. Between them these economies
saved one-third what the Chancellor lost by exempting three
of the most harmful and popular foods — sweets, ice cream
and crisps — from VAT. Mental hospitals have, on the other
hand, received a little more attention. The local welfare
services in the throes of their Seebohm reorganisation have so
far had to battle hard for even minimal resources to meet the
huge volume of continuing need. Mrs Willmott shows how
great the variation is in the standard of such local services
between one local authority and another. This kind of
geographical discrepancy, in his case between regions, is
taken up again in Chapter 10 by Vivian Woodward. He shows
that what many of the poorest people in the poorest regions
such as Scotland (if it can be called a region, not a country)
need is employment — more jobs for more men and women
alike.

In the final chapter Charles Elliott puts the problems of
poverty in Britain, grievous as they are, into international
perspective. Even the low-paid worker looks well-off by
comparison with his counterpart in the bottom 20% of
incomes in a country like India or Brazil. What makes matters
worse is that the poorer the country, the greater the
inequality. Britain's aid to the developing countries has done
nothing to lessen these internal disparities. It is high time that
it should. This would mean that aid should no longer be tied

to British manufactures but tied instead to a policy, of favouring the poor rather than the rich in the generally poor countries. Mr Elliott suggests that one of the best forms of aid we could give would be through trade, that is by allowing more imports of manufactured goods from the poor countries. This would mean allowing obviously uncompetitive industries — some textiles, leather goods, furniture — in Britain to be closed down, and concentrating on the retraining of their employees for other industries where productivity is higher. *Our* wealth and *their* wealth could both be increased by such a strategy.

Priorities for policy

This is a summary of the findings. What do they suggest for domestic policy? Once again I must stress that I can only express a personal view. While all would recognise that painful choices have to be made, some of the authors would have different priorities from the three I am putting forward. For me the most crying need of all is a greater measure of justice for women who are dependent to a greater or lesser extent upon social security. The Women's Liberationists, whether or not they would go so far as to call themselves that, have concentrated their energies on lowering or, occasionally, demolishing the barriers to equal opportunity for women in jobs and in the education that precedes these. That was where all the emphasis was in the consultative document on *Equal opportunities for men and women* published by the government in September 1973. The objective was to 'remove unfair discrimination against women in such important areas as employment and training'. Few would now deny that need. But what about removing unfair discrimination against women who cannot work? On that the consultative document was silent.

The fact is that Beveridge (perhaps too little influenced by his wife, formidable woman though she was) injected sex discrimination into the system of social security at its very roots. It was a contributory system, with whole ranges of entitlements depending upon the necessary numbers of contributions being made by people in employment. Housewives as such were not thought of as being in work, or, if they were, they were not paid by anyone except their husbands. The survey reported in Chapter 6, small as the scale was, suggested that the 'wages' paid by husbands to their wives have not been increasing as fast as more ordinary wages. That, if true, is bad enough. But still more humiliating is the plight of the woman who cannot claim any benefits as of right because, being employed only by her husband while confined to caring for children jointly produced, she is not thought of as belonging to the labour force upon whom Beveridge was focusing. Many such rights that she does have are derived through him, and if he leaves home her rights go with him. As Douglas Houghton said: 'The more one goes into the figures and gains actual experience, the more one realises the social *in*security of women – all sorts and conditions of women: married women; widows; single women; unmarried wives; unmarried mothers; deserted, separated and divorced wives; women at work; women at home . . . Every woman should have social security in her own right and be free of the qualifying conditions and hazards of being dependent upon her husband's contributions' (Houghton 1968).

This being the background, it was perhaps hardly surprising, at any rate with hindsight, that the chief conclusion from the Bethnal Green survey should be that women were more the sufferers than men. Of the households in poverty two-thirds were headed by women, and with the women were all the children who suffered likewise. As well as the mothers living on their own with dependent children whose needs are paramount, are all the older women who are alone, having outlived their husbands. As Tony Lynes points out, at the end of 1971, 'of 1,537,000 single pensioners on supplementary benefit 1,330,000 were women', and the proportions are probably not very different now. The occupational pension schemes which the government so much favours will not help them much and the Social Security Act of 1973 continues in the time-honoured way to discriminate against women.

This is a large subject in itself, and a large range of measures will be needed before the discrimination against *non-working* women is removed. The most obvious immediate necessity of all is that family allowances, the main benefit that women and children can get as of right, should be increased at least to the same proportion of average earnings that they were in 1968, and preferably higher. But that should only be a beginning. As the Mothers' Union stressed in its report published in mid-November, on the same day as the Royal Wedding and the State of Emergency, one-parent families need much more protection from society because they have less protection from within the home. A separated, deserted or divorced wife with young children should be able to get the equivalent of widows' benefits. It is also certainly not too late to restructure pensions beyond the minimum so that women get a fairer deal than they have. One bargaining counter that could be thrown in is a change in the indefensible anomaly in the Beveridge system which allows women to draw a pension at the age of 60 and men at 65. This is sex discrimination against men, who do not ordinarily live nearly as long as women anyway, and one which costs the Exchequer well over £100 million a year.

The next set of recommendations is of a lesser order altogether, but with the merit that for this reason the changes will be easier to carry through. Atkinson and Trinder mention several times the 'hidden constants' in social security. One, to stretch the term a bit, is to do with the frequency with which reviews of benefits are conducted. The rhythm is the same annual one which governs the formal Budget. The rates are now raised only in the autumn. The interval is too great. With prices rising as fast as they have been, the real value of the pension was reduced between the autumn of 1971 and 1972 by no less than 46p, and by as much in 1973 − a very large fall-away for a person for whom every penny counts. Now that a threshold clause has been accepted as part of the policy for earnings in Phase III of the Incomes Policy similar action should be taken for social security benefits. Atkinson and Trinder propose an escalator clause which would ensure that if, for example, the pensioner price index rose by more than 2% since the last review there would be an automatic increase in all benefits, just as (at a different level) should now happen with wages. The most indefensible constants of all are probably the various earnings rules which

actually have the opposite effect, being harassment of people
out of work, as other rules harass other people into working.
This seems all the more ridiculous now that in some areas
there are serious labour shortages. Why force anyone *not* to
work? Why force people to remain solely dependent on the
state when this is not what they want to be? First for the
chop should be the retirement condition for pensions. The
permitted earnings have stayed the same since 1971. Its
abolition would cost £135 million (PQ, 22 October 1973)
but at least £40 million of this would return to the
Exchequer in extra taxes. To restore the 'disregards' for SB
to the relationship with wages they used to have, along with
the change recommended by Lynes for the invalidity benefit
earnings rule, would between them only cost a few millions,
and should surely be done.

The third subject is the by now hoary one of take-up:
many people have not got and are not getting the benefits to
which they are entitled. There is a little further evidence
about this in Chapter 6. The scheme for rent rebates and
allowances is a most important new addition to the array of
the Welfare State. Author after author points out what a
difference it could make to many poor families if they did
claim their allowances or rebates. Yet in Bethnal Green at
any rate only about half the eligible families did so in 1973.
The other half left untouched the money they could have
had. The national record for family income supplement is no
better.

The matter cannot and must not be left. The will is there
to spread the benefits – and not just Common Market
butter – less thinly; the administrative and other means must
be found of raising the take-up levels a great deal higher. One
large problem is the terrifying complexity of the system, or
rather lack of it. There were in 1972 as many as 14 separate
means-tested schemes administered by the central government and 32 administered by local authorities (PQ, House of
Lords, 22 February 1972), ranging from supplementary
benefits and free welfare foods to family income supplement
and legal aid; from rate rebates and free school meals to
higher education awards and home helps. Even the experts
are baffled by it all; what hope has the ordinary woman or

man of finding the way? It is a labyrinth that dozens of well-intentioned and humane Ministers and Departments and countless thousands of national and local government civil servants, nearly all closeted in their own watertight departments, have devised for the collective confusion of the public.

To get one Department of State working with another is always a task for Sisyphus, and still more so to get the local officers of the central government working together with the local authorities. But that is just what is so desperately needed, in order that the poor person, multiplied as he is by millions, should no longer have to have his income enquired into by A, B, C, D, E etc. etc. down a long line of authorities with slightly or sometimes very different rules about the income limits that determine eligibility. What has been done with family income supplement (FIS), disappointing as the general take-up has been, is to the right pattern. With FIS goes a kind of 'passport' which entitles the family to a variety of benefits. Free prescriptions and school meals, welfare milk and help with dental and optical charges — a range of benefits crossing the usual departmental boundaries — are available to FIS recipients without the bottomless box of forms having to be opened again on each occasion to produce yet another for the applicant to fill out. If this model cannot be emulated, and with a much wider coverage, giving a cachet to a more general passport, there are no longer even any counterparts to Paul Chambers or Michael Sadler in the administrative service of the country, and this it is barely possible to believe. No one would want to wait for tax credits before attempting to reduce the complexity.

Another kind of reform should be a little easier to bring off in particular spheres and perhaps even more urgent. The administrative authorities should stretch themselves to do the work for the citizen. An exmaple is given in Chapter 6. The Bethnal Green survey showed that some people would be better off if they had not applied for supplementary benefit but had instead gone to the Town Hall for rent and rate rebates. The Supplementary Benefits Commission is, of course, aware of the issue and it is only a question of developing by dint of relentless innovation the administrative

drill by which people who could be better off with the Town
Hall in fact become better off, without in passage from one
to the other raising a bedlam of anxieties for the individual at
the receiving end of this myriad Welfare State. Our suggestion
is that the Commission should refer all people getting less
than £1.50 to the Town Hall for decision about whether they
would be advantaged or not were the responsibility to be
transferred from the one to the other. There may be better
ideas than this. We do not from the outside know. All we are
convinced about is that this is the kind of administrative
simplification which needs to be mightily striven for. In
saying this we do not for a moment rule out the more obvious
steps that could be taken like door-to-door canvassing,
mobile citizens' advice bureaux, writing individually to every
known ratepayer. I will end the introduction with an etc. But
before giving way to the other authors I would like to
acknowledge the grant received from the Leverhulme Trustees
to cover the cost of the survey in Bethnal Green reported in
Chapter 6.

References

D. Bull, (1971) *Family poverty*, Duckworth in association with the
Child Poverty Action Group.
F. Field, (1971) 'Poverty — facts and figures', in *Poverty* no. 20 Winter
1971, Child Poverty Action Group (Series updated for 1971 and
1972; 1973 figures for wages not available).
D. Houghton, (1968) *Paying for social security*, Institute of Economic
Affairs.
C. Jencks (et al.), (1973) *Inequality*, Allen Lane.
Mothers' Union, (1973) *Families without fathers*.

1 Income Poverty

*Hardly a day, certainly not a week, has gone
by during the year without some mention of
Mr Heath's Incomes Policy. Its phases have been
like the phases of some new moon in our sky
which circles Britain three times a year.
Almost everyone has been influenced for good
or ill by this particular moon. How have the
low paid managed? This is the question with
which Mr Trinder opens the body of the book.*

2   Incomes Policy and the Low Paid
CHRIS TRINDER

This chapter is the first of two on people with low incomes
and in full-time employment. That low pay is one of the
causes of poverty has been well documented by official and
unofficial sources (National Board for Prices and Incomes
1971, Field 1973). But it is especially fitting that it should be
the first subject of this Report because of the government's
Incomes Policy. Governments usually attempt to influence
post-tax income by taking away money in taxes and giving
benefits in addition to earnings: in 1972—3, however, the one
in power attempted to influence on a large scale the
distribution of *pre-tax* earnings. This distributional aim may
have been incidental, as it was with previous incomes policies.
The main objective was to check prices. But whatever the
reason, this development means that the Report should begin
with the effects of the Incomes Policy on the low paid.

   The first of a chain of White Papers on Incomes Policy put
redistribution as one of its three central objectives. These
were stated to be: 'faster growth of national output and real
income, an improvement in the relative position of the low
paid, and moderation in the rate of cost and price inflation'
(*A programme for controlling inflation: [the first stage]*

1972).

While recognising that the first and third of the above objectives are undoubtedly important and may bear on what happens to the low paid, it is still natural in this particular Report to look specifically, on the evidence available up to the end of October 1973, at the second objective and the extent to which the effects so far have lived up to the declaration of intent. The Stage II Pay Code was consistent with that declaration. The pay limit formula (£1 plus 4%) was designed so as to favour low-paid industries. If an industry had, for example, average wage rates of £22 a week it was permitted a maximum increase on these rates of an average of 8.5%, whereas if the industry had average wage rates of £33 a week it was permitted average increases of only 7%. Also there was scope for redistribution within bargaining groups. The pay limit formula did not say how the total had to be divided up (except that no one person could get more than £250 a year). And terms of employment could be improved outside the pay limit. Incomes Data Services claimed in January 1973 that 'moving towards equal pay, the three-week annual holiday and the 40-hour week may be of some real benefit for some lower paid workers' (Incomes Data Services 1973a). Help for the low paid was therefore the intention: was it fulfilled?

Background
Before presenting the analysis it should be said how the Policy evolved. The Conservatives when elected stated that they did not believe that an Incomes Policy was any solution for the problems of inflation or low pay. Like other leaders of other governments in the past, they soon changed their minds. By the summer of 1972 they had opened tripartite talks with representatives of the Confederation of British Industry and the Trades Union Congress and throughout the next few months were involved in a long series of consultations in an attempt to hammer out a voluntary incomes policy. On 6 November 1972, with voluntary agreement still eluding them, they introduced the first stage of the statutory Incomes Policy (henceforth called the Standstill) which came into operation with immediate effect. The Standstill

proposals (contained in the Counter-Inflation Temporary Provisions Act 1972) empowered the government to apply a Standstill on most prices, pay, dividends and rents for a period up until the end of January 1973, with provision for an extension for a further 60 days. Pay was defined to include basic, overtime, and piece rates, and the Standstill was applied to everything except promotional increments. Improvements in the terms of employment, such as the shortening of hours or lengthening of paid holidays, were prohibited. And companies were forbidden to declare dividends in excess of the previous year.

The Standstill on pay ended on 31 March 1973, except for postponed settlements for which an earlier date was permitted, but in either case the regulations of the second stage of the Incomes Policy (henceforth called the Stage II Pay Code) came immediately into effect. They remained in force until the autumn of 1973 when replaced by the third stage (which came fully into operation after this chapter had gone to press). The Stage II Pay Code included a pay limit formula which defined pay in the same way as did the Standstill, but which placed a limit on settlements so that the maximum permitted for any bargaining unit was £1 per week per person plus 4% of the group's total wage bill in the previous year, excluding overtime. In addition, no individual's pay rise was to exceed £250 a year. Outside the pay limit formula, however, negotiating was allowed to achieve the following conditions: a reduction in the number of hours in the standard working week to 40, net of meal breaks; an increase in paid holidays up to three weeks, in addition to six days of public holiday and normal days of rest; a reduction in the differential between men's and women's rates by up to one-third of any which existed at 31 December 1972 and which is required by the Equal Pay Act to be eliminated by 1975; an increase in the value of tax-approved occupational pension schemes; and the payment of increments given annually prior to 1972 or arising from promotion (*The counter-inflation programme: the operation of Stage II 1973*).

A Pay Board was set up to implement the Stage II Pay Code and at the time of writing had issued its first general report (Pay Board 1973). The Pay Board distinguished different types of settlement and explained that major settlements (those affecting 1,000 or more employees) had to be reported to the Pay Board and were not allowed to be implemented until the Pay Board gave its approval; that other settlements (affecting 100 to 999 employees) also had to be reported but were allowed to be implemented without prior approval; and that employers of 10 to 99 employees were required to keep records to be produced on request. The settlements dealt with in the report, however, covered only a small proportion of the labour force (4 million out of 22 million workers). This was because the report referred to only the first two months of operations. More frequent general reports would have been desirable since the evidence for later dates from other sources, for example that reported by Incomes Data Services for July, was no substitute for a full account from the Pay Board itself.

Operation of the Pay Board
(up to 31 May 1973)

Major settlements	Number of settlements	Number of employees affected (000s)
National agreements	54	889.9
Wage Board or Council Order	9	261.5
All others	258	2,407.8
Other settlements	1,383	438.7

NOTE   The figures refer to settlements dealt with.
Of the settlements received, 199 major settlements and 971 other settlements were still outstanding.

In addition to the Stage II Pay Code, regulations were imposed to restrain prices, rents, dividends and profits. Prices and rents are discussed in the next chapter. And on the regulations for dividends and profits it is far from easy to say anything firm. The regulations stated that no company was allowed to raise the amount distributed in any account year by more than 5%. But undistributed profits are still assets to a company, and can therefore add to capital gains. As part of the debate about corporation tax, Meacher noted the complexity of the relationship between profits, dividends and capital gains (Meacher 1971), and there is little hope of disentangling it for 1973 until 1973 is well past. One cannot do much, to start with, without knowing about total profits. The nominal profit regulations were that net profits from sales in the home market were, in general, not allowed to exceed the average level of the best two of the five previous years, with price reductions usually being required when the limit was exceeded. However, when announcing the proposals for Stage III, the Prime Minister officially recognised that in practice companies had been finding ways of evading the profit regulations (for example, the splitting up of a company into two or more separate companies and the attributing of some of the profits to each). In view of these and other complications I shall focus here on incomes from employment.

One further point should be stressed to prevent doubt. The Incomes Policy applied to *all* employment incomes. In other words, it applied to all types of job irrespective of whether incomes were determined by national or plant level collective bargaining, statutory wage-fixing bodies, or without collective agreement; it applied to all levels of wage and salary earners; and it applied to those working full or part-time. I will try to make it clear when I am referring solely to men manual workers, when to all men wage *and* salary earners, and when to women.

Weekly wage rates

Any assessment involves several indicators (wage rates, earnings, and terms of employment) and must examine individual settlements as well as overall evidence. In this section I discuss weekly wage rates negotiated in individual settlements. This requires a definition of 'low paid', that is, specifying how many workers are in that state and who they are. The government has never said what it thinks constitutes 'low pay' and unfortunately has no motive for being precise.

I have therefore to define the term myself. Low pay I define
as weekly earnings below two-thirds of the median earnings
for all adult men working full-time; by 'all' I mean all levels
of salary earner as well as wage earner. Median earnings (for
men) were around £33 a week in 1972; men were therefore
low-paid if they worked full-time and yet still earned less
than £22 a week. In 1972 my definition had the convenient
property of almost coinciding with the earnings of the lowest
decile (the bottom 10%). For example, in April 1972 my
definition would have given a figure of £22 a week in round
terms; the lowest decile gave £21.90. However, unlike the
lowest decile measure, which was the criterion adopted by
the Prices and Incomes Board in their 1971 *Report on Low
Pay*, my definition does not *necessarily* involve 10% of the
labour force (men) being always low-paid merely because of
the definition adopted. My definition of 'low' is not as
arbitrary as it might seem. The Prices and Incomes Board
apart, there is some support for a decision to count as 'low'
anything below two-thirds of the median earnings. According
to Behrend's survey evidence, for example, people in general
often adopt a similar view to this (Behrend 1972).

Because I cannot consider all the settlements made, what I
have done is to pick out eight for illustration. From Table 2.1
one can see the size of the absolute and percentage increases
in men's weekly wage rates in each of them. These increases
do in some cases allow for other improvements in conditions
of employment which had to be included in the costing.
Ford's increase, for example, had to take account of the
equivalent value in terms of earnings of two days extra
holiday. Making these adjustments does not however change
the general conclusions which are all that is drawn from the
evidence anyway.

From the evidence in Table 2.1 it can be seen that the
low-paid men (wage rates less than £22 a week before the
settlement) received larger percentage increases in weekly
wage rates than did the better-paid men workers. However, in
absolute terms the low paid still fared worst, and in particular
the lowest-paid workers in the lowest-paid industries fared
worst of all. For example, the settlement for laundry workers
increased the men's £13 weekly rates by only £1.20. The

Table 2.1 Men's weekly wage rates in 1973

Settlement	Number of employees covered (000's)	Wage rate before increase £	Absolute amount of increase £	Percentage increase %
Civil Service[1] (1.4.73)	210	19.38 22.56 48.00 86.00	1.90 2.15 2.92 3.69	9.8 9.5 6.1 4.3
Hairdressing[2] (1.1.73)	140	13.30	1.65	12.4
Laundering[3] (20.11.72)	104.5	13.00	1.20[5]	9.2
Ford[2] (1.4.73)	52	35.00	2.20[5]	6.3
Vauxhall (9.4.73)	27	37.60	2.40[5]	6.4
Retail				
Bespoke Tailoring[3,4] (6.8.73)	12	15.32	1.61	10.5
Corn trade (2.4.73)	11	18.00	1.72	9.6
Baking[4] (1.4.73)	6	17.80	1.60	9.0

NOTES
1. Non-industrial grades 2. Hourly-paid employees
3. Wages Council 4. England and Wales only
5. All grades received this cash amount
6. The first line refers to a 20-year-old clerical officer whose pay is age-related; the second to a machine operator 21 years or older; the third to an executive officer; and the fourth to a principal

effect of this was to increase the absolute differential between the minimum pay rates in the higher and lower-paid industries. Ford and Vauxhall workers, for example, had men's weekly wage rates increased by £2.20 and £2.40 respectively (whatever the grade of employee), whereas the Wage Council settlements for Laundry workers and Hairdressers increased rates by substantially less than £2. This was also the pattern for the settlements of the other lower-paid industries featured in Table 2.1. Moreover, in addition to the above, of 28 Wage Council settlements (on which many of the low-paid occupations depend) only 6 raised men's minimum weekly rates by more than £2 a week. The evidence in Table 2.1 in this respect thus seems to be indicative of a general trend (Incomes Data Services 1973e).

The 'overall effects' (just discussed) are the product of two factors: the extent to which redistribution occurred 'between' and 'within' groups. Redistribution 'between' bargaining units affects the relative size of the total wage bill available for distribution in the higher and lower-paid industries. It was noted earlier that the pay limit formula (£1 plus 4%) did potentially redistribute income in favour of low-paid industries. It should be noted here, however, that despite this, a 12.4% increase for hairdressers on a wage rate of £13.30 a week meant only a £1.65 increase in pay in absolute terms, whereas a 6.4% increase for Vauxhall workers on wage rates of £37.60 a week meant a £2.40 increase in pay in absolute terms. Therefore the low-paid industry would of course still have substantially less to distribute in absolute terms. Redistribution 'within' bargaining groups affects the relative size of the increase going to higher and lower-paid workers within any one negotiating unit. The distinction between absolute and percentage increases is again important here. Frank Figgures, Chairman of the Pay Board, cited the Civil Service settlement as a 'notable' example of redistribution 'within a bargaining group' in favour of the low paid (for some of the details of the settlement see row 1 of Table 2.1). To the extent that the low-paid Civil Servants got more than £1 plus 4%, Figgures was correct. However, a 20-year-old employee whose salary was age-related on £19.38 a week still received an increase

of under £2 a week. Finally, in order to say whether the low
paid have benefited (if one considers that they have) as a
result of the Incomes Policy, one would need also to say
what would have happened, hypothetically, if free collective
bargaining had prevailed, and this is a task which I do not
attempt. Nevertheless, the extent to which one considers the
actual settlements have favoured the low paid still depends
crucially on one's viewpoint. In percentage terms the low paid
have fared relatively better at the level of weekly wage rates,
but in absolute terms they have still often fared worst.

Outside the pay limit
In this section I examine the changes in the terms of
employment which were permissible outside the pay limit. I
will again concentrate on the low paid. As noted earlier,
permission to reduce hours to 40, improve holidays up to
three weeks, and move towards equal pay, all being outside
the pay limit, were expected to have improved considerably
the relative position of the low paid. Low-paid occupations
ordinarily have longer hours, above the 40-hour standard
working week, and less than fifteen days paid holidays, and
women also figure disproportionately in them. The Pay
Board report shows, however, that in fact (except for equal
pay) surprisingly few settlements took advantage of these
opportunities. Incomes Data Services stated in July that 'the

Outside the pay limit	*Number of settlements*
Reduction in hours	8
Improvements in holidays	29
Occupational pensions or death benefit schemes	12
Movements towards equal pay	220

Source: Pay Board 1973

figures given for settlements including improvements outside
the pay limit came as rather a surprise. Apart from the moves
towards equal pay, few of the Code's provisions were used in

settlements up to 1.6.73' (Incomes Data Services 1973b).
Therefore, although the Pay Board did not publish the figures
for the potential number of settlements that could have
taken advantage of the opportunities outside the pay limit, it
does seem likely that there were many low-paid workers who
although eligible for benefits did not get them. I have picked
out five settlements as illustrations (see Table 2.2) and I
explain in the text the extent to which this evidence is
exceptional or typical.

Table 2.2 Improvements outside the pay limit 1973

Settlement	Equal pay	Hours reduced	Holidays increased	Pensions and other improvements
Ford	already existed	already at 40	not eligible	yes
Vauxhall	already existed	already at 40	not eligible	yes
Corn trade	yes	already at 40	yes	no
Laundering	yes	already at 40	not eligible	no
Hairdressing	no	no	no	no

On holidays an Incomes Data Services Study in May 1973
concluded 'there are still 9 industries where the entitlement is
less than three weeks for workers with maximum service and
all are covered by Wages Councils' (Incomes Data Services
1973c). They all had only ten days and covered one-and-a-
half million employees. The Hairdressers' settlement, for
example, left the annual holiday entitlement at only ten days
for all employees. It is not, however, only in industries in
which *all* employees receive less than three weeks annual
holiday entitlement that improvement could have been made.
In the Corn trade settlement the five-year service quali-
fication for entitlement to three weeks was abolished. Yet

many other settlements which could have made similar changes during 1973 did not in fact do so. The Bakery settlement, for example, left the holiday entitlement at two weeks for those with less than two years service. As for the reduction of weekly hours: the Pay Board reported only eight settlements during the first two months of Stage II. The settlement for provincial Hairdressers, for example, had no reduction in their 42-hour week, and the Agricultural workers' reduction in hours from 42 to 40 did not come into effect until January 1974.

But as a rule settlements did take advantage of the permission to move towards equal pay. In the Corn trade, for example, women's rates were increased from £14.20 to £17.09, whereas the corresponding ones for men were only raised from £18 to £19.73. These higher increases for women brought their rates up from 75% to 83.3% of the equivalent male rates. However, this example highlights the obvious point that the extent to which a move towards equal pay reduces the numbers of low paid (defined in the way I have) depends on the level of the corresponding male rates. Both here and in the Laundry industry even the full implementation of equal pay would do little to reduce the numbers earning less than two-thirds of men's median earnings (Incomes Data Services 1973d). Moreover, some of the rises were not exactly generous. Ladies' hairdressers had minimum rates raised by only £1.15 from £10.25 to £11.40 (even a £1 plus 4% increase would have been £1.40).

One point not mentioned so far is the extent to which those workers who got the benefits were not low paid. This is especially important for pension schemes since it remained true at the end of the year as at the beginning that few low-paid industries had occupational pension schemes of any kind. For any industry which did, the general rule was that employee pension contributions could not be reduced, and that benefits could only be increased for the same level of contributions if the employer made up the difference. Ford's for example did this, thus increasing the value of the pension by 12½p a week for each year of past and future pensionable service. These future cash payments of course still had a present discounted value (there is less need to save for retirement out of current earnings). However, an important exception to the general rule was the gas workers. Here a company revalued its pension scheme and found that it contained a surplus. This allowed them to make use of paragraph 109 (i) of the Price and Pay Code where it states that employee contributions cannot be reduced 'unless the revaluation of the scheme shows a surplus' (*The price and pay code* 1973). Therefore, some gas workers had their contributions reduced (with pension benefits remaining the same) and this added 45—50p a week directly to their gross pay during 1973. There were also other improvements in the terms of employment during 1973. Ford workers, for example, received increases in lay-off and redundancy pay, and Vauxhall workers received three days 'bereavement leave' for the first time (Ford's had had this since 1969). Incremental pay rises went on as before, along with pro-motion, and these were certainly prejudiced against the relative position of low-paid industries. The general con-clusion of this section is therefore that improvements outside the pay limit did not (apart from those for women) make much of a change for the low paid.

What has happened to earnings?
This final section differs from the previous two in two respects. It is concerned not with negotiating groups but with the overall distribution. It is, secondly, concerned with the level of *earnings* rather than wage rates. The one may not vary with the other. This is due to differences, for example, in the availability of overtime, in incremental pay rises and promotion, and in movements between jobs. Earnings drift, therefore, during a period of wage restraint, may upset any attempt to benefit the low paid. The chief source of evidence is the New Earnings Survey for which information is collected each April, with publication of the results in late autumn. No attempt has been made here to separate out that part of the increase in earnings which occurred between April and November 1972 from that part occurring between November 1972 and April 1973. Similarly, no attempt has been made to project the increase in earnings which occurred up to the end of the second stage of the Incomes Policy

(October 1973). Any attempt to divide up 'wage drift' separately for each stage of the Incomes Policy would be a complex business (Office of Manpower Economics 1973). The conclusions of this section are therefore based on a snapshot picture taken in April 1973 and compared with similar ones taken in the April of preceding years. Evidence for April 1973 is only useful for a preliminary look at the effects of the Incomes Policy, since the second stage had scarcely begun.

It may be helpful to begin by outlining the main features of the pre-1973 surveys, concerning in particular the wage explosion of 1970 and after (see Table 2.3) (Department of Employment, 1971, 1972, 1973). The impact of the wage explosion of 1970 on the low paid has been widely disputed. The TUC in its 1971 Economic Review challenged the then prevailing view that the rapid wage inflation in 1970 had widened the gap between higher and lower-paid men manual workers. The 1972 Review argued that the TUC view was confirmed by the 1971 New Earnings Survey which showed that earnings of the lowest decile of full-time adult men manual workers (whose pay was not affected by absence) had increased as a percentage of the median from 67.3 in April 1970 to 68.2 in April 1971. It may be true that the high level of unemployment in 1971 removed many of the lowest paid from the sample and that therefore any improvement was illusory. But even if the TUC were correct for 1970–1, this slight improvement in the relative position of the lowest decile was offset by changes in 1972. By April 1972 the lowest decile had gained verv little: the group was back to 67.6% of the median in April 1972 compared to 67.3% in April 1970. The deterioration continued. By April 1973 the relative position of the lowest decile had declined to exactly what it had been in April 1970. This was for adult men manual workers, but from column 1 of Table 2.3 it can be seen that also in terms of the lowest decile of all adult men working full-time (whose pay was not affected by absence), the position in April 1973 was almost identical with that of April 1970. The picture for all men is just as bleak when looked at in terms of my definition of low pay. In April 1972, median earnings for men were around £33 a week; thus

*Table 2.3 Weekly earnings 1970, 1971, 1972, 1973 of
adults[1] in full-time employment in Great Britain
whose pay was not affected by absence*

		ALL		MANUAL ONLY		NON-MANUAL ONLY	
		Men %	Women %	Men %	Women %	Men %	Women %
Weekly earnings[2]							
Lowest	1973	65.6[3]	67.4[3]	67.3[3]	69.2[3]	61.6[3]	65.6[4]
decile as	1972	65.5	65.6	67.6	68.9	61.7	64.0
% of the	1971	66.1	66.6	68.2	70.2	61.7	65.0
median	1970	65.4	66.4	67.3	69.0	61.8	64.2

		ALL	
		Men	Women
Numbers[3]	1973	1.1	3.4
low paid	1972	1.1	3.4
(millions)			
Numbers[4]	1973	1.5	
affluent	1972	1.5	
(millions)			

NOTES 1. Defined as over 21 for men and over 18 for women.
2. Includes overtime pay.
3. Defined as two-thirds of men's weekly median earnings.
   £'s (round terms)—see text—
       1972 median earnings £33 a week; low paid £22
       1973 median earnings £38 a week; low paid £25
4. Defined as ·one-and-a-half times men's weekly median
   earnings. £'s (round terms) 1972 = £50; 1973 = £57.

Source: Department of Employment 1970, 1971, 1972, 1973.

the low paid earned less than £22 a week. In fact 1.1 million
men were then low paid. In April 1973 median earnings had
risen to £38 a week; thus the low paid earned less than £25 a
week. And in fact 1.1 million men were still low-paid.

On both cut-off points for low pay a low-paid man worker
received only a marginally greater percentage increase in
earnings over the period 1970—3 than that gained by workers
higher up the scale, and there were no signs (in April 1973)

of this substantially changing. Between April 1972 and April 1973 the increase for the low-paid men from £22 to £25 was 15.5%; the increase in men's median earnings from £33 to £38 was 14%; and the increase for those men earning one and a half times median earnings from £50 to £57 was 13%. Even the percentage gains in wage rates made by the low-paid worker at the level of individual settlements appear to have been substantially eroded by 'earnings drift'.

Turning to women workers one sees from Table 2.3 that the position of the lowest decile of all women workers did improve over the year. This is as would be expected from the large number of settlements which moved towards equal pay outside the pay limit. (Table 2.2 shows that equal pay was more likely to be already in operation in the higher-paid industries). However, if we look at the extent to which these gains benefited women in manual or non-manual jobs, it can be seen that the former hardly improved their position at all during the year. Nevertheless, the gains for some women were real enough, even though the total number of women falling below the line we have decided on was no less (3.4 million in both 1972 and 1973: see Table 2.3).

The commentary so far has been about what has happened during the first and second stages of the Incomes Policy. However, a review of low pay in 1973 would not be complete without comment, however speculative, on the proposals for Stage III which were announced by the Prime Minister in October and which came into effect in November. The main proposals on pay were that pay increases for a group could go up to either 7% or an average of £2.25 a week per person, whichever the negotiators preferred — this without taking account of the 1% that could be added on for 'flexibility', and extra payments for 'productivity', for working 'unsocial' hours, for rectifying 'anomalies', for living in London, etc. The individual maximum was in any case set at £350 a year. In terms of the low-paid worker (now on £25 a week) a £1 plus 4% increase would have allowed him an extra £2 a week: the Stage III pay limit formula allows him £2.25. However, for the person on £33 a week, for example, the 7% formula permits £2.31 whereas £1 plus 4% permitted £2.32 (the £2.25 option is no benefit either). The Stage III formula

therefore does marginally increase the potential gains for the
low-paid worker, but not for those earning a little more. At
the same time, it does allow up to £2 a week on the top limit
of those now allowed to earn £350 rather than £250 — in
other words the high paid. In addition to the above changes,
the government also introduced threshold safeguards. These
enable pay to be increased by an additional 40p a week
(maximum) if, in Stage III, the increase in the retail price
index reaches 7% (from the October 1973 base), and by up
to another 40p a week for every full 1% rise above that level.
It is worth noting, too, that in the final version of the Stage
III code published on 31 October increases outside the pay
limit for the furthering of equal pay in collective agreements
were again permitted. However, none of these benefits are
automatic — it all depends on individual agreements.

On profits Stage III aimed to close the loopholes. In
general, only companies which were already in operation in
April 1973 could be counted as separate enterprises. The rate
of dividend increase is continued to be limited, in general, to
5% per annum. (*The price and pay code for Stage III: A
consultative document* 1973). These are welcome changes, as
is the last point: a suggestion by the Prime Minister that a
board be set up to look at the problems of low pay, and in
particular that survey evidence of what the general public
think should be given due weight both in this and on the
other aspects of future policy.

Conclusion

My purpose has been to consider how far one of the
government's prime objectives in its Incomes Policy — an
improvement in the relative position of the low paid — has
been achieved. In order to sum up it may make better sense
to start by referring back to the last section rather than to
the first. I did not follow that order in the body of the
chapter, despite the obvious argument for it, because I
wanted to highlight the Incomes Policy which had bulked so
large in the economic and social history of 1973.

If the full figures for 1973 were published in 1973 most of
my problems would vanish. This not being so I have had to
make do with what is available, deficient in many ways

though it be. As it happens, the most important single piece
of evidence about earnings is in the New Earnings Survey.
This deserves the name of 'new' much more than most
official data. The gap between collection and publication of
the statistics is only about six months. But the gap does mean
that not until November 1973 when this chapter went to
press, can anyone say anything really comprehensive about
earnings in the previous April; and the only comparison that
can be made is with April in the previous year. The Incomes
Policy did not start until November 1972 and even then only
with a Standstill to begin with, so that the comparison which
can be made covers half a year with and half a year without
the Policy. It is therefore impossible for anyone to say which
of the differences between April 1972 and April 1973 were
accounted for by the Incomes Policy and which by other
influences altogether. That said, the main conclusion which
does stand out from the best figures there are does not speak
all that well for the weekly earnings of the low paid. It looks
as though a small move towards a greater equality between
1970 and 1971, which was made much of at the time by the
TUC, was reversed in later years, with 1973 being no better
from that point of view than 1972. I am talking of men.
Women — or at least non-manual women — can claim to have
made some slight relative improvement, which may have been
due not just to the impact of legislation on equal pay, but
also to the encouragement given to it by the Incomes Policy.

What has happened since April 1973 is bound to be more
speculative. I have had to piece together what bits of
evidence I could find in order to take a view about the rest of
the year up to the time of writing. Once again, the first
report of the Pay Board is out of date. Mainly from the
evidence collected by Incomes Data Services we have tried to
see the kind of thing that has been happening to wage
settlements. The £1 plus 4% formula, with a ceiling increase
of £250 pa, was inherently egalitarian. £1 meant more to a
man on £20 a week than to one on £1,000 a week, and the
ceiling ought to have restrained increases for the very well
off. But the information that I have on actual wage
settlements does not suggest that the effects were all that
large, mainly because people in higher-paid industries usually

received larger increases than in the lower paid, at any rate in absolute terms. In percentage terms, however, there was some narrowing of the gap between the higher and the lower paid as far as wage rates go. But actual earnings are another matter. There has probably been no similar relative gain to the low paid in terms of wage drift above the formula (except for the push given to equal pay).

Moreover, this conclusion does not have to be qualified if account is taken of improvements permitted in the terms of employment outside the pay limit formula. Some lower-paid workers moved closer to higher-paid workers in terms of the length of paid holidays but on the whole the low paid did not improve their relative position much here either. The main verdict on the egalitarian objective must therefore be that justice has not yet been seen to be done.

References

A programme for controlling inflation: The first stage, (1972) cmnd. 5125, HMSO.

H. Behrend, (1972) 'Public acceptability and a workable incomes policy' in F. Blackaby (ed.), (1972) *An incomes policy for Britain*, Heinemann.

Department of Employment, (1970) 'New earnings survey', *Department of Employment Gazette*, vol. LXXVIII no. 11.
        (1971) 'New earnings survey', *Department of Employment Gazette*, vol. LXXIX no. 11.
        (1972) 'New earnings survey', *Department of Employment Gazette*, vol. LXXX no. 11.
        (1973) 'New earnings survey' *Department of Employment Gazette*, vol. LXXXI no. 10.

F. Field (ed.), (1973) *Low pay*, Arrow.

Incomes Data Services, (1973a) *Incomes data report 153*.
        (1973b) *Incomes data report 165*.
        (1973c) 'Holidays', *Incomes data study 52*.
        (1973d) 'Women's pay', *Incomes data study 56*.
        (1973e), 'Panorama' *Incomes data study 57*.

M. Meacher, (1971) 'The indulgence of Mr Barber', *The Times*, 3 April 1971.

National Board for Prices and Incomes, (1971) 'General problems of low pay', *Report 169*, cmnd. 4648, HMSO.

Office of Manpower Economics, (1973) *Wage drift – review of literature and research*, HMSO.

Pay Board, (1973), *Report 2 April–31 May*, HMSO.

The counter-inflation programme: the operation of Stage II, (1973) cmnd. 5267, HMSO.

The price and pay code: Consultative document, (1973) cmnd. 5247, HMSO.

The price and pay code for Stage III: A consultative document (1973) cmnd. 5444, HMSO.

Knowing something about what people earn, as
we now do, the next question to ask is about
the value of the pay packet or cheque. This
depends primarily upon how much goes in tax
and national insurance; the cash benefits for
children; housing benefits; and on the
extent to which prices have risen. Professor
Atkinson and Mr Trinder set out to take them
all into account.

3   Real Incomes of People at Work
TONY ATKINSON and CHRIS TRINDER

In this chapter we translate the changes in earnings during
1972–3 into 'real disposable income' to show what the pay
packet bought in the autumn of 1973 compared with a year
earlier. Before the war this task would have been relatively
easy to do. Most workers were below the tax threshold,
family allowances had not been introduced, rent rebates were
rare, and rate rebates not invented. Today the relationship
between gross earnings and disposable income is a more
complex one. We have to allow for the taxation of wages in
different forms, family benefits, and housing benefits and
rising rents. We have above all to allow for the extent to
which any gain in disposable income in money terms was
eroded by inflation. Each of these will be dealt with in
separate sections.

   We are again primarily concerned with what has happened
to the low-paid worker and how his experience compares
with that of other workers. We shall define 'low pay' in the
same way as in the previous chapter, so that our starting
point is with a 'low-paid worker' who earned £22 a week in
round terms in November 1972. The relative effect on the
low-paid worker of changes in taxes, benefits, and prices will

of course depend upon the other income levels chosen for comparison. What we have done is to pick out as illustrations two other main levels of income: the 'average worker' (with around £33 a week in November 1972) and the 'affluent worker' with earnings of one and a half times the average (with around £50 a week in November 1972).

Take-home pay
As explained in the previous chapter, the full implications for earnings of the first and second stages of the Incomes Policy were not known at the time of writing. The analysis has therefore been carried out on two different assumptions about the changes in gross pay for the low-paid, average and affluent workers. The first, naive, assumption is that the increase in earnings received by each group of workers followed precisely the Stage II formula: £1 plus 4% over the year. For the three levels of pay that we are considering this would have meant:

	November 1972	*Increase in £s*	*Increase in %*
Low-paid worker	£22	1.88	8.5
Average worker	£33	2.32	7.0
Affluent worker	£50	3.00	6.0

This is the bottom limit. Earnings for most people have risen at least this much and for many people they rose by a good deal more. Our second assumption therefore allows for 'earnings drift' of 7% above the formula for all three income levels alike. The earnings of the low-paid worker would on this basis have risen by 15.5% and those of the average worker by 14%. The assumption that the extra earnings drift was the same percentage for all three income levels is tantamount to saying that the free movement of earnings did not give the low-paid worker the same relative advantage as the Stage II formula. Some support for this is provided by the New Earnings Survey evidence for the changes between April 1972 and April 1973, as discussed in the previous chapter (Department of Employment 1973). This is what happened to earnings. What then did it mean for real disposable resources?

Of deductions from gross pay the first is income tax. As Turner and Wilkinson among others have emphasised, income tax has become increasingly important for the low paid (Turner and Wilkinson 1971). This is because the tax threshold has failed to increase in line with rising earnings. For example, in 1938 the tax threshold for a married man with one child was over one and a half times the average earnings. Even the 'affluent worker' would not have been subject to income tax at that time. After the war the tax threshold fell to three-quarters of average earnings, and since then it has steadily declined until with the introduction of the new unified tax system in April 1973 it was only 49% of average earnings. As a result, a much larger proportion of the working population fall into the tax net.

So any increase in earnings is likely to be taxable, and now that we no longer have the reduced rates of income tax this is payable at the full basic rate of 30%. For example, if we take the average worker with two children aged 11 and 16 and assume that his earnings rise in line with the Stage II formula, then his tax bill rose from £3.16 a week in November 1972 to £3.86 a week in October 1973. Moreover, the effect was even more marked for the low-paid worker with two children. He was previously below the tax threshold but became subject to tax as a result of his Stage II increase; the consequence was that his increase in take-home pay was reduced by income tax alone from 8.5% to 6.6%. The impact of tax for a range of different family circumstances is shown in the column headed 'After tax' in Table 3.1. It should be emphasised at this point that the net effect of different tax and social policies depends very much on individual circumstances and that the examples given here and in subsequent tables do not by any means exhaust the range of possibilities. These examples should therefore be regarded as purely illustrative, the task of providing definitive results requiring a much more detailed analysis than space permits here. Nevertheless, despite these reservations, Table 3.1 does bring out the important general point that there has not simply been increased wage taxation reducing gains in after-tax pay for everyone, but that this increased wage taxation has borne differently on different groups of workers. To take extremes, the 'affluent' single worker had a 2.5% smaller increase in gross earnings than did the 'low-paid worker' with one child, but the difference in after-tax pay was only 0.7%.

During 1973 the new unified tax system was introduced in April (Board of Inland Revenue 1973). The changes for the average person were the abolition of earned income relief — which had puzzled taxpayers for so long — and the offsetting adjustments to the basic rate of tax and the personal allowances. The net effect of the changes made little difference to the tax bill of the ordinary worker; in fact as a result of rounding, there was a very slight reduction in the tax due, the average worker paying about 4p a week less in tax. At the same time there were changes for higher rate taxpayers (surtax payers) and those with investment income. The effect was to soften the impact of Stage II for those with an income of £5,000 a year or more. A man with earnings of £5,000 a year, receiving the maximum permitted increase in gross pay of £250 (5%) a year, gained 5.6% in terms of after-tax pay. For those with substantial investment income there was also the valuable concession which allowed the first £2,000 per annum to be treated as earned income. A person with investment income of £15,000 a year paid £27 or so a week less in tax. Although almost unnoticed, the 1973 tax changes gave a large bonus to those with large incomes that far exceeded the Stage II norm.

Returning to our main concern, we have also to allow for the effect of higher national insurance contributions. National insurance contributions are of considerable importance as far as redistribution is concerned since the basic charge is a declining proportion of earnings (a situation which will be improved but not ended by the 1973 Social Security Act). The automatic effect of a general increase in earnings is, therefore, to place a relatively heavier burden on the lower paid. If the contribution conditions had remained unchanged, men on £22 a week would have paid an extra 5p on their graduated national insurance stamp as a result of their Stage II increase, whereas men on £50 would have paid nothing more, being above the 1972 ceiling for graduated contri-

Table 3.1 Increases in take-home pay 1972—3

Low-paid worker (£22 a week in 1972)	Stage II formula (8.5% increase in gross earnings)		With earnings drift (15.5% increase in gross earnings)	
	After-tax	Take-home pay	After-tax	Take-home pay
	%	%	%	%
Single person	7.0	7.4	12.7	13.0
Couple	6.6	7.0	12.0	12.3
Couple with 1 child	6.2	6.5	11.3	11.5
Couple with 2 children	6.6	6.9	11.5	11.7
Couple with 4 children	8.5	9.0	14.8	15.2

Average worker (£33 a week in 1972)	Stage II formula (7.0% increase in gross earnings)		With earnings drift (14.0% increase in gross earnings)	
	After-tax	Take-home pay	After-tax	Take-home pay
	%	%	%	%
Single person	6.1	6.2	12.2	12.3
Couple	5.9	5.9	11.8	11.8
Couple with 1 child	5.6	5.6	11.2	11.3
Couple with 2 children	5.4	5.4	10.8	10.8
Couple with 4 children	5.3	5.3	10.6	10.5

Affluent worker (£50 a week in 1972)	Stage II formula (6.0% increase in gross earnings)		With earnings drift (13.0% increase in gross earnings)	
	After-tax	Take-home pay	After-tax	Take-home pay
	%	%	%	%
Single person	5.5	5.0	11.8	11.7
Couple	5.3	4.8	11.5	11.4
Couple with 1 child	5.2	4.7	11.2	11.0
Couple with 2 children	5.0	4.5	10.9	10.7
Couple with 4 children	4.9	4.4	10.7	10.5

NOTE
The children are assumed to be aged 7 (one-child family); 11 and 16 (two-child family); and 7, 9, 12, and 14 (four-child family).

butions. In 1973, however, this potentially regressive effect was partially offset by the new contribution conditions coming into force in October, which reduced the flat-rate contribution and increased the graduated element (Department of Health and Social Security 1972, 1973). As a result, the contributions payable by the low-paid worker as a result of his Stage II increase and the new level of contributions, amounted to £1.56 a week in all (if not contracted out), an increase on the beginning of the year of only 4p, whereas the affluent worker had an increase of 33p a week.

The combined effect of income tax and national insurance contributions is summed up under the heading of 'Take-home pay' in Table 3.1. These columns show that with one exception households with children had a smaller percentage increase in take-home pay than households without children. The exception was the low-paid worker with four children, since a Stage II increase in gross earnings would not have made him liable for income tax, and his national insurance contributions decreased over the year as a proportion of gross pay. The next section examines how far this relative worsening of the position of families was offset by changes in family benefits.

Family benefits
There are at present two main cash benefits for families with children: family allowances and family income supplement (FIS). There are also child tax allowances, but these have already been taken into account in working out the income tax payable. Family allowances are a universal benefit payable to all families with two or more children, and they represent a valuable source of family support. However, unlike other social security benefits, the value of the allowance has not been increased regularly (the last increase was in 1968). Their value has therefore been eroded by inflation. The allowance per child recommended by Beveridge in 1942 was some 10% of average earnings, but the present allowance of £1 (90p for the second child) is only some 3%. Since family allowances have been allowed to remain unchanged while income rises they contribute less and less each year to the family's disposable resources. This

process continued during 1973 and reduced still further the
relative net gain to families compared to households with no
children. This is shown by the columns in Table 3.2 headed
'Income after family benefits' (with the exception of the
low-paid worker with four children eligible for family income
supplement and discussed below).

The other main source of financial provision for children is
family income supplement (FIS). FIS is a benefit provided
for families with the man in full-time work but whose total
income is still below a specified level. The size of the
payment is one-half of the amount by which the family's
gross income falls below the prescribed amount, subject to a
maximum payment. In contrast to the family allowance, the
value of this benefit has been increased twice in the course of
the year. In April 1973 there was an increase in the
prescribed income eligibility levels and in October 1973 there
was a further increase, coupled with a raising of the
maximum payment for families of three or more children
from £5 to £6. Whether these changes led to an improvement
for low-income families depends on whether the increase in
the prescribed income eligibility levels was sufficient to keep
up with the increase in earnings. Of the families we are
considering, only one, the low-paid worker with four
children, would have been eligible for FIS. The income for
such a family in November 1972 would have been £22 plus
family allowances of £2.90, so that it was £1.10 below the
FIS eligibility level, entitling it to a payment (rounded
upwards) of 60p a week. By October 1973 income on the
Stage II formula would have risen to £23.88 plus £2.90, but
the FIS eligibility level would have risen to £29 so that the
FIS entitlement would have been £1.20 a week.

In assessing the impact of these improvements in FIS it is
important as always to bear in mind take-up — or the fact
that all those entitled to FIS do not necessarily claim. The
official estimates of the proportion of eligible families who
were claiming initially placed it at around three-quarters,
which was less than the budgeted figure of 85%. More
recently, evidence to the select committee on the tax credit
scheme revealed that in March 1973 only about half the
numbers eligible were thought to be claiming. In fact, one of

the least noticed features of the tax credit discussion is the official recognition of the problems caused by the inadequate take-up of means-tested benefits (*Proposals for a tax-credit system* 1973). In Table 3.2 we have therefore shown the net benefit with and without FIS for the family which is eligible.

The final source of state provision for families. is the means-tested family benefits in kind, of which free school meals, welfare foods, school uniform grants, and maintenance grants are examples. As prices rise, the value of the benefit in kind increases. Free school meals, for example, become more valuable with increases in the cost of feeding children at home or giving them sandwiches, or if the price of school meals rises (in fact the price of school meals was frozen as part of Stage II). These benefits in kind are, however, provided only subject to an income test and therefore the number of families qualifying for them would be reduced during the year unless the income eligibility levels were increased in line with earnings. For school meals, for example, the income limits for eligibility were increased sufficiently in September 1973 for the low-paid worker with four children to remain eligible for four free school meals in October 1973. But again it obviously cannot be assumed that people claim the benefits to which they are entitled.

Housing benefits and rising rents
In their analyses of the circumstances of low-income groups the Department of Health and Social Security make use of the concept of *disposable resources*, defined as net income of a household minus housing costs, the latter being regarded as an 'unavoidable' element in the household budget. For our purposes this concept is useful: it allows us to separate the changes in housing costs in recent years from other factors affecting low-income groups. So in this section we examine the rise in housing costs over the year and try to see what was left to the households by way of disposable resources.

Any such analysis would become enormously complicated if one were to allow for the wide variety of types of tenure, let alone other variations in individual circumstances. Tenure certainly matters. The experience of owner occupiers is very different from that of tenants, and of council tenants from those in furnished private accommodation. For any full account of owner occupiers we should need to count capital appreciation on the income side of the account. But at this stage it would be extremely difficult to estimate for 1972—3 with any precision. We focus therefore on tenants, without trying to throw any light on the interesting question of differences according to their type.

A tenant not eligible for a rent rebate, or one who is eligible but does not claim, had to face an increase in rent in the year. Its precise magnitude varied from area to area and according to the type of accommodation. No average figure is available. In what follows we conservatively assume a 50p increase in weekly rent over the year. This was the procedure adopted by the Chancellor of the Exchequer when he announced an increase in rent rebates as from 1 October 1973. Peter Willmott discusses the increase in rents over the year in more detail in Chapter 7. The net change in disposable resources allowing for an increase of this magnitude is shown in the column for resources in Table 3.2 headed 'Resources — not claiming rent rebate'. In these calculations allowance is also made for rate increases which are assumed to have risen by 10% during the year, but rates and rate rebates are discussed further in the next chapter.

The position for a tenant receiving a rent rebate is more complicated, since the change in his disposable resources depends on the interaction between his increased earnings, the rise in rent, and the change in the rent rebate formula. Two changes in this formula were announced during 1973. The first was announced by the Prime Minister as part of Stage II and involved a £3.50 increase in the needs element of the formula. The second increase was announced by the Chancellor in July and came into effect from 1 October. This gave a £1.50 a week increase in the needs element of the formula for a single tenant, £2.50 for a married couple and an additional 25p for every dependent child. Therefore, if we take a 'low-paid worker' with two children, his rebate in November 1972 with rent of £4 was £1.95 a week, whereas a year later, on the assumption of earnings increasing in line with the Stage II formula, his rebate had become £3.19. In other words, his rent went down by 74p a week.

Table 3.2 Increase in disposable resources 1972–3

	Stage II formula			With earnings drift		
	Income after family benefits	Resources + not claiming rent rebate	Resources + claiming rent rebate	Income after family benefits	Resources + not claiming rent rebate	Resources + claiming rent rebate
	%	%	%	%	%	%
Low-paid worker						
Single	7.4	5.1	10.2	13.0	12.4	15.5
Couple	7.0	5.0	11.4	12.3	11.9	16.2
Couple with 1 child	6.5	4.5	10.6	11.5	11.0	14.9
Couple with 2 children	6.6	5.0	11.2	11.2	10.9	14.5
Couple with 4 children	10.2	10.0	15.3	12.1	12.5	16.7
*	7.9	7.0	13.6	13.8	14.8	18.5
Average worker						
Single	6.2	4.5		12.3	11.8	
Couple	5.9	4.4		11.8	11.5	
Couple with 1 child	5.6	4.1	6.0	11.3	10.9	11.1
Couple with 2 children	5.2	4.0	8.0	10.5	10.2	12.7
Couple with 4 children	4.8	3.5	7.5	9.6	9.3	11.6
Affluent worker						
Single	5.0	3.7		11.7	11.3	
Couple	4.8	3.7		11.4	11.1	
Couple with 1 child	4.7	3.5		11.0	10.7	
Couple with 2 children	4.4	3.4		10.5	10.3	
Couple with 4 children	4.1	3.1		9.8	9.7	

NOTES

*The first row refers to a family claiming FIS and the second to a family which is not claiming. In other cases there is no eligibility for FIS.

+Assuming rent and rates per week as follows:

November 1972: Single person £3 rent and 90p rates

Couple or couple with 1 child £3.50 rent and 95p rates

Couple with 2 children £4 rent and £1 rates

Couple with 4 children £4.50 rent and £1.05 rates

October 1973: All rents had increased by 50p and all rates by 10%

The estimated changes between 1972 and 1973, set out in Table 3.2, suggest a number of conclusions. From the column for income after family benefits it is clear that there has been a worsening in the relative position of families (with the exception of the small minority receiving FIS). For low-paid workers the single man had an increase of 7.4% (on the Stage II formula) compared with only 6.6% for the married man with two children. The column for resources brings out the importance of knowing how many families claim the rent rebates to which they are entitled. The low-paid worker with two children would have an 11.2% increase in disposable resources if he had claimed a rent rebate, but an increase of only 5% if he did not claim. The debate about the poverty trap has focused attention on the high marginal rates of 'tax' as earnings rise and benefits are withdrawn, but this may be less important (particularly with the increases in the income limits for many benefits) than the problem of non-take-up. The increasing emphasis in government policy on means-tested benefits has meant that what was previously a matter of a few pence a week can now make a substantial difference to living standards. Those who do not claim are likely to fall rapidly behind.

Have disposable resources kept up with rising prices?
The final step is to convert disposable resources in money terms into purchasing power: it is true that the resources of the low-paid worker with two children have gone up by 11.2% since the autumn of 1972, but everyone knows that prices have gone up as well. The usual way of measuring the rate of inflation is by the change in the retail price index. It is this which gets most attention in the newspapers. But the retail price index is unsatisfactory for our purposes. This is partly because it includes housing expenditure, whereas we have already allowed for this in arriving at the index of disposable resources, but more importantly it is because the retail price index does not allow for the fact that inflation affects different groups differently, depending on how they spend their money. Some items rise in price more than others (some actually go down) and households which spend a lot on items which rise in price will be affected more seriously

by inflation.

In 1973 there were two main reasons why the above points are likely to have mattered particularly. First, there were very substantial increases in food prices. The retail price index (excluding housing) rose by 6% between autumn 1972 and mid-1973 whereas food prices rose on average by 12.4% — meat and bacon prices rose by 22.7% and fish by 18.6%. As a result, households spending a large part of their budget on food were hit harder than those for whom food was a relatively less important item of their expenditure. The variation in the proportion of income spent on food is in fact quite marked. While the average household spends 26% of its budget on food, this conceals a range which varies from 20% for a couple with an income of £2,500 a year to a figure of 35% for low-income families with three or more children (Department of Employment 1972). For the latter type of household the rise in food prices was nearly twice as severe a burden. The second reason why prices went up at different rates for different goods was because of the introduction of VAT in April 1973 in place of purchase tax and selective employment tax. This tax change caused a rise in the price of 'necessary' items such as prams and cots (+£1.50), toothbrushes (+2p), beds (+55—85p), house repairs (+£1.65 on a £20 job), and lino (+20—33p on a £15 roll). The fact that there was at the same time a fall in the price of fishing rods (–35p), cameras (–50p), golf balls (–1p) and colour televisions (–£15—23) provided little consolation to the low-income family who could not afford to buy any of these items (Customs and Excise 1973). These effects are due to the fact that VAT is levied at the same rate on a broad range of goods, whether luxuries or necessities, whereas purchase tax was levied at a higher rate on luxuries.

The effects of inflation during 1973 must therefore have been more serious for the low-wage family spending most of its budget on food and other necessities, than for the average household represented by the retail price index. Despite this, the government does not publish a separate price index for low-wage groups. There is a pensioner index which is discussed in the next chapter, but the Cost of Living Advisory Committee, which five years ago recommended the introduction of the pensioner index, did not consider that there was at that time a strong enough case for compiling a special index for low-income households with children. They did suggest that the matter be reviewed in the light of experience with the pensioner index, but no progress has been made. In view of this we were forced to construct our own price indices for different groups. In doing this weights for the different goods were obtained from the Family Expenditure Survey 1971 (the latest published results, available at the time) and they varied according to differences in income and differences in household composition. While these weights are undoubtedly subject to error and could be refined in a number of respects, they should be sufficiently accurate for a first-time look at the question whether inflation has indeed affected low-income households and large families more severely than the rest of the population. The answer they suggest is that there were noticeable differences in the extent of price increases. Whereas the retail price index (excluding housing) rose by 6% between autumn 1972 and mid-1973, the index for a low-paid worker with four children rose by 6.4%.

Since this chapter was written before the end of 1973 the full extent of inflation during the year was not known. Therefore the price indices referred to in the previous paragraph were calculated over the eight months mid-October 1972 to mid-June 1973 and were then extrapolated on two alternative assumptions. The first assumption is the over-conservative one that there was no further inflation (column headed 'Minimum inflation' in Table 3.3). The alternative assumption is that the remaining four months had the same rate of inflation as did the previous eight months (column headed 'Extrapolated inflation' in Table 3.3), which is probably rather closer to the truth. Both assumptions show how inflation has eaten into living standards during the year. On the most optimistic set of assumptions (earnings drift combined with minimum inflation), the average worker has enjoyed some increase in real disposable resources, but on more reasonable assumptions the gain was small. And the Stage II formula would have meant a fall in real resources for the average worker with no children, even on the minimum inflation assumption.

Table 3.3 Changes in real disposable resources 1972-3

	Stage II formula		With earnings drift	
	Minimum inflation	Extra-polated inflation	Minimum inflation	Extra-polated inflation
	%	%	%	%
Low-paid worker				
Single	4.2	1.5	9.2	6.3
Couple	5.1	2.2	9.7	6.6
Couple with 1 child	4.0	1.0	8.1	4.9
Couple with 2 children	4.9	2.0	7.9	4.9
Couple with 4 children	8.4	5.2	9.7	6.5
Average worker				
Single	−1.1	−3.6	5.9	3.2
Couple	−1.2	−4.3	5.6	2.9
Couple with 1 child	0	−2.8	4.8	1.9
Couple with 2 children	1.8	−1.0	6.3	3.3
Couple with 4 children	1.4	−1.4	5.3	2.4
Affluent worker				
Single	−1.7	−4.2	5.5	2.9
Couple	−1.7	−4.2	5.4	2.7
Couple with 1 child	−2.0	−4.5	4.9	2.2
Couple with 2 children	−2.3	−4.9	4.2	1.5
Couple with 4 children	−2.8	−5.5	3.3	0.5

NOTE
It is assumed that rent rebates and FIS are claimed where a family is eligible

Turning to the low-paid worker, we can see that his net gain was small where his earnings increased according to the Stage II formula and inflation continued throughout 1973 (the one exception is the four child family claiming FIS). Since these are the most plausible assumptions for many low-paid workers, the picture is not an encouraging one. The low-paid worker with one child may have done better than his counterpart on £50 a week who lost £1.50 in real terms, but the low paid are unlikely to have achieved a significant improvement in living standards. Even assuming that the redistributive element of the Stage II formula was reflected in actual earnings its effectiveness was blunted by the effects of taxation and of differential price increases. Finally, it should be emphasised that the figures given in Table 3.3 rest on the optimistic assumption that families are claiming the rent rebates to which they are entitled; where this was not so the increase in real disposable resources was even less.

Conclusion

This chapter has looked at the impact of Stage II on the real incomes of the working population. Since the analysis has been based on a number of assumptions, and may need to be revised when more data are available, the detailed figures should not be given too much weight. They serve none the less to bring out a number of important points. First, although the Stage II formula was designed to give larger percentage increase to the low paid there were other forces working in the opposite direction. The low level of the tax threshold, the failure to increase family allowances, and the faster increase in the price of necessities all meant that the advantage to the low-paid worker was eaten away. If the government is sincere in its desire to help poor households then its incomes policy must take into account everything which affects their standard of living. Secondly, the analysis suggests that households with children have on the whole tended to fare worse, reflecting the fact that family allowances have remained unchanged. The government clearly ought to consider whether their real value should be restored. Finally, there is a strong case for the publication of official price indices for different groups (in addition to the pensioner index), since the retail price index may well mask divergent movements for different types of household. At present rates of inflation even quite small differences in budgets can rapidly lead to serious anomalies.

References

Customs and Excise, (1973) *Your guide to the VAT price changes,* HMSO.

Department of Employment, (1972) *Family expenditure survey 1971,* HMSO.

(1973) 'New earnings survey', *Department of Employment Gazette,* vol. LXXXI, no. 10, HMSO.

Department of Health and Social Security, (1972) 'National insurance contributions', *Leaflet NI 195,* HMSO.

(1973) 'National insurance contributions', *Leaflet NI 204,* HMSO.

Proposals for a tax-credit system (1972) cmnd. 5116, HMSO.

The Board of Inland Revenue, (1973) 'The new unified tax system', *Leaflet IR 19,* HMSO.

H.A. Turner and F. Wilkinson, (1971) 'Real net incomes and the wage explosion', *New Society* 25 February 1971, vol. 17, no. 439.

The third of the opening trio of chapters turns to the people who are not able to work and are dependent upon support from public funds. The main questions are the same as in the previous two chapters — how much money have people received, and how much has it been worth?

4 Real Incomes of Other People
TONY ATKINSON and CHRIS TRINDER

The last two chapters have been concerned with those in work; in this chapter we turn to those who are not and who depend principally on social security benefits. Have the latter kept up with the former? What role do means-tested benefits play in supporting those who are out of work, and how has this changed in 1973? Have old people been protected against the rise in prices? This chapter is therefore about the standard of living of those *not* able to work. In the first section we look at the main national insurance benefits and how they have changed in relation to earnings. In the second we look at the principal means-tested benefit — supplementary benefit (SB) — and the numbers dependent on it for support. The third is about housing benefits, in particular, rent and rate rebates. And the fourth section is about the still larger question of how people have fared when account is taken not only of benefits but of what benefits will buy, of how inflation has affected the purchasing power of the old, the sick, and the unemployed.

National insurance benefits
National insurance (NI) benefits provide for a wide variety of circumstances. Under the original legislation they covered retirement, widowhood, sickness, unemployment, industrial

injuries, maternity, orphanhood and death. In recent years they have been extended to cover disability, invalidity, and those people who did not qualify for retirement pensions when national insurance was introduced. Without trying to deal with everything we focus here on four main types of household. *Pensioners* are the largest single group receiving NI benefits (7,793,000 in December 1972). Virtually everyone now retiring qualifies for a full flat-rate NI pension. This is paid at the age of 65 (60 for women) to those who satisfy the retirement condition, and at the age of 70 (65 for women) to those who do not satisfy it. The *sick* are eligible for the flat-rate NI benefit and may in addition qualify for a short-term earnings-related benefit payable for six months. The *unemployed* are subject to the same conditions as the sick except that entitlement to NI benefit ceases after a year; payment is conditional on registration for employment. Finally, *widows* are entitled to a short-term benefit for six months, including an earnings-related supplement where the husband was in work; and to a longer-term benefit at a flat rate if they have dependent children or are over 40 years of age (a reduced rate applies between the ages of 40 and 49).

For most people in these groups the NI benefit makes up a large part of their support (and for some, their only support). All are therefore critically dependent on the regularity with which the levels of benefit are reviewed, especially during a period of inflation. However, when the national insurance scheme began in 1948, regular reviews were thought unnecessary and in the first ten years there were only two general increases in the benefit rates. Only in recent years has the procedure been changed: the Wilson government made biennial reviews the established pattern, and for the past three years they have become annual. In the year October 1972 – October 1973 the single pension was increased by £1 from £6.75 a week at the end of 1972 to £7.75 a week from October 1973; and the pension for a couple went up from £10.90 to £12.50 a week. These were increases of nearly 15% in the rates for single persons or adult dependents and were described by Sir Keith Joseph as the 'largest ever' (Department of Health and Social Security 1972, 1973a).

Comparing the levels of NI benefit with average gross

*Table 4.1 National insurance benefits 1972, 1973, and
the Beveridge target*

*National insurance benefits as a percentage of
average earnings*

	Autumn 1972 %	Autumn 1973[2] %	Beveridge target[3] %
Single pensioner	20.5	21.9	27.0
Pensioner couple	33.0	35.4	45.0
Sick or unemployed man with two children[1]	45.8	48.4	63.5
Widow with two children[1]	40.5	43.5	45.0

NOTES
1. Including family allowances
2. Assuming average earnings increased according to the Stage II formula
3. Proportions as in 1938

earnings, projected on the Stage II formula assumption, then the benefits from NI have shown a relative increase (see Table 4.1). For example, the pension for a single person went up from 20.5% of average earnings in October 1972 to 22% of average earnings in October 1973. In addition to the increase in the NI benefit levels, the government also gave pensioners a bonus of £10 each during December 1972, and again in December 1973. This no doubt provided more political capital than a corresponding increase in the pension, although a great deal must have been lost by refusing the bonus to 7,000 pensioners because their earnings in the relevant week exceeded the eligibility limit (the government later relented). The most recent precedent for this type of measure was the £4 Christmas bonus given to pensioners in 1964, but if it were to become an annual event the bonus for a single pensioner would be equivalent to a payment of approximately 20p per week throughout the year. In broad terms, therefore, the government does appear to have tried to give pensioners a fair share in terms of rising money incomes. However, it is also worthwhile comparing the present benefit levels as proportions of earnings with the Beveridge recommendations. By this standard the present benefits fall a long way short for all except widows. The single pension would have to be raised to at least £9.50 to reach the Beveridge target (see Table 4.1).

Households headed by a man who is sick or unemployed, or by a widow, may be entitled to short-term benefit in addition to the flat-rate amounts taken into account in Table 4.1. The fact that these additional benefits are earnings-related suggests that they are protected automatically against inflation. However, payment is based on earnings in the previous tax year so that they will not necessarily keep up with acceleration in wages. There is also a maximum to the supplement permitted. The maximum rate payable was at last raised in January 1974 from £7 to £8.47. But the striking fact is that before this rise the ceiling had remained constant ever since the benefits were introduced in 1966. This is an example of one of the 'hidden constants' in the social security system, or elements which have remained constant while the general level of benefits has been increased. Another example is the earnings rule by which the retirement pension is reduced if a man aged between 65 and 70 (a woman between 60 and 65) earns more than a specified amount. This rule has been applied at a level of £9.50 since 1971, but if the limit had been increased in line with the pension it would now be some £12.25 a week. Similarly, in 1971 a very welcome increase of 25p a week was added to the pension of those over 80. In the post-October 1973 regime this addition has remained unchanged; if the same proportionate addition had been maintained it would now be 35p a week. A further 'hidden constant' is the death grant. When introduced in 1948 this grant was £20 but twenty-five years later it is still only £30, an increase which no more reflects the rising cost of a burial than anything else.

A final question is the extent to which people actually receive the benefit. In general there are no serious problems about take up; but there are problems about eligibility, particularly for the unemployed. The maximum duration for NI unemployment benefit is one year, and once exhausted there is no further entitlement until the person has re-qualified by working for three months. As a result of the high levels of unemployment in the past few years many of the unemployed have exhausted their entitlement. For example, in May 1973 only 41% of unemployed men were receiving NI benefit compared with an average of over 50% for the period 1961—70 (Department of Employment 1973a). For about half the unemployed men at any one time, and for an increasing proportion over the period 1972—3, NI has failed to provide a source of income support. As a result they were dependent on supplementary benefit.

Supplementary benefit
Supplementary benefit (SB) is the 'safety net' of the social security system. For those receiving NI benefit who have no other major source of income it provides supplementation. For those not entitled to NI benefit, such as the long-term unemployed or single women with children, SB is a misnomer since it provides their only, or principal, source of income. In May 1973 there were nearly three million households receiving SB.

	Households (000s)
Retirement pensioners and widows over 60*	1,781
Others over pension age	95
Sick and disabled without NI benefits	164
Sick and disabled with NI benefits*	130
Unemployed with NI benefits+*	73
Unemployed without NI benefits+	262
NI widows under 60*	61
Women with dependent children	231
Others	22
	2,819

NOTES
+ Provisonal
* SB recipients also receiving NI benefit

The first striking feature of the figures opposite is their size. Beveridge hoped that SB would form a 'minor part of the work of the Ministry of Social Security'. This hope is a long way from being realised, and indeed the number dependent on SB has been growing steadily. For example, at the beginning of the 1960s the number was well under two million. Although this growth stems partly from the larger population 'at risk', there has also been an increase in the proportion of NI recipients. In the early 1960s the proportion of pensioners also receiving SB was around 22% but by 1972 it had increased to 28%.

The regular review of the levels of benefit became established rather earlier with SB than with national insurance. There have been annual increases for the past eight years. However, the size of the increases has been less encouraging. In particular, the October 1973 increase gave those receiving the 'ordinary' rate (as distinct from the long-term rate) a smaller increase than the corresponding one in NI benefit. An unemployed man with two children received a rise in NI benefit from £15.10 a week to £17.10, but the SB scale – assuming that the children were aged 6 and 12 – rose only from £15.65 to £17.10. If, therefore, he was claiming SB his net gain in disposable income (in money terms) was only 9.3% (for further details see Table 4.2). One of the features of the October 1973 changes in SB was the structural change involving the incorporation of the previous long-term addition into a new 'long-term weekly rate'. The 'long-term' recipients (pensioners and persons under pension age, apart from the unemployed, who have received SB for a continuous period of two years or longer) received a larger increase. For example, the long-term rate shows an increase of £1 for a single person and £1.60 for a couple, or exactly the same amount as the increase in NI benefits.

A second change in procedure which was brought into force during 1973 by the National Insurance and Supplementary Benefits Act was in the exceptional circumstances additions (Department of Health and Social Security 1973b). These may be given to cover needs such as heating, special diet, extra laundry or domestic assistance. Before the 1973 Act the Supplementary Benefits Commission had powers of discretion which allowed them to set exceptional circumstances additions against the long-term addition, but in a High Court case in February 1973 it was established that such deductions should not be automatic. In response to this the government introduced legislation to remove powers of discretion: from 1 October 1973 exceptional circumstances additions given for all purposes (except heating) had the deductions automatically applied. For example, a person who before 1 October 1973 received SB of £6.55 a week plus the 60p long-term addition, and who had an exceptional addition for special diet of 40p a week which was not set against the long-term addition, received a total payment of £7.55 a week. From 1 October 1973 this same person received only the £8.15 new long-term weekly rate (because the 40p for special diet was automatically offset). Therefore, the total SB payment rose by only 60p a week and the person did not derive the full benefit from the October 1973 £1 increase in the SB long-term scale rates.

With SB as with NI there are elements which have not been increased regularly in line with scale rates. This applies again to the earnings rule. Under SB a person required to register for work can have up to £1 of earnings disregarded, and those not required to register for work, such as a claimant's wife, can earn up to £2 before it is deducted from the scale rates of benefit. These allowances have remained unchanged since 1966. At that time they represented 24.7% and 49.4% respectively of the scale rates for a single householder, whereas now they have fallen to 14% and 28%, which is only approximately half their 1966 value. Another example is the rule for the treatment of capital. In 1966 the figure for the total disregarded was £300 and it has remained so ever since.

Rent and rate rebates
In the previous chapter we made use of the concept of disposable resources defined as net income minus housing costs. In theory those receiving SB have their housing costs met in full and therefore SB recipients are not usually affected by rent and rate increases. So we will focus on those not receiving SB. Let us take as an example a single pensioner living in a flat with a rent at the end of 1972 of £3 a week

and rates of 90p a week (these figures are taken from an example given by the Department of Health and Social Security in its evidence to the Tax Credit Committee). If the pensioner whom we are considering has only a small amount of income besides the retirement pension, then he is likely to qualify for both rate and rent rebates.

In order to qualify for the maximum rate rebate the pensioner's other income had to be less than £5.25 a week. The pensioner would still have received some rebate if his income was a little above this amount. But we will assume that the pensioner had £5 a week of other income and therefore did meet the eligibility condition for the maximum rate rebate. Rates are normally due twice a year and therefore in 1972 with rates of 90p per week the pensioner's half-yearly rate bill would have been £23.40. In this case the pensioner would be required to pay £3.75 (the fixed charge whatever his rates) plus one-third of £19.65 (the remainder of the rate bill after deducting £3.75) giving a total of £10.30 over the twenty-six week period, or 40p per week rather than the full 90p. During 1973 the net position of the pensioner was affected in two ways: by the adjustment in the income limits for eligibility for a rate rebate, and by the increase in the full rate payment. The adjustment in the income limits for eligibility for a rate rebate occurred in April 1973, and because the adjustment was more than the £1 increase in the pension, the pensioner would have remained eligible for a maximum rate rebate in October 1973, provided that his other income did not rise above £5.75 a week. The 1973 increase in rates was caused by a number of factors, including the effects of inflation in increasing the cost of providing local services; one particular factor in 1973 was the rating revaluation. Although the rating revaluation did not by itself lead to a rise in rate bills (the rate in the £ being adjusted to allow for the higher rateable values), some ratepayers did face higher increases than others, and in view of this, the Chancellor of the Exchequer announced in the Budget that the government would meet half the cost above 10% of any increase in domestic rate bills which were attributable solely to the effects of the revaluation. Nevertheless, the pensioner would still have been liable for one-third of the increase in the rates up to at least 10%. On the assumption that the pensioner's rates did increase by 10% during 1973, the pensioner was then required to pay one-third of £21.99 (the remainder of the 1973 half-yearly rate bill after deducting £3.75) plus the fixed charge of £3.75, giving a total of £11.08 over the twenty-six week period, or 43p a week. The net effect is therefore that the pensioner would have been liable for an additional 3p a week (a 7.5% increase) if the remainder was met by an increase in the rebate.

With a total income at the end of 1972 of £11.75 a week the pensioner was entitled to a rent rebate. In fact his rent would have been made up of the 'minimum rent' (in this case 40% of £3 = £1.20) plus 17% of the excess of his income over the needs allowance (£1.25), giving a total of £1.41, so that the rebate would be £1.59 a week. As is clear from this calculation, the rent rebate depends on three different factors: income, rent, and the needs allowance. During 1973 all three have changed. To examine the likely net effect, let us assume that the pensioner's other income remained unchanged, and that his rent went up by 50p a week during the year. Given these assumptions, the effect of the increases in the needs allowance by £3.50 a week as part of Stage II and the further increase in October 1973, was that the pensioner's total income in October 1973 was below the needs allowance by £2.75, and his rent was therefore the minimum of £1.40 minus 25% of £2.75. This gave a total of 71p and meant that his net rent had gone down over the year. Even if his other income had gone up by 10%, his net rent would still have fallen. However, the discussion up to this point has been based on the crucial assumption that those eligible for rate and rent rebates do in fact claim them, and it is to the problem of take-up that we now turn.

For rent rebates and allowances no estimates are yet available about take-up; however, there is growing evidence that many people who are entitled to receive rate rebates do not do so. The *Circumstances of Families* report showed that in 1966 only 10% of families with incomes below assistance level had applied for a rate rebate, even though it is likely that most were eligible. When the rate rebate scheme began in 1966 there were 932,000 rebates granted, but since then the number has declined to 808,000 in 1971–2. Although the Minister said in 1971 that there was insufficient data to provide a reliable estimate of the take-up rate, there had earlier been an official forecast that one and a half million ratepayers would have been eligible. So the likelihood is that the take-up rate is 60% or less. An example of recent evidence for a specific area is Molly Meacher's survey of Islington. This survey showed a rate rebate take-up rate of only 19% (23% among pensioners) and these findings were *after* an extensive advertising campaign (Meacher 1972). These findings are perhaps best regarded as no more than straws in the wind. But they do suggest two general points which should be of concern to policy makers. First, that if experience with rent rebates shows a take-up rate no better than that indicated for rate rebates, then on that ground alone the government's housing policy requires serious reconsideration. Secondly, they are relevant to the planned reform of local government finance; if after this reform rates are to remain and are to be accompanied by a more extensive rebate system, then unless the take up is greatly improved, the reforms may place a considerable burden on many people with low incomes.

What the benefits will buy
Table 4.2 (column 1) shows the increase in money resources for the different households that we have been considering. As in the previous chapter we want to know what the money will buy, or in other words, the increase these households have had in terms of purchasing power. It is again not possible to do more than take a few cases, and the experience of other households may well be rather different. In each of the examples we are concerned with the level of disposable resources — that is net income minus housing costs — and for this purpose we need a price index for all items excluding housing. For pensioners we can use the official pensioner price index (Department of Employment 1973b). For the other types of household special indices have to be constructed. For an unemployed man with two children, the index for the low-paid worker used in the previous chapter seems appropriate; for single-parent families there is in-

Table 4.2 Purchasing power and benefits autumn 1972,
autumn 1973

	Increase in disposable money income[1] %	Minimum inflation %	Increase in purchasing power %	Extrapolated inflation %	Increase in purchasing power %
Single pensioner claiming SB[2]	14.0	7.3	6.7	11.0	3.0
Single pensioner with £5 other income not eligible for SB[3]	16.8	7.3	9.5	11.0	5.8
Single woman with two children* receiving SB for more than two years[2]	11.9	6.1	5.8	9.1	2.8
Unemployed man with two children* claiming SB[4]	9.3	6.1	3.2	9.1	0.2
Single woman with two children* receiving SB for less than two years[4]	9.1	6.1	3.0	9.1	0.0

* assumed to be aged 6 and 12

NOTES 1. Not allowing for any discretionary addition
2. Recipient of long-term addition (1972) and long-term weekly rate (1973)
3. Recipient of national insurance pension and rent and rate rebates
4. Not eligible for long-term addition or long-term weekly rate

sufficient evidence about their patterns of expenditure to construct a special index, and so the index for the low-paid worker is again used.

In Table 4.2 the two alternative assumptions made in the previous chapter about the rate of price increases are again adopted, and the resulting real increase in disposable resources for the different types of household is shown in columns 2 and 3. From these results we can clearly see that there has been discriminatory treatment of different categories of social security recipients. It is the 'long-term' recipients who have gained most in terms of increases in money incomes and in terms of purchasing power, and those not receiving the long-term rate may well have enjoyed no improvement at all over the year in terms of real disposable resources.

The results in Table 4.2 show the value of the benefits from 'peak' to 'peak', or in other words, the value of the benefits just after the 1972 increase compared with their value just after the 1973 increase. However, with the present rates of inflation, the loss of purchasing power between reviews is a serious matter. Therefore, in Table 4.3 we have calculated the real value of the supplementary pension at different dates over the period 1966—73 and have shown the decline in purchasing power between reviews. In addition to bringing out the small size of the actual gain in terms of purchasing power (less than 10% between 1966 and 1972), this also demonstrates clearly the need for frequent reviews. For example, the real value of the pension was reduced between autumn 1971 and autumn 1972 by no less than 46p. This reduction is a very large amount for a person trying to manage on £6 or so a week, yet the review period is the same as it was in the second half of the 1960s when inflation was a less serious problem: between 1966 and 1967 the fall in purchasing power was only 14p. Therefore, there is a strong case for a more frequent review of supplementary and other benefit levels, or for an automatic escalator clause of the kind used in many other countries. An escalator clause would mean, for example, that if the pensioner price index rose more than 2% since the last review, there would be an automatic increase in all benefit levels to take account of the price rise. The proposal about the 40p threshold for Stage III of the Incomes Policy makes such a change for non-wage earners all the more difficult to resist. The Chancellor of the Exchequer would lose the chance to play Lord Bountiful, but old people would gain a form of security in social security which would be of great value.

Table 4.3 The pensioner and rising prices

Purchasing power of single person's supplementary pension in terms of autumn 1972 prices

Autumn		£s per week
1966	after increase	6.53
1967	before increase	6.39
	after increase	6.74
1968	before increase	6.41
	after increase	6.82
1969	before increase	6.46
	after increase	6.78
1970	before increase	6.29
	after increase	6.77
1971	before increase	6.11
	after increase	6.76
1972	before increase	6.30
	after increase	7.15
1973	before increase—minimum inflation	6.66
	extrapolated inflation	6.44
	after increase—minimum inflation	7.60
	extrapolated inflation	7.34

NOTE
Supplementary pension includes long-term but no other additions

Conclusions

Although in broad terms the increase in social security benefits was probably enough to preserve the standard of living of those not in the labour force, the level of benefits as a percentage of average earnings is still well below the Beveridge target. The analysis in this chapter has also brought out a number of other disquieting events, or non-events, of 1973. First, the increase in the benefit given to the 'short-term' recipients of supplementary benefit, such as the unemployed, was significantly less than the increase given to pensioners. One can only hope that this does not reflect any revival of the old distinction between the 'deserving' and the 'undeserving' poor. Secondly, the main benefits have increased at least as fast as rising prices, but there are elements in the system which remain constant for long periods and therefore tend to reduce the actual benefit derived. The government should make sure that all social security benefits are protected against inflation. The last point is that at present rates of inflation annual reviews do not give sufficient protection. Automatic reviews would be better. Benefits would then increase whenever the rise in the cost of living exceeded a specified percentage.

References

Department of Employment, (1973a) *Department of Employment Gazette*, vol. LXXXI, no. 8, HMSO.
   (1973b) 'Pensioner index', *Department of Employment Gazette*, vol. LXXXI, no. 9, HMSO.
Department of Health and Social Security, (1972) 'National insurance benefit rates from October 1972', *Leaflet 196.72*, HMSO.
   (1973a) 'National insurance benefit rates from October 1973', *Leaflet 196.73*, HMSO.
   (1973b) *Review of social security benefits and associated changes*, cmnd. 5288, HMSO.
Molly Meacher, (1972) *Rate rebates and means-tested benefits*, 'CPAG Poverty Research Series 1.
Ministry of Social Security, (1967) *Circumstances of Families*, HMSO.

The previous three chapters have been mainly
about what happened to poorer people in 1973.
Decisions were also taken in the year about
what should happen in the future. Tony Lynes
discusses the significance of the Social
Security Act which has passed into law in
1973, and also the very important proposal
for tax credits on which a select committee
of the House of Commons reported in
1973 — this against the background of the
many smaller changes made in the
system of social security since the last
general election.

5   Policy on Social Security
TONY LYNES

The changes in the social security system made or proposed
in, or up to, 1973 fall under three headings: minor changes
which while important to those directly affected have not
radically altered the main structure; the more radical changes
for retirement pensions provided for in the Social Security
Act 1973, and due to be implemented in April 1975; and the
tax credit scheme, which has yet to be embodied in
legislation but is expected to commence in 1978 if the
government's plans are not frustrated. I will deal with these
three changes in turn, starting with the measures already
enacted and implemented since 1970.

The Conservative Party's 1970 election manifesto contained a section headed 'Care for those in need' — a title
which aptly reflected the school of thought within the party
which favoured a more 'selective' approach. But in the debate
between 'selectivists' and 'universalists' during the preceding
years the identification of selectivity with means testing had

become less marked. The underlying intention to reduce public expenditure by concentrating benefits on those most in need, found practical expression increasingly in proposals for benefits payable to particular categories whose claim to priority rested on grounds other than individually proved low income.

The specific measures enacted between 1970 and 1973 embodied this approach. They were mostly of two kinds: new or increased benefits for selected groups of recipients regarded as having a particularly strong claim to help from the state; and the reduction or partial withdrawal of benefits payable to those whose claim was regarded as the opposite. In principle, one cannot reasonably quarrel with this policy, if all that is required is gradual adaptation of the existing system to accommodate changing needs and priorities. Even within this limited perspective, however, the effectiveness of 'selectivity' depends on the basis of selection, both of those to whom more help is to be given and of those from whom benefits are to be withdrawn. If the legislation of the past three years is examined from this point of view there are grounds for questioning whether the priorities it reflects are the right ones.

The attendance allowance
The most important of the new benefits, and the one about which, in terms of priorities, there can be the least doubt, is the attendance allowance for disabled persons; 'a tax-free allowance for adults and children over the age of 2 who are severely disabled, either physically or mentally, and have needed a lot of looking after for at least six months' (Department of Health and Social Security 1973). The principle of compensation for the cost of attendance was already found in the industrial injuries and war pension schemes, but its extension to those disabled through other causes is a big step forward, not only because it brings much-needed help to a substantial number of severely disabled people (the number of persons receiving the attendance allowance in July 1973 was about 100,000) but also because the underlying principle of compensation for the expenses resulting from disability, once accepted, is bound to

be extended to cover a wider range of needs and broader categories of disabled people. Already the allowance has been extended to cover those in need of attention either by day or by night (originally only those requiring both day and night attendance qualified).

An important feature of the attendance allowance is the fact that, unlike other national insurance benefits, the allowance is not dependent on attachment to the labour market or payment of a minimum number of contributions. Only the needs of the disabled person are taken into account, not his present or past employment status. Disabled housewives qualify, as do those disabled from birth or childhood. This is so obviously sensible that it would hardly be worth commenting on but for the fact that in the past all national insurance benefits have been subject to contribution conditions, even where such conditions were neither necessary nor appropriate; the most absurd example being the £25 maternity grant which a substantial minority of mothers still cannot claim because neither they nor their husbands have paid the required number of contributions. Generally it is those most in need (eg unmarried mothers) who do not qualify. Yet Ministers solemnly defend present practice in the name of the 'contributory principle'. One must be thankful, therefore, that the attendance allowance is entirely free of contribution conditions.

Invalidity benefit

The same cannot be said of the new invalidity benefit payable in place of sickness benefit after twenty-eight weeks of sickness. The benefit consists of two elements: an 'invalidity pension', equivalent to the basic flat rate retirement pension (£7.75 for a single person from October 1973); and an 'invalidity allowance', which varies with the age at which incapacity began from 50p for those aged 45 or over, to £1.60 for those under 35. No invalidity allowance is payable to a person falling sick when already within five years of pension age (ie a man aged 60 or over or a woman aged 55 or over). Since invalidity benefit replaces sickness benefit it is only paid if the contribution conditions for sickness benefit are satisfied. Hence it does not help those who have never been able to work and to pay contributions. It does, however, go some way towards cushioning the long-term sick against the sudden reduction in their benefit resulting from the fact that the earnings-related supplement of up to £8.47 per week (from January 1974) is payable only from the third to the twenty-eighth week of sickness. For a single person the cushion is decidedly thin: instead of sickness benefit of £7.35 per week plus the earnings-related supplement, he gets from £7.75 to £9.35 depending on his age. Those with dependants do better. A man with a wife and two children gets sickness benefit of £15.60 plus earnings-related supplement; whereas after twenty-eight weeks his invalidity benefit amounts to between £19.20 and £20.80. The rules regarding the wife's earnings also become less stringent once invalidity benefit is in payment. If she earns more than £4.55 while he is drawing sickness benefit, he loses the whole of the dependent wife's allowance of £4.55; but invalidity benefit is reduced only if the wife earns more than £9.59, and even then the reduction is gradual.

Invalidity benefit, therefore, is intended primarily to meet the needs of *families* where the breadwinner's earnings are interrupted by a long period of sickness. The benefit rates can hardly be described as lavish; indeed many families in this situation will still be dependent on supplementary benefit or, at best, will have their income raised marginally above that level. Only if the wife can go out to work or the family has other financial resources will their total income reach a level which could be regarded as adequate. Compared with the situation that existed up to 1971, in which the long-term sick were entitled only to the basic flat-rate sickness benefit, the new arrangements, as far as they go, are a welcome improvement; but they do not go very far.

The very limited increases given to single persons by the change from sickness to invalidity benefit is only one of the scheme's limitations, but a significant one, since it reflects the generally unsympathetic attitude towards the single. It is true that a single person who has been sick for over six months and is not in hospital is likely to be living with relatives, but it does not follow that he should be compelled to rely on them for financial support.

Many of those entitled to invalidity benefit found that the increase in their income in September 1971 was illusory, because their supplementary benefit was reduced by the same amount. The official estimate was that the proportion who would get no net increase for this reason was about a third (*Hansard*, 13 July 1971). This give-and-take effect is, of course, a normal feature of the supplementary benefit (SB) scheme, which, in principle, is intended to raise the recipient's total income to a minimum level represented by the SB scale. There are, however, exceptions. For example, if the attendance allowance is awarded to a disabled person in receipt of SB, an equivalent amount is added to the normal supplementary benefit scale in assessing his needs. Similarly, the first £2 of a disablement pension is ignored in calculating the amount of SB payable. No such exception is made for invalidity benefit, which is taken into account in full. This is not because the supplementary benefit scheme treats long-term and short-term sickness alike, but because it defines long-term claimants as those who have been drawing SB for *two years*. During that period they can receive more than the basic supplementary benefit entitlement only if they can show that they have special needs. Even after two years the automatic addition to the normal benefit rates to take account of long-term needs is only 90p or £1 for a single person and £1.20 for a married couple.

Like sickness benefit, invalidity benefit is payable only to those certified as incapable of work. It thus acts as a disincentive to those who after a long period of illness would like to take on some part-time work but are not fit enough to be 'signed off' by the doctor. An exception is made for work undertaken as part of the treatment of the illness, but even this applies only where the weekly earnings do not exceed £4.50. The idea of partial incapacity is not recognised in the national insurance scheme, and it is regrettable that the introduction of invalidity benefit was not used as an opportunity for remedying this serious defect.

The combined effect of sickness, invalidity and supplementary benefits upon the sick and disabled can be summarised as follows:

(a) For short spells of sickness (up to two weeks) the

only insurance benefit payable is the basic flat-rate benefit of £7.35 for a single person or £11.90 for a married man whose wife is not working, plus allowances for children. Even this is not paid for the first three days of sickness unless there was an earlier spell of sickness or unemployment in the previous thirteen weeks (until 1971, benefit for the three 'waiting days' was paid in arrears if the period of incapacity lasted for two weeks, but this provision was abolished by the Social Security Act 1971).

(b) From the third to the twenty-eighth week of incapacity, an earnings-related supplement is added. For those with a good earnings record in the relevant tax year the total benefit payable is substantially above SB level, though still far below their normal net earnings unless supplemented by the employer. Those with low earnings or periods off work in the relevant tax year, on the other hand, get little or nothing from the earnings-related scheme and are likely to have to claim SB.

(c) After twenty-eight weeks invalidity benefit commences, payable at higher rates than flat-rate sickness benefit, but in many cases lower than the combined flat-rate and earnings-related benefit. Those with working wives do relatively well at this stage; single men and women are reduced to near or below SB level.

(d) Those claiming SB get a small addition after two years (counting from the date when they claimed SB not from the onset of incapacity) if they are not already receiving it on a discretionary basis.

(e) For those incapacitated for work from birth or childhood but not severely enough disabled to qualify for an attendance allowance, there is only SB.

(f) Rehabilitation of the long-term sick is discouraged by rules preventing a gradual return to work while drawing sickness or invalidity benefit (SB can be paid to a person in part-time work but only £1 or £2 of earnings are disregarded in calculating the benefit payable).

(g) Neither sickness nor invalidity benefit provides for the additional expenses resulting from disablement, though the attendance allowance may be payable in the more extreme cases.

What this summary shows is that there are wide variations of treatment, not only between one category and another but even within the same category, and that these differences are largely unrelated to the real needs of the sick and their dependants. The introduction of invalidity benefit has done something to improve the situation of the long-term sick who before 1971 were entitled only to the basic flat-rate sickness benefit, but most of the anomalies remain. A House of Lords amendment to the 1973 Social Security Bill required the Secretary of State for Social Services to review social security provision for chronically sick and disabled persons and to lay a report before Parliament by 31 October 1974. One can only hope that the review will lead both to further improvements and to a more rational structure of benefits.

Benefits for the unemployed
With the relatively high levels of unemployment experienced in the last few years, one might reasonably have expected 'selectivity' to operate in favour of more adequate unemployment benefits. The unemployed, however, rank among the less 'deserving' objects of state support. Being by definition capable of work, they arouse the greatest fears about the disincentive effects of social security. As Paul Dean, Under-Secretary of State for Health and Social Security, put it in a recent debate: 'One has to be careful that one does not get into a position where it becomes comparatively easy for a small number of people to sit back and rely on benefit, when jobs are available for them and when they could be earning their living. This is one of the reasons which make a strong case for a distinction between the unemployed and the chronically sick and disabled.' (House of Commons Standing Committee F, 17 May 1973, col. 63). Selectivity, therefore, tends to operate against the unemployed, both by denying them the benefits conferred on other social security beneficiaries and by imposing deterrent penalties on those suspected of being 'voluntarily unemployed'.

The most blatant discrimination against the unemployed is that their insurance benefit is limited to 312 days (i.e. fifty-two 6-day weeks), after which they are entitled only to means-tested SB. This restriction is not new. What is new is the decision to treat the unemployed, even while still entitled to unemployment benefit, less generously than the sick. For the first twenty-eight weeks sickness and unemployment benefits are identical. After that the unemployed revert to the basic flat-rate benefit. There is nothing comparable to invalidity benefit for the long-term unemployed, though the needs of a family whose breadwinner has been unemployed for six months are likely to be as great as if he had been sick — perhaps greater, since he will not have had the benefit of an employer's sick pay scheme and will probably have exhausted any savings he may have had.

Those unemployed for shorter periods do not necessarily qualify for unemployment benefit. They are disqualified, normally for six weeks, if they left their last job voluntarily without just cause, were sacked for misconduct, or have refused a reasonable offer of work. Moreover, if the insurance officer suspects that a man *may* have committed one of these 'offences' he can suspend his benefit pending investigation. An unemployed person who is disqualified or has his benefit suspended on these grounds can apply for SB. Until 1971 it was the practice of the Supplementary Benefits Commission (SBC) in such cases to reduce his SB by 75p per week, using its discretionary powers which permit reductions where there are 'exceptional circumstances'. This practice was defended on the grounds that a person disqualified under the insurance scheme might otherwise be just as well off on SB. An attempt to impose a bigger penalty by Act of Parliament, taking the matter out of the Commission's hands, had been made by the Labour government in the National Superannuation Bill which was killed by the 1970 election. The Conservatives were more successful, and the Social Security Act 1971 imposed a reduction of 40% of the SB scale rate for a single person, or £2.85 per week at current benefit rates. Sir Keith Joseph, the Secretary of State, announcing both this change and a number of measures to reduce the SB entitlement of strikers and their families, admitted that he had not consulted the SBC about these provisions of the Bill (*Hansard,* 29 March 1971), and it seems reasonable to infer that they did not have the Commission's approval.

It is not surprising that the SBC should have felt some misgivings about the policy foisted on it by the government. Although the 75p deduction made by the Commission might seem to indicate that its attitude to the workshy was unduly lenient, this was certainly not so. The Commission's officers are authorised to refuse benefit altogether in cases where jobs are known to be available and there are no dependants who would suffer hardship as a result. According to official statistics, there were about 15,000 such cases in 1971 (Department of Health and Social Security and Department of Employment 1973). The Commission also uses its discretionary powers to cut off benefit in large numbers of cases after four weeks' warning, solely on the ground that the claimant, having been given this warning, has not re-applied at the end of the four weeks. Draconian as these measures may seem, they at least have the merit that the Commission can decide when they can be imposed without serious risk of hardship. The 40% reduction, however, is virtually automatic. In theory, the Commission can use its discretionary powers to make only a 75p reduction in exceptional cases where the 40% reduction would cause hardship; but in practice its officers are far too busy to examine each case individually for this purpose. What makes the 40% reduction particularly objectionable is the fact that it is imposed not only where the insurance officer has decided that the conditions for disqualification are satisfied, but also where unemployment benefit is merely suspended on the basis of a suspicion which several weeks later may turn out to have been without foundation.

Apart from these specific objections to the penalty imposed by section 1 (2) of the Social Security Act 1971, the Commission must have been disturbed by the effects on public opinion of measures of this kind, which brand large numbers of unemployed men as workshy and reinforce prejudice against the unemployed generally. Such prejudices were further encouraged by the appointment of the Committee on Abuse of Social Security Benefits under the chairmanship of Sir Henry Fisher. The Fisher Committee's report, published in March 1973, was on the whole moderate in tone and in places openly critical of the methods used to curb 'abuse'; but few people will read the report, compared with the very large numbers who will have seen the appointment of the Committee as confirmation of the belief that abuse of the system is rife.

Whether the workshy really exist or not, it is certainly true that 'for certain groups, particularly those with large families, more, or nearly as much, money may sometimes be obtained by remaining out of work as by gaining employment' (Hill *et al.* 1973). The key to this problem is to be found not in the social security system as such, but in the plight of the low-paid worker and his family and the failure of successive governments to ensure that their income, from wages and family allowances (or other social benefits such as family income supplement (FIS)), is sufficient to provide a reasonable standard of living. This failure is discussed in Chapters 2 and 3, but it is important to stress here that until it is remedied it is futile to expect social security to be adequate for the unemployed. As long as substantial numbers of workers and their families are living in poverty, governments will continue to insist that they remain in poverty during periods of unemployment.

Earnings-related supplements
Flat-rate sickness and unemployment benefits are supplemented after the first two weeks by an earnings-related benefit payable for up to twenty-six weeks. The individual's annual earnings are divided by 50 to arrive at a weekly earnings figure on which the supplement is calculated. The first £10 of weekly earnings are ignored for this purpose. This means not only that employees with very low earnings derive little benefit from the scheme but that those with fluctuating or intermittent earnings are treated unfairly. To take an extreme case, a man who earned £20 a week in 1972–3 but was able to work for only twenty-five weeks, would have a weekly earnings figure of £10 and would not be eligible for any earnings-related supplement if he was again sick or unemployed during 1974, in spite of having contributed to

the scheme for half the previous tax year. Still more unfair is the effect in such cases of the rule that the earnings-related supplement when added to the flat-rate benefit must not exceed 85% of the weekly earnings. Where the earnings figure is artificially low because of gaps in the earnings record for the previous year, the 85% ceiling, intended to prevent benefit from exceeding normal net earnings, merely imposes a further penalty on those unfortunate enough to experience periods of sickness or unemployment in successive years.

When earnings-related supplements were introduced in 1966 there may have been some justification for sacrificing equity to simplicity in order to get the scheme into operation as quickly as possible. Eight years later, one would hope that some means would have been found by which the initial inequities would be reduced if not eliminated. Instead, with effect from May 1973, the method of calculating the supplement was changed in a way which made it even less satisfactory, by regulations which attracted little attention when they were approved by Parliament in June 1972. The effect of the change is that weekly earnings for the tax year ending on 5 April, instead of being used for calculating the supplement from the beginning of May, are not taken into account until January. A person who is sick or unemployed towards the end of 1974 will receive a supplement based on his earnings in the year to 5 April 1973. This has one important advantage: it will no longer be necessary to produce evidence of the previous year's earnings when claiming the supplement, since the necessary information will be obtained from the Department of Health and Social Security computer. But in a period of rising earnings it will also mean a significant reduction in the amount of benefit payable between May and December each year compared with what would have been payable under the old formula.

In one respect the scheme has become more responsive to the needs of the lower paid than when it was first introduced. The lower limit of the band of earnings on which the supplement is calculated was originally £9 per week and is now only £10, despite the much greater proportional increase in average earnings. This means that a larger proportion of the low-paid worker's earnings are taken into account than when the scheme started in 1966.

Earnings-related contributions, on the other hand, are still levied on earnings over £9, with the result that contributions paid on earnings between £9 and £10 per week do not earn any supplement – a singularly indefensible situation. This, however, is just one more anomaly in a scheme' which is badly in need of a radical overhaul. It is disappointing to find it re-enacted in virtually its present form in the Social Security Act 1973. But this may not be the government's last word on the subject, since the Explanatory Memorandum on the Social Security Bill (Department of Health and Social Security 1972) states that the desirability of further changes in short-term benefits is being considered.

Widows under 50
Until 1971 a widow with no dependent children did not qualify for a widow's pension unless she was aged 50 or over at the time of her husband's death. Similarly, a widowed mother did not qualify for a pension when her youngest child reached the age of 19 unless she was then 50 or over. It was assumed that a woman under 50 could normally be expected to take a job and maintain herself without further help from the state. The result of this rule, however, was that, by being just the wrong side of the age barrier, a widow could lose ten years' pension. In the National Superannuation Bill the Labour government had proposed to introduce a more flexible arrangement by which a widow aged between 40 and 50 on the operative date would receive a scaled-down pension. Like the attendance allowance for the disabled, this uncontroversial proposal was taken over from the defunct Bill and enacted by the Conservative government. The reduced pensions were paid from April 1971.

The over 80s
Two more examples of the policy of selective benefits for the 'deserving' must be mentioned – the 'old persons' pensions' for those aged 80 and over who did not previously qualify for a retirement pension, and the 25p 'age addition' paid to all retirement pensioners over 80. The problem of the 'non-pensioners' had long been an embarrassment to both Labour

and Conservative governments. In a non-contributory scheme it would be absurd to exclude a relatively small group of very old people from the benefits payable to other people over pension age. In a contributory insurance scheme, however, it is not easy to justify paying the same benefits to those who have not contributed as to those who have, especially when the decision not to pay contributions was in many cases made voluntarily by the individuals concerned. Whatever the merits of the case, public sympathy was strongly on the side of those old people who had been left out of the national insurance scheme in 1948; hence the undertaking in the 1970 Conservative election manifesto to 'give some pension as of right to the over 80s who now get no retirement pension at all'. The word 'some' was a clear recognition of the difficulty of treating the non-pensioners in the same way as those who had earned pensions by their contributions. In the event, it required two Acts to fulfil even this limited pledge. The National Insurance (Old persons' and widows' pensions and attendance allowance) Act 1970, provided a reduced pension (£3 for a single person and £4.85 for a couple, compared with the full pension rates of £5 and £8.10) for those left out of the scheme in 1948. The government then discovered that an unknown number of other people over 80, for one reason or another, had not qualified for a retirement pension. The National Insurance Act 1971, therefore, extended the old persons' pension to cover all the over 80s not already getting a pension.

Judged in the light of the government's selectivist philosophy, the old persons' pension is open to the criticism that many of the neediest recipients were already getting supplementary pensions of over £3 a week and therefore gained nothing. The 25p age addition introduced by the National Insurance Act 1971, on the other hand, benefited all the over 80s, since a similar increase was given in the supplementary pension scale for them. Had the government been genuinely concerned to provide for the needs of very old people, however, it would hardly have regarded an addition of 25p per week as adequate. Nor would it have left the addition unaltered in the two subsequent reviews of pension rates, in which the basic pension has been raised by

29%.

Considered as a whole, the structural changes in social security provision between 1970 and 1973 have done little to remedy the deficiencies of the system. Apart from the attendance allowance, the policy of selectivity has not been notably successful in helping those most in need. What it has done is to confer some additional benefits on 'deserving' groups such as the very old and some (but by no means all) of the long-term sick, while penalising those regarded as less deserving — particularly the unemployed and the 'workshy'.

The Social Security Act 1973

The aspect of social security which arouses far more public interest than any other is what is done for the elderly. Most people will live to be retirement pensioners even if they have never received any other social security benefit. And most people have relatives who already are pensioners. Numerically, pensioners are far more important than any other category of social security beneficiaries. At the end of 1971 there were over seven and a half million pensioners, compared with about a million people drawing sickness or invalidity benefit and 400,000 drawing unemployment benefit at any one time. Pensioners are also by far the biggest group of *long-term* beneficiaries and account for over two million of the three million weekly payments of SB.

For all these reasons the provision of adequate pensions is bound to figure prominently in any plan for the future development of the social security system. Given the inadequacy of both the existing flat-rate pension and the 1961 graduated pension scheme, the need for a new and more effective approach is particularly urgent. The present government's solution is the Social Security Act 1973.

The Act provides for the continuation of flat-rate pensions as under the existing scheme. It does virtually nothing for the existing generation of pensioners. They will benefit from the annual review to which the government is now committed, but this undertaking had already been put into effect before the 1973 Act was passed. The only new right conferred on them by the Act is a guarantee that the annual increases will be sufficient to maintain the purchasing power of the

pension, but this is less than governments of both parties
have achieved in recent years. Indeed, the accepted con-
vention is that the flat-rate pension should rise roughly in line
with average earnings, thus more than maintaining its
purchasing power, though it is true that the increases given in
1967 and 1969 fell short of this objective.

Since the failure to help existing pensioners was the most
serious criticism of the Labour government's national superannuation scheme it may seem surprising that the Conservatives have done no better. The main object of the Social
Security Act, however, was to encourage the growth of
earnings-related occupational pension schemes, and a major
expansion of the flat-rate scheme would have conflicted with
this aim. More and better occupational schemes may produce
bigger pensions in the future, but they are no help to those
who have already retired – and even in the future the higher
benefits will emerge extremely slowly by contrast with the
national superannuation scheme which was to have matured
in twenty years.

A fundamental difference between state and occupational
pensions is that the former are financed on a pay-as-you-go
basis, while the latter are in general funded, the contributions
being invested to provide pensions for the present generation
of contributors when they reach retirement age. Thus, if
more money is channelled into occupational schemes, the
immediate effect is merely to increase the size of their
accumulated funds. In the state scheme, on the contrary, an
increase in contributions makes possible an immediate
improvement in pensions already in payment. In theory there
is no reason why both state and occupational schemes should
not be expanded simultaneously, thus helping both present
and future pensioners. The cost of doing this, however,
would be very high.

Even in their present form, the new arrangements coming
into effect in April 1975 will involve a considerable increase
in contributions for employed persons and employers,
especially for those not at present covered by occupational
schemes. From that date, all employees who are not members
of a recognised occupational scheme will have to be brought
into the State Reserve Pension Scheme – a fully funded

scheme operating on commercial principles and financed by contributions of 4% of earnings up to about one and a half times the national average (2½% payable by the employer and 1½% by the employee). Some occupational schemes providing benefits at the minimum level required for recognition by the Occupational Pensions Board may be able to manage with total contributions of less than 4%, but usually the cost will be considerably higher. Assuming that a contribution of only 4% has to be added to the basic contributions payable under the Act, which will in future be wholly earnings-related, the total contribution rate will be 16.75%. The way in which this is divided between employee and employer will vary, but in employments covered by the reserve scheme the employer will pay 10% and the employee 6.75%. The present contribution rate for a man earning £40 a week and not contracted out of the graduated scheme is just over 6%, while his employer pays 6.9%, so their combined contributions will rise by over 3.75% in 1975, from less than 13% to 16.75%, most of the increase falling on the employer. For a man earning only £20 a week the present contribution rates are: employee 7%, employer 8.75%: total 15.75%. Even at this very low level of earnings, therefore, the new contributions will be 1% higher, though the whole of the increase will fall on the employer. Whether it is the employer or the employee who pays, however, it is clear that by imposing these higher contribution rates to pay for future pensions the government has made it difficult, if not impossible, to raise more money through the contribution system to finance an increase for existing pensioners.

Whether it would be justifiable to condemn very large numbers of the present retired generation to poverty in order to provide adequate pensions for those retiring in the next century is, to say the least, doubtful. The Social Security Act 1973, however, is unlikely to achieve even this distant aim. Neither the standards required for recognition of an occupational scheme nor the benefits offered by the reserve scheme can be regarded as offering a reasonable standard of living to future generations of pensioners. Many occupational schemes will provide far more than the minimum laid down in the Act, but others will not, while the number of

employees in the reserve scheme will certainly run into
millions, despite the efforts of the insurance industry to
persuade employers to set up occupational schemes.

The minimum annual pension to be provided by a
recognised occupational scheme is, for men, 1% of reckonable earnings throughout the relevant period of employment.
For women, the minimum pension is only 0.7% of reckonable earnings, to allow for the fact that women can draw
their pensions five years earlier than men and, on average, can
expect to live longer. These rates apply only to schemes in
which pensions are increased after payment of them begins
(of the permitted methods of calculating the increases, the
simplest and the one most likely to be adopted is a fixed
increase of 3% per annum); where no post-retirement
increases are given, the minimum pension rate is higher —
1.25% of reckonable earnings for men, 0.9% for women.
Table 5.1 shows the minimum pension payable at age 65 for
a man or 60 for a woman in a scheme giving post-retirement
increases, as a percentage of earnings at retirement, assuming
that the earnings of the particular employee have risen
annually by 6% or 9% (the latter figure being nearer to the
experience of recent years).

*Table 5.1 Minimum Pension payable by recognised
occupational scheme as percentage of earnings at retirement*

Age at start of scheme	Number of years' contributions	Pension as percentage of earnings at retirement, if earnings have risen by	
		6% pa	9% pa
Men			
54	10	8	7
44	20	12	9
21	43	16	11
Women			
49	10	5	5
39	20	8	7
21	38	11	8

Sources: Hansard, Written Answers, 1 March 1973, cols. *427–8*, and
2 March 1973, cols. *463–4*.

To see what these figures mean in terms of total pension, the flat-rate pension must be added. For a man whose earnings throughout his career are equal to the national average for male industrial workers, assuming that the flat-rate pension remains roughly 20% of average earnings, his minimum pension after contributing to an occupational scheme for 43 years would be either 36% or 31% of his pre-retirement earnings, depending on whether the annual rate of increase of earnings is 6% or 9%. At present earnings levels, this would give a pension in the region of £12–13 a week for a single person. The supplementary pension rate is £8.15 plus rent, but the first £1 of an occupational pension is disregarded. Assuming that SB rates continue to rise roughly in line with average earnings, therefore, a man who had earned the average wage and contributed to a recognised occupational scheme offering benefits at the minimum level, from 1975 until his retirement in 2018, would quite probably find that his total income was below supplementary benefit level. Men earning less than the average wage will be still more likely to find themselves in this situation, while women, whose earnings are in general lower, will fare worst of all.

In schemes giving no post-retirement increases, the pension will start at a higher level but its real value is likely to be seriously eroded by inflation within a few years. Where post-retirement increases are given, a rate of increase of 3% per annum is unlikely even to maintain the purchasing power of the pension, still less to maintain its value relative to average earnings. The longer the pensioner lives, therefore, the less adequate his pension will become and the more likely he will be to have to apply for SB.

The reserve scheme differs from most occupational schemes in being based on the principle of 'money purchase': the amount of pension earned by each year's contributions depends on the number of years during which the money will earn interest in the reserve pension fund. Contributions paid by men and women in their twenties are worth twice as much as contributions of the same amount paid by those in their forties. In schemes which place the same value on contributions regardless of the age at which they are paid, there is a considerable degree of redistribution in favour of those

entering the scheme towards the end of their working lives.
The absence of this redistributive element in the reserve
scheme makes it particularly unattractive to older employees.
A man aged 54 at the commencement of the scheme could
expect to earn a pension of about 4% of his pre-retirement
earnings, compared with the 7% or 8% minimum occupational pension shown in Table 5.1 for a man of this age.
For a woman aged 49 in 1975, the reserve scheme pension
would be about 3% of pre-retirement earnings, compared
with the 5% she could expect from an occupational scheme.
For younger workers, on the other hand, the reserve scheme
is more attractive than an occupational scheme offering only
the minimum benefits required for recognition. Every £1 of
contributions paid into the reserve scheme fund for a man
aged 21 earns nearly twice as much pension as a recognised
occupational scheme would have to provide in respect of the
same amount of earnings. Anybody contributing to the
reserve scheme for the whole of his working life from age 21,
therefore, will probably finish up with a bigger pension than
he would have got from an occupational scheme at the
minimum level, though the difference is unlikely to be more
than about 5% of his pre-retirement earnings. Those retiring
in the next 30 years, however, will get even smaller pensions
from the reserve scheme than the minimum payable by an
occupational scheme. Given the choice, older employees
would no doubt prefer to be in an occupational scheme, but
the Social Security Act leaves the power of decision with the
employer. For an employer whose work force is predominantly middle-aged, setting up an occupational pension
scheme is expensive, and he may well prefer to contribute to
the reserve scheme.

At the end of 1971 five million of the seven and a half
million retirement pensioners were women, another half
million women under 60 were drawing widows' benefits, and
112,000 women over 80 were getting the old persons'
pension introduced in that year. Out of 1,537,000 single
pensioners on supplementary benefit 1,330,000 were women.
One of the most glaring deficiencies of occupational pension
schemes is their failure to provide for the needs of women,
whether in retirement or in widowhood. The Social Security

Act 1973, does little to remedy this deficiency. Discrimination against women is found both in the reserve scheme pension formula and in the minimum pensions required for recognition of occupational schemes. Any earnings-related pension scheme is bound to be unfair to women as long as women's earnings are themselves unfairly low compared with men's. Unequal pay means unequal pensions. But the Social Security Act goes further than this and enshrines the principle that even with equal pay women will still get smaller pensions than men. The government attempts to justify this on two grounds: first, that women are allowed to draw their pensions at 60 while men must wait until they are 65, and secondly, that women live longer than men. The earlier retirement age for women dates back to 1940, when it simply meant that women were entitled to draw the flat-rate pension five years earlier than men. With the introduction of earnings-related pensions based on contributions paid, earlier retirement has become decidedly less advantageous and the case for reverting to a single pension age for men and women is now very strong. If the government insists on maintaining the existing situation, it should also ensure that the pension drawn by a woman at 60 is as generous, in relation to her earnings, as that drawn by a man at 65. The more logical solution, however, would be to have the same normal retirement age for women as for men.

The second argument used to justify the lower pension rates for women in the Social Security Act 1973 — their greater expectation of life — has some force if the provision of pensions is seen purely as a commercial operation. It costs more, on average, to provide a pension of a given amount for a woman than for a man: therefore, for equal contributions, women must get smaller pensions. Social insurance, however, is not a commercial operation but a pooling of risks by the whole community. Viewed in this way it is no more logical to pay lower pensions to women because they live longer than to pay lower unemployment benefit to manual workers because they are likely to experience more unemployment than white-collar workers. Indeed the fact that women have to manage for a longer time on their pensions makes it more important, not less, that those pensions should be adequate.

Moreover, the assumption that a woman is likely to live longer than a man is at best a very crude one. It leaves out of account all the other factors influencing longevity which cause women in some social class and occupational groups to have a *lower* expectation of life than men in other such groups.

So far as the basic flat-rate state pension is concerned, married women will continue to be treated as appendages of their husbands, entitled to a small dependant's pension by virtue of the husband's contributions. If they go out to work, they will be allowed, as at present, to opt out of the main part of the weekly social security contribution. Those who choose to pay full contributions are anyway unlikely to earn a worthwhile pension, since women's earnings are generally low and they are likely to have substantial gaps in their contribution record for periods off work due to child-bearing and other exigencies of family life. The possibility of crediting contributions during periods when a woman is prevented by domestic ties from taking paid employment was considered and rejected on somewhat unconvincing grounds by the Labour government in 1969 (Department of Health and Social Security 1969). The present government shows no sign of even having considered the question.

The provisions of the Social Security Act 1973 concerning widows are equally inadequate. Under the reserve scheme, as in the existing graduated pension scheme, a widow will receive half her husband's pension entitlement at the date of his death, together with any subsequent bonuses declared by the Reserve Pension Board. This is much less generous than the Labour government's proposal to allow a widow to inherit the whole of her husband's pension entitlement, including a notional entitlement in respect of contributions up to his sixty-fifth birthday if he died before that age. Because reserve scheme widows' pensions will be based only on contributions actually paid, it will be many years before they begin to reach significant amounts, and even then they will not be enough to assure the widow a decent standard of living. Nevertheless, the reserve scheme is far ahead of most occupational schemes in this respect. The Act requires a recognised occupational scheme to provide a widow's pension of half the husband's personal pension entitlement, but with only the same inadequate protection from inflation that applies to pensions awarded at normal pension age, despite the much longer periods for which widows' pensions may be payable. If the husband dies before normal pension age the employer has the option of commuting the widow's pension for a lump sum, and many employers will prefer to do this as a matter of administrative convenience, whether it is in the widow's interests or not. Even these limited requirements, however, go further than the provisions of most existing occupational schemes and many employers are having to amend their schemes in this respect — a small but welcome improvement.

The provisions of the 1973 Social Security Act dealing with preservation of occupational pension rights are similar to those proposed by the Labour government and will go some way towards ensuring that employees who change their jobs do not lose their pension rights, but the protection offered is far from complete. In particular, periods of employment of less than five years are not covered by the preservation requirements, except in respect of the minimum benefits required for recognition of the scheme (or equivalent rights in the reserve scheme). In this, as in so many other respects, the Act reflects the government's anxiety to set standards low enough to accommodate the majority of existing occupational schemes, regardless of whether those standards are adequate to meet the needs of future generations of pensioners. The consequence is that the reserve scheme, like the present graduated scheme, has had to be made unattractive enough not to offer serious competition to the insurance industry. Indeed, the reserve scheme is not even to be allowed to compete on equal terms, since its members will not qualify for tax relief on their contributions as they would if they were contributing to an occupational scheme.

It is conceivable that the 1973 Act may be repealed within the next few years and a new start made, priority being given to the provision of adequate pensions to those already over retirement age. Assuming that this does not happen, however, can anything be done to improve their relative position in the context of existing policies? It is possible that the pressure of public demand could become so strong that the government would be compelled to raise the flat-rate pension substantially, despite the increases in taxes or contributions that would be necessary. Another possible way out of the moral dilemma created by the decision to channel into funded pension schemes the money that could otherwise have been paid to the existing generation of pensioners, would be to compel these schemes to invest a substantial proportion of any increase in their accumulated funds in government loan stock. The money borrowed in this way could be used to pay a special supplement to all existing pensioners. The loan would be repaid out of future taxation. As occupational schemes reached maturity the rate of growth of their funds would decline and less money would be available for the supplement, which would gradually be replaced by the pensions emerging from the occupational schemes.

For the present, however, the only prospect of an improvement in the standard of living of the retired generation, other than the annual increases needed to maintain the present level of inadequacy, is to be found in the tax credit scheme for which they will probably have to wait until 1978 at the earliest.

Tax credits

A Green Paper, *Proposals for a tax-credit system* was published in October 1972 and subsequently considered by a select committee of the House of Commons whose report was published in July 1973. The majority of the select committee reported in favour of the scheme with some important modifications. Three of the Labour members opposed it. In the Queen's speech of 30 October 1973 legislation about tax credit was included.

Tax credits are a device for giving the benefit of income tax allowances to those with incomes below the tax-paying threshold. Tax allowances of the existing type are deducted from income to arrive at the net figure on which tax is payable. Under the proposed scheme, from 1978 (if the present timetable is adhered to) all income will be taxed, but a tax credit based on the individual's family circumstances will be set against the tax payable. If the credit exceeds the liability, the difference will be paid as a cash benefit.

The tax credit scheme was not conceived as a remedy for poverty in Britain so much as a rationalisation of existing taxation and social security arrangements. As the Green Paper explained, it was the outcome of a search for 'a way to simplify and reform the whole system of personal tax collection and, at the same time, to improve the system of income support for poor people'. It is not surprising, therefore, that critics of the scheme have been able to show that other methods would be both cheaper and more effective if the elimination of poverty were the sole objective. One may reasonably question whether the other objectives of the scheme justify the very substantial additional cost involved. But it would be shortsighted to condemn any proposal which could result in a significant reduction of poverty merely because it is not designed solely for this purpose.

The question of cost is, nevertheless, of fundamental importance in considering the probable effects of the scheme. The net cost, with credits based on 1972 income levels, was estimated in the Green Paper at £1,300 million per annum. No indication was given as to how this colossal sum was to be raised. The Green Paper merely said: ' . . . with the growth of the national income, more resources will become available to devote to the task of eliminating poverty: the government consider that, taking all factors into account, and given the right order of priorities, the cost of the scheme would be a manageable one'. But it was also made clear that the rates of credit used in the Green Paper — £4 for a childless single person, £6 for a married couple or single parent, and £2 per child — were merely illustrative: 'no government could commit itself to the precise level of credits to come into operation some years ahead'. Whether the national income grows at the expected rate or not, a large part of the net annual cost will have to be met either by taxation which would otherwise not be necessary or by cuts in other kinds of public expenditure. There is, therefore, bound to be strong pressure to keep the credit rates down to the lowest possible level.

It must also be stressed that the illustrative rates of credit

in the Green Paper are already out of date and will become
more so by 1978. These rates were intended not only to
replace family income supplement (FIS) for all except the
self-employed but also to replace dependency increases for
children in the national insurance scheme. The 1973 increases
in national insurance benefits mean that, to achieve these
results, the credits would have to be about 15% higher — say
£4.60, £6.90 and £2.30. If, as now seems likely, the scheme
is to be incorporated in the 1974 Finance Bill, the credit
rates must also take account of the benefit increases
proposed for October 1974, and the Bill must provide for
further adjustments to preserve their relative value between
1974 and 1978. If this is not done, the scheme will be
fundamentally different from that proposed in the Green
Paper and endorsed by the majority of the select committee.

An important question which the Green Paper left open
was whether tax credits for children should normally go to
the father or to the mother, or should be split between them.
The logic of the scheme demands that where the father is the
main breadwinner the child credits should be set off against
his tax liability in the same way as the credit for himself and
his wife. Child credits, however, are to replace not only tax
allowances, which at present go to the father, but family
allowances and FIS which are normally drawn by the mother.
The select committee therefore recommended unanimously
that the whole of the child credit should go to the mother
and that it should be paid to all mothers, whether their
husbands qualified for inclusion in the tax credit scheme or
not. The government has accepted this recommendation.

The scheme on which work is now proceeding can be
regarded as two separate, though related, entities. First, there
is to be a payment on similar lines to the present family
allowance, but much larger and covering the first child,
whereas family allowances start from the second. The present
combined value of family allowance and child tax allowance
to a standard rate taxpayer varies from £1.15 per week for a
first child under 11 to £1.88 for a third or subsequent child
aged 16 or over. A credit of £2.30 per child would therefore
leave the standard rate taxpayer considerably better off. For
a family with a very low income and only one or two

children, the maximum FIS payment of £5 is worth more than £2.30 per child, but the difference would be more than made good by the tax credit in respect of the parents. Those who would benefit most would be families who are entitled to FIS but do not claim it, since it can be assumed that the take-up of tax credits, as of family allowances, would be very nearly 100%. This part of the scheme, therefore, provides a form of child endowment, unencumbered by means testing and universal in application. Now that it is clear that payment will be made to mothers it can be welcomed unequivocally.

The second and more controversial part of the government's proposals is the replacement of the tax allowances for single persons and married men by tax credits, normally payable to the husband in the case of a married couple. This part of the scheme would cover employed persons (other than those with very low earnings) and recipients of national insurance benefits. The main groups excluded would be the self-employed, those wholly dependent on supplementary benefit, and others (mostly young people) with earnings of less than, in current terms, about £9 per week. The introduction of tax credits would be accompanied by two major changes in the tax system, which must be seen as integral parts of the proposals. Short-term national insurance benefits, at present tax-free, would in future be taxed, and the present cumulative PAYE system under which an employee's tax liability is based on his annual income, would be replaced by a non-cumulative system under which tax liability would be assessed on each week's or month's earnings separately.

The first of these changes — the taxation of short-term benefits — is logical enough and becomes administratively possible as a result of the second. In most cases, the tax credit will exceed the tax payable on the benefit and there will be a net increase in the income of a sick or unemployed person compared with the present situation. This will not always be so, however. Professor Kaldor drew the attention of the select committee to the situation of a person who is unemployed for half the year but earns enough in the remainder of the year to absorb the whole of his tax allowance. He will get little benefit from the change from tax allowances to tax credits but will suffer tax on his unemployment benefit. (Select Committee on Tax-Credit 1973, vol. II). The Tax Credit Study Group of officials working on the scheme agreed that there was the possibility of a maximum loss of some £50 from this effect of the Green Paper. They estimated that the total numbers who would be worse off from the effect would not exceed a quarter of a million a year. The majority of the select committee did not see this as a weakness of the scheme, since the tax payable on a given income ought to be the same whether the income consisted of earnings plus benefit or of earnings alone; but they pointedly added 'We are not expressing any view on what the level of unemployment benefit ought to be'. (*Ibid.* vol. I). The fact is that, however anomalous it may be in principle, paying short-term benefits tax-free helps to diminish the drop in living standards caused by sickness or unemployment. To remove this anomaly without at the same time (if not sooner) taking effective steps to remedy the inadequacies of the benefits themselves would cause hardship and resentment.

The adoption of a non-cumulative system of tax deduction is a major element in the proposed simplification of the tax system. Without tax credits it would produce unfair results for those with fluctuating incomes, since they would no longer receive tax refunds in weeks of low earnings. The resulting overpayments of tax could be adjusted by repayment at the end of the year, but this would remove much of the desired simplicity. Part of the case for tax credits, therefore, is administrative. Two members of the select committee, Joel Barnett and Robert Sheldon, argue in a minority report that the non-cumulative system would be inflexible because it depends for its simplicity on most taxpayers paying a single uniform rate of tax, and that it would be difficult or costly in administration either to re-introduce reduced rate bands or to lower significantly the level of income at which higher rate tax begins. (*Ibid.* vol. I). In fact, however, the administrative cost of bringing more people into higher rate tax, involving individual end-year assessments, would not be increased by a non-cumulative deduction system. Reduced rates of tax would present more difficulty but are not, in fact, the best way of helping those with low incomes. Reducing the tax rate on the lowest band of income gives equal benefit to all except those with incomes so low that they do not reach the top of the reduced rate band. A more equitable way of distributing the same total benefit would be to increase the tax credits.

For most of the groups with which this chapter is concerned — those temporarily or permanently out of full-time employment — the tax credit proposals could offer some advantages, provided that the rates of credit are adjusted to take account of increases in national insurance benefits and other incomes. For instance, a large number of pensioners would no longer be dependent on supplementary benefit. The Green Paper estimated the number of national insurance beneficiaries (mostly pensioners) whose income would be raised above SB level at about a million, and the select committee's proposal to give pensioner couples the equivalent of two single persons' credits, if adopted, would take another 100,000 couples off SB. In some cases, the net addition to their income would be small, but a single pensioner with only the basic flat-rate pension would gain £1.98 per week on the basis of the Green Paper's figures.

The proposal to give the same credit to a single-parent family as to a family with both parents present could be particularly valuable provided that some way can be found of bringing the great majority of single-parent families fully within the scope of the scheme (they will in any case receive the child credits). This the Green Paper failed to do, but the Finer Committee, which has already spent four years enquiring into the needs of such families, is expected to recommend a special social security benefit for single parents (other than widowed mothers for whom provision is already made in the national insurance scheme) which would provide them with a qualifying source of income for tax credits. (*Ibid.* vol. II). The result would be that many families now in receipt of SB would be raised above the means-test level by tax credits, while for many others it would become worthwhile for the mother to take a part-time job in order to achieve independence of the SB system. These advantages, however, would depend on acceptance of the Finer Committee's expected recommendations. To introduce tax credits in the present situation would increase the pressure on mothers to take full-time work, since a part-time job might not bring them up to the level of earnings required to qualify for tax credits.

The fact that those receiving neither a wage nor a national insurance or similar benefit are to be excluded from the tax credit scheme means that the gaps in the coverage of national insurance will apply also to tax credits. Even if single-parent families are covered as a result of the Finer recommendations, the long-term unemployed and the congenitally disabled will still be left out. To the extent that their needs are provided for by the SB scheme, paying them a tax credit would not increase their total income. For these groups, however, as for single-parent families, the existence of a tax credit scheme would at least open the possibility of raising their incomes above SB level by means of a modest flat-rate benefit to which the tax credit would be added, if no better solution of their problems has been found by 1978.

There are no doubt good reasons why such a radical change in the fiscal system must take five years to bring fully into effect. But this should not be used as an excuse for doing nothing to improve the situation of low-income groups in the meantime. In particular, the decision to pay child credits to the mother makes them virtually indistinguishable from family allowances and removes any administrative obstacle to earlier implementation of this part of the scheme. Similarly it would be intolerable if the introduction of a single-parent family benefit were to be delayed until 1978.

A final verdict on the tax credit scheme must await the publication of a Bill incorporating the government's detailed proposals. It would be a fundamental error, however, to see the scheme as a substitute for adequate social security benefits designed to meet the needs of particular categories of beneficiaries. At the rates proposed in the Green Paper, the credits would be a useful supplement to the less than adequate benefits provided by the social security system at present. In particular, they would significantly reduce the number of people dependent on SB. This is a worthwhile achievement in itself; but two million people on supplementary benefit is still two million too many, and those taken off SB would in most cases receive only a small net increase of income, far from sufficient to remove them from being means-tested for a variety of other benefits and rebates. Higher rates of tax credit would be possible in theory but, because the increases would go to all those covered by the scheme, not only to those with low incomes, the cost would be prohibitive. Tax credits, in fact, may alleviate the problems of poverty in Britain but cannot solve them.

References

Conservative Party, (1970) *A better tomorrow,* Conservative Central Office.

Department of Health and Social Security, (1969) *National superannuation and social insurance,* cmnd. 3883, HMSO.

(1972) *Explanatory memorandum on the Social Security Bill 1972,* cmnd. 5142, HMSO.

(1973) *Family benefits and pensions,* Department of Health and Social Security.

Department of Health and Social Security and Department of Employment, (1973) Committee on abuse of social security benefits: *Report,* cmnd. 5228, HMSO.

Hansard, 13 July 1971, vol. 821, col. 194.

29 March 1971, vol. 814, col. 1153.

M.J. Hill, R.M. Harrison, A.V. Sargeant and V. Talbot, (1973) *Men out of work,* Cambridge University Press.

Proposals for a tax-credit system, (1972) cmnd. 5116, HMSO.

Select Committee on Tax-Credit, (1973) *Report and proceedings of the Committee,* vols. I and II, HMSO.

The focus is now on one locality, Bethnal Green. A small survey was made towards the end of 1973 in order to find out who was feeling the pinch most. One out of three families there were in poverty, and the chief sufferers were women and children.

6 Poverty in Bethnal Green
LUCY SYSON and MICHAEL YOUNG

If we had been able to we would have liked to have made a national survey to gather first hand evidence about standards of living in 1973, and to make it the first of a series so that comparisons could be made from one year to another. This remains a hope for the future. But it seemed sensible to start with a small survey in order to test out in one place the kind of questions that might be asked, before trying to enlarge the scale. The place we chose was a parliamentary constituency in east London where surveys have previously been made by the Institute of Community Studies (Townsend 1957; Young and Willmott 1957; Marris 1958; Willmott 1966).

We did not choose it because it *is* typical, since it most obviously is not. But at least one of its peculiarities *was* an asset. Bethnal Green belongs to an East End which is almost as much of a working-class city within the larger city as when it was described by Walter Besant at the beginning of the century.

> People, shops, houses, conveyances — all together are stamped with the unmistakeable seal of the working class . . . perhaps the strangest thing of all is this: in a city of two million people there are no hotels! This means, of course, that there are no visitors. (Besant 1901).

The main subject being what it was, there would have been

little point in setting out on a house-to-house search in South Kensington or North Oxford. In Bethnal Green we were bound to find some of the people we were looking for. This was especially so because it has more old people than usual and definitely not people who have come to take the waters or breathe in the sea air — 20% of pensionable age in 1971 compared with a national figure of 16%. This is one consequence of the vast migration forced upon Bethnal Green in this century. The population fell by two-thirds — from 108,184 in 1931 to 36,765 in 1971. Older people, if poor, are less prone to migrate than younger.

Housing authorities themselves have been partly responsible for the exodus. The Greater London Council (and the LCC before) has rehoused many people outside the borough boundaries since 1931 and replaced very many old houses within them. The proportion of households living in Council properties, the Greater London Council and the London Borough of Tower Hamlets sharing the stage, has therefore been rising steadily — 73% in our sample, 66% two years previously at the time of the Census. This means, without for a moment pretending that the new flats are at all popular, that as far as housing standards go Bethnal Green should be better off than many other districts.

Since this is only one place, and an unusual one, it hardly needs to be said that one cannot generalise from it. What is true here is not likely to be true of the country as a whole. And there is a further reason for caution on the same score. We cannot make any great claims for our informants being representative even of the district. The sample, of households not individuals, was selected at random from electoral registers in the approved way to avoid bias (Gray 1971). But in Inner London it has been proving more and more difficult in recent years to get a high response in surveys of any kind on any topic. To start with we picked 500 addresses. At some of them no interview could even be attempted: the houses were empty hulks or had been demolished since the electoral register had been made up ten months before. At a few other addresses there were no domestic households, but pubs, shops and institutions. We made definite contact at 417 addresses but at some places there was more than one household, so that 443 households became the maximum we could have netted. 161 of these refused and 282 agreed to answer our questions so that our response rate on this basis was 64%. That left 52 places where no decisive contact was made: in some cases appointments were made only to be broken, in others the occupants were on holiday during the period mid-August to mid-September when the survey was made; in others again, despite repeated calls (an average of over five for each such address), there was still no answer at the door.

We compared our households with the 1971 Census to see if the low response seemed to mean we had a biased sample. On some main criteria — the size of households and the number of single-person households above and below retirement age — there was no difference between the proportions in our sample and the Census figures for the total population of Bethnal Green. But we still cannot be sure that the people in our 282 households were between them typical of the place. We must therefore think of them as individuals more than representatives, but individuals who are all citizens of the country as well as residents in one part of it, under the dominion of the same National Insurance Scheme, the same National Health Service, the same Supplementary Benefits Commission, and along with these institutions, of general policies, which well beyond Bethnal Green go far to determine who is in poverty, and how they are treated when they are.

The information we were after was about households, because these are the financial collectives in which most people live, being to some extent at any rate rich or poor not individually but together. This meant, obviously, that we collected our facts about gross and net incomes per week during the previous five weeks from husbands and from wives where either was earning, or for that matter where they were not and were dependent on social benefits. It was more difficult to know what to do about subsidiary earners, most of whom were children who had left school and had begun to earn themselves. We *could* have tried to find out how much they earned and how much they contributed to the general housekeeping money. We decided not to for the simple reason that this was not the practice of the Supplementary Benefits Commission (SBC). Its Means Test does not, like the old Poor Law or the Unemployment Assistance Board in the 1930s, take account of all the income of such an earner, or even of his actual contribution to the family exchequer, but by rule of thumb assumes that he or she contributes a standard amount to the rent. Since we intended, for reasons we shall present in a moment, to judge whether people were poor by the same criteria as the Commission uses, we had to conform to their rules, so that information about the actual behaviour of subsidiary earners, if we had it, would not have altered the amount of 'poverty' one way or the other. But this does mean that we (like the Commission) are bound occasionally to count as poor some people who would not be if they were credited with the actual sums their children were giving them instead of the notional sums they are assumed to, and sometimes even the other way round – to exclude from poverty people who are not helped at all by their children.

How to define poverty
In Chapter 2 Chris Trinder defined low pay for 1973 as being less than £25 per week. We could have adopted the same criterion for poverty, but decided not to. We did not want to depart too far from previous practice. The most obvious thing to do is not to invent one's own definition but adhere to that in use by the SBC. The SBC in its own pronouncements studiously avoids the word 'poverty'. The scale rates are 'regarded as covering all normal needs which can be foreseen, including food, fuel and light, the normal repair and replacement of clothing, household sundries (but not major items of bedding and furnishing) and provision for amenities such as newspapers, entertainments and radio and television licences . . . What the scale rates provide is an amount for people to meet all ordinary living expenses in a way that suits them best'. (Department of Health and Social Security 1972). That could almost as well be a prescription for the needs of a millionaire as of a pauper. What matters is the practice: Parliament sets specific SBC levels such that people falling below these for almost any reason as long as they are not in ordinary employment have the right to get their

incomes made up out of public funds. In other words even if the words are not used officially, they are regarded as being sufficiently poor when below that line to have a right to financial assistance.

This has also been the criterion adopted by researchers both outside (Abel-Smith and Townsend 1965) and inside the government (Department of Health and Social Security 1971). It served for them as it does for us for the somewhat paradoxical reason that the standard, despite its high authority, is not one that is universally observed. If it were, and no one at all had an income below the SB level, then accordingly there would be no one by this standard in poverty. The point of being so guided is precisely that plenty of people are below this standard. People do not have to be on the minimum if they do not want to be. Many who would be entitled do not choose to apply for help. Others do, but are kept below by various rules such as the famous 'wage stop' which prevents people with low wages being any better off when dependent on public funds than they were in employment.

The logic of equating SB rates with the poverty line is therefore fairly compelling — one is asking how many people are so poor that they fall below that line. But to make things more complicated the line is in the plural rather than the singular. It would not be a problem if the variations were no more than sufficient to allow for differences in the size of the household — if a person living on his own received up to a certain sum, a couple so much, a dependent child so much, as indeed they do. At the time of the survey the SBC paid £6.55 to a single householder, £10.65 to a married couple, and so much for each child according to his or her age.

The first complication, although one relatively easy to deal with, is about housing costs. Rents paid have varied so much, especially before rent rebates were introduced, that the SBC could not have a realistic overall formula that rents are at any particular level for a family of a given size. It has therefore in the ordinary way, and very humanely, paid whatever the rent actually was (unless this was 'unreasonable') in addition to any other money it gave to people getting full basic scales. This means that with people not getting SB, in order to judge

what would happen if they did apply, one has to do the same
and disregard rent. It can be done in one of two ways — by
taking the actual net income and then comparing this with
the SBC basic scales plus actual rent (which was what
Abel-Smith and Townsend did), or by deducting actual
housing costs from net income and then comparing what is
left with the scale rates (as the government enquiry did)
(Department of Health and Social Security 1971). We
decided in favour of the latter because if one is going to
disregard housing altogether it seemed more sensible to do so
completely, as the official researchers did, on both sides of
the comparison, for the person getting, as well as not getting,
benefit.

The second complication is that the SBC 'disregards'
income earned up to £2 per week or £1 for the unemployed,
small private superannuation payments and small disability
pensions and interest on savings up to a certain amount.
Officials customarily overlook occasional payments made by
relatives and friends.

There was the same trouble about the third and more
serious complication. On top of the basic scales there is a
'long term addition' of 60p a week, or 85p where the
claimant was aged 80 or over, for all people receiving SB who
are over pensionable age or who have been receiving a
supplementary allowance for a continuous period of two
years. At the discretion of SBC officials they may also receive
special allowances for heating, say, or laundry, or diet. What
were we to do about that for the people not receiving
supplementary benefit at all, or receiving it but not any
special allowances to which they might be entitled? The most
satisfactory procedure would probably be to collect in a
survey all the information that SBC officials would require in
order to decide whether or not to award discretionary
allowances, and then to ask the actual officials to award them
or not, though notionally. But they would be unlikely to
agree to do something so hypothetical, even were the survey
itself an official one.

The decision being so difficult, one can avoid this
particular issue altogether, as the government researchers did,
and publish no more than the proportions of people below

SB scale rates and at various levels above them. This is done in Table 6.1 for the 243 households out of the 282 interviewed for whom we had enough information about family finances to be sure of our ground, divided between households headed by males and females since this is a distinction that we want to stress further in a moment.

Such a table does not of course enable anything to be said about the number in poverty until a decision is taken about the line to follow. Abel-Smith and Townsend decided that the disregards and allowances could be said to add 40% to the basic scales; so anyone whose expenditure was below that level was considered in poverty. We have looked for guidance mainly to the actual income of the 63 households in our sample who received SB. 12 were below even the basic SB scale, 40 received up to 20% more, and 8 between 20% and 40% more. 3 were over the 40% level. This suggested to us that the best line to take, the one accounting for 82% of SB households, was the 20% one and in what follows we have therefore regarded as in poverty those falling below that point, even though it means that our results on some topics are not directly comparable with those of Abel-Smith and Townsend.

On sheer numbers below the 20% level a comparison can be made with their figures just to provide some sort of perspective. In Bethnal Green 30.9% of households were in poverty; in the country generally in 1953—54 there were 5.7% and in 1960 12.5%. The years were not the same, nor was the manner of dealing with housing costs. Nevertheless, the figure of 31% of households in poverty (which is 30% of all the people in the households) is clearly a high one, although perhaps no more than one would expect in view of the unusual character of the district, as described at the beginning of the chapter. It is not much higher than the proportion of 25.9% below the same SB + 20% level which was found in a survey made in 1966 in the St Ann's district of central Nottingham (Coates and Silburn 1967).

The most striking conclusion which seems to us to stand out from the Bethnal Green survey is not, however, so much the level of overall poverty as the fact, shown in Table 6.1, that poverty bore more heavily upon women than men. Of the 75 households in poverty 49, or 66%, were headed by females. A fifth of these, as we shall see, were mothers with dependent children, a state of affairs which was itself partly responsible for the fact that of all the143dependent children in our sample households 40% were in poverty — substantially more than of adults. Women and children were the first to suffer from it.

Table 6.1 Households and people above and below
supplementary benefit basic scales in Bethnal Green 1973

	Male-headed households		Female-headed households		All households	
	house-holds %	people %	house-holds %	people %	house-holds %	people %
Below SB	7.5	7.5	15.5	15.9	10.3	9.9
0–20% above SB	8.2	8.2	44.0	50.0	20.6	20.0
21–40% above SB	8.8	9.5	11.9	9.7	9.9	9.6
More than 40% above SB	75.5	74.7	28.6	24.4	59.3	60.5
Total	100.0	100.0	100.0	100.0	100.0	100.0
Total numbers	159	450	84	176	243	626

Income and housing poverty
The one out of three households picked out in this way as being in poverty were all judged by their incomes alone. The fact that there is a Part II to this book shows we recognise that dire lack of money is not the only kind of 'poverty', even if one is beginning to stretch the term a bit to use it as broadly as we shall. Why we did, and do, is because we want to stress that people who are badly off for income, though they are often badly off in many other respects as well, like housing, education and health, are not necessarily so. Our survey was not comprehensive enough to allow us to relate many such dimensions to each other in an overall 'standard of life' — that should be attempted more systematically in

any future enquiry. But we could do it in a limited way for housing, using three customary criteria – the absence of an indoor lavatory, the absence of a bathroom, and the extent of overcrowding. There was no correlation between the two types of poverty as judged in this way. Only 8% of the 75 income-poor households and 16% of the 168 others lacked an inside lavatory. 19% of the poor and 20% of the others had no bathroom, and hardly anyone in either category was living at a density of more than 1.5 persons per room (a kitchen counting as a room for this purpose), this being an official definition of overcrowding. Put another way, two-thirds of the 48 without bathrooms were not poor by the income criteria, nor were four-fifths of the 33 with outdoor lavatories. Thus, very few of the income-poor were particularly badly off for housing, assessed by these indices. The reason, which would not apply to anything like the same extent in many other districts, is that so much of the housing belongs to the two Councils. Except when it is old property recently taken over, this always has basic amenities, and if serious overcrowding came about in such property the tenants would often be transferred to a larger flat. But, as we shall see later, the possession of enough rooms with the right bits of fixed equipment in them is not everything by any means. What many people (including us) would regard as poor quality is not measured only in this way. On a subjective basis, nearly half (47%) of the poor said they were not satisfied with their housing, whether this was because repairs had not been done, there was no playspace for children, or because they did not have the basic amenities we have just talked about.

Who were the poor?
As for the people in income poverty, if they were not in specially bad housing, what more can we say about them? There are obviously many ways of dividing them up. The most straightforward is according to the employment status of the head of household. This is done in Table 6.2, with comparisons being made according to the way households were classified in the data for the 1953–54 enquiry of Abel-Smith and Townsend.

*Table 6.2 Employment status of heads of households
in poverty*

Employment status of head	United Kingdom 1953–4[1][2] (Sample analysed = 3,225)		Bethnal Green 1973[1] (Sample analysed = 243)	
	Number	% in poverty	Number	% in poverty
Retired			47	62.7
Non-working women in one-parent families[3]	223	68.4	11	14.7
Unemployed	10	3.1	6	8.0
Sick (long and short term)	14	4.3	6	8.0
Working part-time	15	4.6	3	4.0
Working full-time	64	19.6	2	2.7
Total	326	100.0	75	100.0

NOTES
1.   'Poverty' is defined as SB scale rates plus 20% in 1973 but SB rates plus 40% in 1953–4.
2.   From Abel-Smith and Townsend 1965, Table 5
3.   That is, single, widowed, divorced and separated women under retirement age and not working or chronically sick or disabled. These were not classified separately from other 'unoccupied including retired' in the 1953–4 enquiry

One difference between the Bethnal Green survey and the others was that in our district there was hardly anyone in poverty because of low pay. This was not because no one was low-paid in Bethnal Green, where 19.6% (23 out of 117) of the male heads of household in full-time work were receiving low pay according to Chris Trinder's definition for 1973 in Chapter 2. But many wives were going out to work (70, or 54% of all married women) and in 11 of the 18 married couples where the husband was earning less than £25 the wife was working. But the figures for our survey, and indeed for the others on the same subject, may be misleading because the assumption behind them all, that families are completely unified for financial purposes, may not be justified. A family is not counted as being poor if the income coming into it from all sources is more than the poverty line. But it is obviously quite possible for some members of such families to be so, especially if the husband spends a large part of his earnings on himself and keeps down the housekeeping money he gives to his wife. Children as well as wives may in such circumstances be the sufferers. This is an aspect of poverty which has never yet been properly enquired into. Very little is known about the relationship of housekeeping allowances to wages.

But it is at least possible, perhaps even more, plausible, that as one of the authors said on a previous occasion 'there may be a tendency for wives to suffer, relatively to their husbands, in any period of inflation . . . Like other un-organised workers, their money income may not advance as fast as prices'. (Young 1952). We were not in this present survey able to go into the subject in any depth but we did ask people whether housekeeping allowances had risen in the previous year. This mattered most, of course, in households where the wife not herself working was entirely dependent upon what her husband gave her. There were 50 of these. Of these wives 20 said their allowance had stayed the same; 4 that it had decreased and 26 that it had increased. This means that nearly half the dependent wives said they had not received any extra 'wages' from their husbands even though most of the husbands said they had themselves got higher wages from their jobs. Since this has been a year of inflation — the general view amongst informants was that whatever the retail price index may say (and it said that the difference was 9p), the £ in September 1973 had fallen in value by at least 25p over the previous year — the failure of housekeeping allowances to respond probably meant that the standard of life of many wives and children fell fairly substantially during the period. The Incomes Policy enforced by their husbands on them was long-term Standstill. Nor could they be helped in any other way save, as Atkinson and Trinder point out, by family allowances, which are paid to mothers. But family allowances have stayed the same since 1968, so that their value has continuously fallen.

About housewives and children in ordinary households we cannot be sure how many were 'poor' even though their husbands were not. About others we can be rather more firm. Going back to Table 6.2 we shall discuss the people in poverty under the chief headings in the table — the retired, the one-parent families, the unemployed and the sick.

Retirement
Old age in Bethnal Green was, as it has likewise been in every other survey, the outstanding cause of poverty; and here as elsewhere this was especially so for women, because there were so many more of them. The superior hardiness of the female sex which is responsible for the fact that women generally live longer than men means that more of them are inferior in purely material terms. The numbers of them in poverty are also swollen by the strange anomaly in the national insurance system whereby women can qualify for a pension by retiring from work at 60 and men not till 65. It is no surprise, therefore, to find that of the 47 retired heads of households in poverty 33 were women, most of them living on their own. In the following examples which are drawn from what some of them told us, we have of course used fictional names so as to conceal identities.

Whether poverty is any harsher for old women than men is clearly debatable. Townsend has shown convincingly, and for the same district of Bethnal Green, that men can easily lose their self-respect, and sometimes their wives' too, when they leave the work which was for them the source of status as

well as income. The fact that women's work is never done
can at this stage of life be a positive advantage. Among our
informants on the one hand is a widower like Mr Gareth who
said that he was less bored in summer because 'I sits in a little
park near by in fine weather'; on the other, a widow like
Mrs Mayne who goes every morning to look after her
daughter's house, and the children in it, while the daughter is
at work. Against that advantage, which is of course largely
lost as soon as disability makes any kind of housework
painful, there are several serious disadvantages. Single women
appear on the whole to be poorer than men, partly because
they do not ordinarily have so much in savings and partly
because occupational pension schemes often leave out
women. More fundamentally, with poverty as with company,
two is better than one. It is accepted by the state that the
overheads of a house are in many ways the same whether it is
occupied by two people or by one — which is why a person
on his own gets a retirement pension of £6.75 and a couple
not double but £10.90 (up to October 1973 when the rates
were raised, though still in the same proportions). But it is
doubtful whether the relative generosity to the people on
their own is enough to compensate for her (or him) having no
one to share with. If it is not enough, this is a kind of
hardship which bears particularly on women, on top of any
special liabilities for those who are frightened by being alone
at night in a house without a man, or unable to do any of the
heavier work once the man who did it has gone.

However any such comparison would balance out in the
end, the plain fact is that more old women were in poverty,
and that it was for many of either sex not exactly an enviable
state to be in, especially in this particular year. 'It's shocking.
I spent 8s. in the old money yesterday and didn't know
where it had gone.' 'I don't know the last time I tasted a
proper piece of meat — it's disgusting the price of food.' 'I
used to manage lovely on my pension but now I can't.' 'The
hospital says I should go on a diet, but how can I afford it?'
Such remarks were common enough. Since food had to come
first and it cost so much, even in the street markets with
which the district is well endowed, there was quite often not
much left over for other things.

Heating, in winter, was a problem for almost all who did not live in centrally heated flats and for some who did where the heating broke down. Mrs Namier gave herself a treat only once a week. 'On a Sunday afternoon I'd have the electric fire on, but other times I couldn't afford to have the fire all the time.' Mrs Ayer said that 'You don't get much gas for your money. It doesn't last more than five minutes.' People like her with slot meters had to pay more per unit than others, but at least they did not have to face large quarterly bills which are not easy to save up for each week. For Mr Tinberger the electricity bill is the biggest worry — 'it's always over £10. I sit in misery sometimes at night when I'd like the light on'. For private tenants who pay the rates separately from the rent there was the same problem. 'I have to pay six-monthly rates in advance' said Miss Halsey, 'and every time they go up I can never get it back from Social Security.' Perhaps this was because she did not know that she could approach the SBC for help, and even get the extra money immediately for the rates on special request.

Most of the old people living below the poverty line had not been able to add to their 'capital' since retirement. Mrs Sparrow was unusual in having bought a carpet on the HP 'I kissed the carpet when it was paid for, and said it's mine.' Others had to make do with the furniture they had even if it did more or less fall to pieces, and put patches over the lino when it finally wore away in front of the sink or by the door. It was the same with clothing, which had to be secondhand — 'I go to jumble sales to keep myself clean and tidy'. Mrs Jasper, aged 72, said she wore the same clothes she had when she finished working many years before.

As we have said, poverty in housing did not by any means go with poverty in income, if judged by the amount of space per person, which is partly because age matters so much. Old people, alone or in couples, had more space because they continued to live in places with room enough for children well after the children had departed. In other respects they were about as badly off (or well off) as other people in the district, except for some special disabilities they suffered. Stairs were the enemy of her arthritis for Mrs Beloff.

I would have liked a downstairs place because of my spinal

arthritis. The downstairs flat has changed three times but
they've put in people who go to work each day. I put in
for it but heard nothing. I've tried ever since I've been here
but now I'm too old and I've given up. They don't care
nothing — it's obvious.

The lack of indoor lavatories and bathrooms could also be
acutely felt. Mrs Chester's chief wish was for a bath. 'I was
told I should have hot baths for my arthritis. I have to
manage with a bucket of hot water. It's just a little bath I
need.'

In blocks high enough and modern enough to have lifts
and bathrooms there were other difficulties — worst of all
perhaps just the sheer vastness of some of them, compared
with the friendliness of the little homes which had been
replaced by the big, in what one man called a 'bloody
concrete jungle'.

> We liked our house. We used to grow marrows on an
> air-raid shelter, and tomatoes. One of our old neighbours
> from there, he's living in one of these blocks now. If he
> opens his front door he sees only an empty corridor. In the
> old days we could natter over the back fence. I said to his
> wife 'Poor old chap, he's got nothing to do'. She said 'He
> can look out of the window, can't he?' I said 'What use is
> that? He can't even mow the grass. The council do it'.

The lift itself may be cause for complaint if it goes out of
order or smells. 'Young couples go in the lift and make it
smell'. Another is the virtual impossibility up in the air of
cleaning the outside of the windows. The charge per flat
could be as much as nine shillings (in the old money that
most of the old people still think in), and then the men did
not come regularly.

Old people, if private tenants, were also more liable to
harassment. Mr Sandell told the story of what had happened
to him a short time before.

> I had a room in the other house. It was a big place, with 20
> rooms in it. The new owner wanted me out and paid
> someone to do it. They sent in about 100 Beatniks one
> night, just to frighten me, and another time they locked
> me out for three nights. They put all the old beds near my
> front door. They'd roll beer bottles down the stairs.

They'd turn my electric off, and I'd come home to find all my food wet and all. They broke up the toilet and the cistern, so that I had to go down the road to the public convenience last thing at night and first thing in the morning. And another time a man knocked on my window at two in the morning and offered me money to get out. He was all done up in RAF uniform and spoke lovely — he must have been paid by the landlord to come and ask me. But he did give me a fright. I wasted all my money on a solicitor but he wasn't no good — he just kept sending on to me the letters from the landlord. I told the police and they said they would watch the place, but they couldn't have or they would have seen what was going on. I took this place in a flash when I finally got the chance, or I'd have had a complete mental breakdown.

We shall be discussing some of the complexities of the social services in a later section. It is worth saying here that what is confusing to the younger is liable to be even more so to older people like Mr Ratchford, who have to grapple first with one authority and then another.

I'm on the Assistance and the Assistance sent me like a rebate — the Assistance stopped the rebate and the council gave me a rebate. They stopped at one end and gave this to me the other like.

The enlargement of the borough, when Bethnal Green was joined with Stepney and Poplar to make Tower Hamlets, had apparently made the local authority seem less local, the department of this and that far away for old people in a borough not well served with buses. 'Bethnal Green used to be a nice little borough. It has gone to pot since we went in with Tower Hamlets because we are subsidising the other areas like Stepney. We don't get nothing now. So I've written to the heads of the government. I say "Don't send your Ministers down here for two minutes to see our problem". I say to them "Come and live here".' Mr Bassett said he had had no reply from Sir Keith Joseph.

One-parent families

The 12 families with dependent children but lacking one parent completely and with the remaining parent not working, were perhaps the worst off of all those in the sample. How badly off? Some might take it as conclusive that all but one of the eleven women and one man who had fallen on hard times had a TV set, some of them old and without BBC-2, others borrowed, none of them colour, but all able equally to receive much the same basic programmes as richer people. If the presence of a TV set is a sure sign that poverty is absent, then it was for these women and children.

On other grounds their plight was more grievous. Mrs Jarrett had not only been deserted by her husband. He had vanished leaving behind him a handsome debt in the form of rent arrears of £125 which, on the old assumption that those whom God and the state had joined were one, the council considered Mrs Jarrett was liable for. Every week, as a remembrance of him, she had to repay some of his debt. (The SBC have only to meet current needs and not rent arrears, so it is up to the person concerned to make arrangements with the local authority accordingly.) She had not had a holiday for ten years. Mrs Farrow spoke for others too when she was asked which of the goods she bought had gone up most in price in the last year, and replied that it was food — about other things she could not say because there was not much else that she could afford to buy. Children's clothes were a problem for almost everyone. When the cast-offs of the eldest were passed down the line a new garment had to be procured from somewhere.

The three widows among the 11 were in one way better off. Although none of them did, they could unlike the others who were dependent on supplementary benefits, work if they wished without losing their widowed mothers' allowances. They also had no slur to carry. But they had other heavier burdens, especially near the time when their husbands died. For Mrs Sullivan there was a special financial one. Her husband's burial insurance had lapsed because he had been out of work (his wife used a word with Victorian overtones, 'idle') a lot before he died, and she had the whole cost to bear herself. 'I had to pay £188 for the funeral before I could get the body removed. I had to get it by 3.30. He died early morning. His body was removed at 6 pm.'

She also had to buy a set of black clothes and when the

mourning period was over there was a financial problem as well in 'coming out of black'. Before October 1973 the SBC did not ordinarily help with funeral expenses. Mrs Sullivan's main complaint about prices was the extent to which potatoes had gone up. An Irish woman, she regularly ate some three pounds a day. She had no bitterness about the 90p by which the SBC topped up her widow's pension, comforting herself and us with the thought that 'if you stay indoors all the time you're well off — you haven't spent your money'. Another wife on equally short commons was quite as philosophic about it. Perhaps remembering how things had been before her husband left she said of the present: 'I know some people get less than me even though their husbands are working'.

As for housing, all these wives were without exception living in council flats. With their broods of young children their claim had been good enough for that. They had something else in common. They were mostly living in the worst council housing, some of the descriptions being the kind that ordinarily are more associated with private property — 'damp', 'leaking roof', 'due for conversion'. Mrs Farrow was in one such place, a flat in a giant tenement which had been taken over by the Council and would be demolished before long. Three out of four windows were already filled with corrugated iron. Tunnels ran through the block at intervals into a common courtyard almost choked with old cars without wheels, and glass, iron bedsteads, cardboard boxes and rotting food. A mass of children were jumping up and down as if it were a sort of trampoline on a mattress which had been thrown away and now had flock spurting out through a dozen holes at each jump. Mrs Farrow said she had been even worse off in the first place she had gone into when her husband left her — a furnished flat which she shared with seven other people. They took it in shifts to use the gas stove. She had to wait until nine at night before it was her turn to cook. 'Then I had a bit of a barney with my landlord. I paid £3.50 for one room. I went out and spent the night with a friend, I was so upset. When I got back in the morning I found he'd let the room. I was lucky to get this'.

Mrs Farrow was fortunate only by the standards of her

own past. The fact that she and the others, though in Council-owned housing were in the worst of it, raises a large question about housing policy in Bethanl Green and indeed throughout the country. All councils have a hierarchy in their housing, which varies in quality more or less with its age, though of course other characteristics matter too. The most modern may be disliked if it takes the form of tall blocks but at least the flats are up-to-date and well-equipped. At the other extreme are tenements built before 1914 which have become as dilapidated as almost anything privately owned. Rents vary pretty closely with the quality of the accommodation. In the past the common practice of housing managers in these circumstances was to assign the roughest and poorest tenants to the roughest quarters. Since so many one-parent families have been among the poorest and the most 'undesirable' they have therefore usually got the worst places to live in (Cullingworth Report 1969, para. 96). Many of them were glad because they then had the lowest rents; they could not afford more.

All that was perhaps understandable enough in the past. It is so no longer. One-parent families can now ordinarily get their rent either paid in full by the SBC or offset by a rent rebate. Really needy people do not have to pay any rent at all. There is therefore no reason any more why such people should go into inferior accommodation. This has, of course, been recognised by many housing managers. They no longer mind what the income is of prospective tenants as long as they have clean rent books, without arrears. Where this is the view, one-parent families will stand as good a chance as anyone else of getting into better accommodation. But what has not been done anywhere, as far as we know, is to lean right over in the other direction and give a positive preference for the better places to the one-parent families. If the intent were to allot according to need, and to make up in a small way for the other hardships endured by such families, this is what housing managers would decide to do now that the new rent policies have gone a long way towards relieving them from the financial pressures which used to compel distribution according to means rather than needs.

One single-parent family in the sample was headed by a

man. He had been unemployed for nearly four years since his wife left him with year-old triplets and two other children. At least he was well-housed, though this had happened before he had been left on his own. 'We had a two-bedroomed place before — all fur growing on the walls. My wife had to take the three babies down the housing and threaten to leave them there if they didn't get us a place.' Although the children were all now eligible for free meals and milk at school — and were receiving them — life was not exactly easy for him.

Only five fatherless families were not in poverty. There were two main reasons. First, none had more than one dependent child, and one thing that stands out clearly from our findings and those of other researchers is that just one child is not enough to push people into poverty. There were 23 two-parent families with one dependent child and none of them were in poverty either — most of the wives were at work. Second, they were all at work. One was working part-time but very recently separated, waiting for her divorce and having her rent paid by her ex-husband. The others were working full-time. If they had been men they would all have come into the 'low-paid' category — only one was earning more than £20 a week — and none of them could, by this reckoning, be called well off, but compared with single-parent families with more than one dependent child and where work was out of the question, they were in a far better position.

Not that this was exactly enviable. One son had become diabetic after his father's death and needed a great deal of care. A mother had her three teenage daughters in one bedroom. It was not worth trying to move because the two elder, both now at work, might get married.

The unemployed

Women, then, were the most likely to be poor in Bethnal Green, whether because they lived longer or were having to manage on their own, or because they did not go out to work, having young children who could not be left, and depended on their husbands for housekeeping money which in many cases did not rise despite inflation and growing needs within the family.

There is another group, though, which cannot be left out
of this description. These are the unemployed, six of whom
were interviewed and all of whom fell below our poverty line.
All but one was married and these five had twenty
dependants between them — four wives and sixteen children.
The man who was unemployed because his wife had left him
has already been described above with the single-parent
families. None of the others had been unemployed as long as
he, but only one had been out of work for less than three
months. Only the single man could be described as relatively
well off: he could get work whenever he wanted but
sometimes he could not be bothered. When asked how many
jobs he had had in the past five years he said 'I've been
working for myself on and off like. Employers — I'm not
bothered with. I'm so much in work and out of work — I
don't think I can go back that far. Five years — it's like a
lifetime.' He was a steel erector and must have been well paid
when in work — he had a car, colour television and a
telephone and had not bothered to apply for a rent rebate.
'Laziness, I'm on my own and a single fellow and you just
take everything as it comes.'

For the others unemployment brought harsher changes.
Mrs Baines had a husband who had been waiting for nearly a
year for a place at a government training centre and had had
to stop her own part-time job two or three months before the
interview. 'I can't go too potty on shopping' she said,
understating the problem of keeping her three small children
adequately clothed. But 'there's people worse off than us'.
Her husband was one of those suffering from the wage
stop — their total income was less than the basic SB
scale — yet they had not been advised by the SBC to apply
for a rate rebate which could have cut £1.37 off their £2.20
weekly rate bill, even though this would not, according to the
rules, have affected their SB level (Department of Health and
Social Security 1972).

Mrs Hockney, whose four children were aged between
eight and four, had her housekeeping cut by £12 a week
when her husband became unemployed three months before
the interview. He was at a government training centre — he
wanted to learn a more remunerative trade than van

driving — and the family was on exactly the SB scale rates.

Two others had become unemployed more recently — within the previous four months — and were existing on unemployment benefit plus family allowances only. Mr Cleaver, with two children and a tendency to bronchitis, was thinking of applying for SB. 'It depends how the money lasts out.' He was living at below SB rates and was not even receiving a rent rebate — he would have got his whole rent of £4.64 rebated — nor a rate rebate, which would have saved £1.40 of his £2.24 rates bill each week.

The sick

One other group remains to be described. These are the sick and disabled. In our sample there were eight heads of families who were sick, either short or long-term — that is for more than six months. It is, of course, the long-term sick who have the worst time financially as well as in other ways. 'People in bad health also tend to get offered very low-paid jobs — £16–£17 a week' said Mr Flowers, whose job as a postman ended when he had a heart attack three years ago. He had not worked for fourteen months before we saw him but he had no dependent children to support and because he was receiving a Post Office pension he was the only one of the long-term sick not poor. The short-term sick person who wasn't poor, though only just, was Mrs Pierce, a separated woman who was receiving half-wages from her employers as well as the family income supplement that had been awarded when she was still well.

All the other six households whose head was sick were also poor. Mr Seers, whose wife had just brought their ten-day-old daughter back from hospital, had had an accident at work: this gave £9.60 extra on top of the ordinary benefit and he had not felt it necessary to apply for supplementary benefit too. He would not have been eligible at the basic scale rates, though he might have been for discretionary allowances. He certainly was eligible for rent rebate but 'they sent me a form four or five years ago and asked me to fill it in. I filled it in but I never heard no more about it. I got no rent rebate'. He was a GLC tenant and so must have been talking about the GLC scheme which started before the government introduced the national scheme, and thought that once out, always out.

Mr Carn was separated with two teenage daughters. His special problem was that he was epileptic and employers found it upsetting. He had been unemployed for three months during the past year and although he was now working — in a rather low-paid decorator's job at £25 a week after tax — he was off sick again at the time of the interview and was clearly worried because the only way to increase his pay was through working extra hours to earn a bonus. He did not feel up to that.

The other four in poverty were the long-term sick. Two were women on their own — one single and one widowed. Mrs White was probably the best off. She opened the door in her petticoat, explaining she'd just been putting her grandchild to bed. She lived alone but she and the 'other Granny' were both baby-sitting that night, reported our interviewer. Miss Woolley was much sadder. Her poor sight and bad leg had made her leave her packer's job ten years before. She said she was 'just existing' and was definitely worse off than most people in the area 'because of my disability'. 'Otherwise I'd have been working. You see, I've had a pin on a plate in the hip nine years ago, two operations on a knee and a knee-cap removed a year ago. And with my sight so bad and the street is so bad to walk along and all the old neighbours have gone . . . ' She was not registered as disabled. 'No, I was thinking of doing it to get me ticket on the buses, but never bothered. Might as well wait until next year, now' (she was 59).

But is it worse to be alone and sick or to have others in the family and not to be able to support them properly? Here is another of our interviewer's comments on what he found in one family. 'Mrs Glover in a nervous state as well as being physically ill. Eldest daughter (there were three children) protective and helpful. Husband left home, but no formal separation or divorce. Appears that he retains tenancy of the flat. Mrs Glover is visited by a social worker who has been of some help, but both according to her and judging by appearance, not enough.' Here the marital and financial instability coincided with the physical problems of chronic rheumatism and bronchitis.

The last family was different again. Mr Baker had a damaged spine and one of his five children had only one arm and arthritis in one leg. But his wife, clearly the moving spirit, was one of the few we encountered who had a really good idea of what benefits were available, but was still poor.

We have been describing only people under retirement age. There were, of course, many old people who also had trouble of one sort or another — often arthritis and chest troubles. Three-fifths of the pensioners in our sample mentioned a health problem big enough to be described by them as a 'disability'.

Take-up

There is only one other important subject to cover for which there is space left, and that is the take-up of the chief means-tested benefits. We shall not deal with them all — for one thing there are too many — but instead pick out rate rebates, rent rebates, supplementary benefit (SB) itself, with a brief word on family income supplement (FIS).

Separate assessments had to be made for each of these because, to the confusion of most people in Bethnal Green as elsewhere, there is not one single method of calculating means for each of these schemes. Each scheme has its own rules and its own critical level below which aid can be given. Rent rebates and allowances are described by Peter Willmott in the next chapter. All that needs to be added here is that since our survey was conducted before October 1973 when the level of needs allowances was raised, our calculations are based on the old rate of £14 gross income for a single person, and £18.25 for a married couple or an individual with dependent children, and £2.75 for each dependent child. With rate rebates the means test was more stringent. In order to be eligible for a full rate rebate, the gross income of a ratepayer had at the time of the survey to be less than £13.50 for single, widowed, divorced and separated people, and £16.50 for a married couple plus £2.75 for each dependent child. Nobody could have their whole rate bill rebated. £3.75 had to be deducted from the half-yearly rate bill and two-thirds of what remained could be rebated. The SB levels have already been indicated — they are still more stringent than the rate rebates. FIS moved the other way, the total income that people on it could get being slightly higher. A family with one dependent child had to have less than £21 gross (in August 1973) to qualify for FIS; for the next three children £2.50 was added for each child, and after that an extra £2 for each further child. FIS is discussed at the national level in Chapter 3. Figures for this benefit are not included in the table below, since the numbers were too small. Only two families were found in the sample who seemed to be eligible for FIS. They were both receiving it. So were two other people, one of whom had stopped working in order to look after her children; the other was sick and off work. Since from April 1973 onwards the benefit was awarded for twelve-month periods, these women were clearly still receiving the award which had been made when they were still at work.

Table 6.3 shows who were eligible for the other benefits discussed in detail (rent rebates and allowances, rate rebates and supplementary benefits) and who, of those who were eligible according to our calculations, was actually receiving them.

There have not been any enquiries before covering these three benefits at once so we cannot make comparisons, except for rate rebates which were examined by Meacher in her study in Islington in 1971 (Meacher 1972). 19% of those eligible claimed these rebates after an advertising campaign. Bethnal Green in 1973 could not get anywhere near that level. Although no other specific comparisons can be made, the general conclusion must be the same as Meacher's. The level of take-up was not high — apart from another benefit not specifically referred to in the table, cheap butter. 73% of eligible people were getting butter tokens. This was because they were available only to people receiving SB and FIS, and when they were introduced at the beginning of July 1973 everyone already receiving SB or FIS was given a form at their local post office and those who filled it in were sent tokens through the post. Since then people who have become eligible for these benefits (worth 5p per fortnight for the beneficiary and each dependant) have been issued with them automatically, though some people have returned them

Table 6.3 Eligibility and take-up of three means-tested benefits in 243 households headed by men and women Bethnal Green, 1973

| | Rent rebate or allowance | | Rate rebate | | Supplementary benefit | | |
	% eligible	% receiving of those eligible	% eligible	% receiving of those eligible	% below scale rates	% receiving of those eligible	Total numbers
Above poverty line							
Men	26.1	31.4	5.2	14.3	—	—	134
Women	73.5	48.0	50.0	5.9	—	—	34
Total	35.7	38.3	14.3	8.3	—	—	168
Below poverty line							
Men	96.0	70.8	88.0	13.6	48.0	33.3	25
Women	96.0	58.3	90.0	0.0	26.0	61.5	50
Total	96.0	62.5	89.3	4.5	33.3	48.0	75
All sample							
Men	37.1	47.4	18.2	13.8	7.5	33.3	159
Women	86.9	54.8	73.8	1.6	15.5	61.5	84
Total	54.3	51.5	37.4	5.5	10.3	48.0	243
Numbers	132	68	91	5	25	12	—

saying they did not want them. At the time of writing, it seemed that this scheme was intended to last until December 1973 and tokens were being issued only for that period. But this apart, there is no doubt that in general low take-up evidently remains a quite vital problem.

The other general conclusion is once again about women. More households with female heads were eligible for benefits and except for SB, for those below the poverty line, lesser proportions actually received them. Almost everyone was in a muddle about what they were and were not entitled to, but if anything, women seemed more confused than men, perhaps partly because the widows amongst them had for most of their lives left dealings with official bureaucracies to their husbands. One widow, Mrs Heston, thought rent rebates 'was only for council tenants'. Mrs Box, another, said she had not applied for a rebate 'because my daughter lives here and people not on their own don't receive one'. Mrs White, yet another, was 'waiting to see what happens about rent reductions'. This last caused monumental muddles, because at the same time as the 1972 Housing Finance Act was coming into force for rent rebates it was doing the same for 'fair rents' for council property, and on top of that some rates were being altered as a result of the revaluation of property. When rents and rates were taken together the payments by some people went down. When this happened some thought it was the result of a rent rebate they had received without having applied for it.

This is not the place to discuss *how* take-up could be improved, nor the more fundamental question *if* it can be without some great simplification of the dozens of different means tests, except to make the one obvious point that anything that can be done to help the poor by the various administrative authorities working more closely together obviously should be done. The initiative need not then come from the under-informed citizen. In looking at the facts we had collected from our sample in order to form a judgment about the eligibility of each household for each benefit, we noticed that some people at present getting SB would have been better off if they had *not* claimed SB and had gone straight to the Town Hall for full rent and rate rebates. People whose whole rent and rates are being paid by the Supplementary Benefit Commission (SBC) cannot at the same time get full rent and rate rebates – this has perhaps helped to spread the impression that people getting SB are not entitled to anything more.

The critical group pinpointed was not, however, the people getting all their rent and rates paid, but only part of them because they were only getting partial benefit from the SBC. There were, for example, a number of people with war widows' pensions or disability pensions – higher than the basic rates for retirement pensions – and, on top of that, only a small supplement to bring them up to the SBC standard. If they only receive a small supplement they only get a small part of their rent and rates covered. What we found was that some of them — in eight households to be precise — would have been slightly, or some very considerably better off, if they had given up their supplementary benefit altogether and gone instead for a rent and rate rebate from their local authority. The National Union of Mineworkers has made the same point about retired miners with occupational pensions (Child Poverty Action Group 1973) although the Child Poverty Action Group, commenting on this, also stressed that the person who wants to move from the SBC to the Council should clearly take account of the discretionary SB allowances he or she might forfeit as well as the basic scale amounts.

The remedy is for once firmly in the hands of the authorities. There should be no need for individuals to act, unless the authorities refuse to. The SBC should be requested to examine the circumstances of all the recipients of benefits who are or would be getting from it say less than £1.50 a week and, if it seems that they would be better off on rate and rent rebates or rent allowances, refer the person concerned straight over to each local Council. Thousands of poor people — mainly people living alone — could benefit as a result and the take-up rates on the least-used scheme — rate rebates — would improve quite considerably. Even more would benefit if all old age pensioners not on SB were written to individually about the advantages which rate rebates and full rent rebate or allowance (instead of the 60% allowed by the SBC) might bring them. The Claimants Unions could also do a lot to stir up interest in what is still clearly the much misunderstood new scheme of rent rebates or allowance. There is no doubt that they can make a large difference. There were 20 families above our poverty line of SB scale rates plus 20% who were receiving either a rent rebate or a rent allowance. 6 of these were receiving SB at such a level that it would have made no difference to them whether they were getting a rebate or not. And even without a rent rebate or allowance 7 of these families would have remained above the line. But the other 7, who had an average rebate or allowance of £2.03 per week, would all have been well below our poverty line (2 below even SB scale rates) had they not been receiving rebates or allowances.

Conclusion

We mentioned right at the beginning of this chapter the caution that should be used in interpreting the results of this little enquiry in one place that certainly cannot represent the whole country. But Bethnal Green is not some City of Dreadful Night; it is very much part of our country, as much England in its way as Barnsley or Bath, and in our findings there is therefore no comfort for anyone in or out of the East End. It is disturbing that one-third of the households and two-fifths of the children, were living in poverty in the autumn of 1973. But what stands out most sharply of all is the plight of women. Even when married, if they were tied to the home by young children and unable to work themselves, there was very far from any guarantee that their 'wages' from the husband would keep pace with his. When not married but with children dependent on them, their lot was still less enviable. Widowed mothers have been given a somewhat better deal since the war. The committee on one-parent families chaired by Morris Finer, after four years of deliberation, is due to report very soon. Let us hope it will draw attention to the plight of divorced, separated and unmarried mothers who as we have seen, are still too often doubly unfortunate, at the bottom of the welfare state's schedule of priorities. In old age, too, there are more women surviving on what the state gives them, and many of them surviving in loneliness after their husbands have died. A great effort has been made over many years to secure equal pay and conditions for women who are at work; it is time for at least as large an effort on behalf of all the women who are not working.

References
B. Abel-Smith and P. Townsend, (1965) *The poor and the poorest*, Bell.
Walter Besant, (1901) *East London*, Chatto & Windus.

K. Coates and R. Silburn, (1967) *St. Ann's: poverty, deprivation and morale in a Nottingham community*, Nottingham University.

Cullingworth Report, (1969) *Council housing: purposes, procedures and priorities*, HMSO.

Department of Health and Social Security, (1971) *Two-parent families*, HMSO.

(1972) (Supplementary Benefits Commission) *Supplementary benefits handbook*, HMSO.

S. Gray, (1971) *The electoral register*, Office of Population Censuses and Surveys.

P. Marris, (1958) *Widows and their families*, Routledge.

Molly Meacher, (1972) *Rate rebates*, Child Poverty Action Group.

Child Poverty Action Group, (1973) *Poverty* no.26, Summer 1973.

P. Townsend, (1957) *The family life of old people*, Routledge.

P. Willmott, (1966) *Adolescent boys of East London*, Routledge.

M. Young and P. Willmott, (1957) *Family and kinship in East London*, Routledge.

M. Young, (1952) Distribution of income within the family, in *British Journal of Sociology*, vol. III, no.4.

2 Other Dimensions of Poverty

People in bad housing are the most visible of the poor. The inside can be imagined from the outside. If their material conditions are grim in this one crucial respect it is difficult for anything else to make up for their deprivation. The importance of the government's policies for housing does not therefore have to be underlined.

7 Housing
PETER WILLMOTT

The richest families often have two or even three homes — spacious, well-maintained and equipped with central heating and extra bathrooms — while some of the poorest are crammed into one or two rooms, crumbling and damp, with no bathroom at all and sharing with others the kitchen and WC. Such contrasts illustrate the 'housing problem'. They are a reminder that, as with any dimension of poverty, the deprivations of the poor are not just a matter of absolute standards. In every age the 'worst off' (itself by definition a relative term) will judge themselves, and be judged by others, in terms of what the 'better off' have. One cannot sensibly examine poverty without also discussing inequality (Townsend 1973). To talk about the poor — in this instance, the housing poor — is inevitably to talk about the distribution of housing, about which sort of people have and do not have access to a home at what would nowadays be considered a decent minimum standard and at a price they can afford (Eversley 1973).

It is clear that the general standards have improved in recent years: from 1961 to the end of 1972 about four and a quarter million new homes were built in Britain; the proportion of households in England and Wales with less than the recognised minimum number of bedrooms (roughly one for a married couple, one for each single adult, and one for each pair of same-sex children) fell from 11% in 1960 to 6% in 1971 (Office of Population Censuses and Surveys 1973); the 1967 and 1971 House Condition Surveys showed that the percentage of unfit dwellings in England and Wales had fallen from 12% to 7%, and of those without a bath from 13% to 8% (Department of the Environment 1973). But as these percentages themselves confirm, some people have been left out of the advance. They are the housing poor, and, though this chapter will discuss other aspects of what happened in housing during 1973, the crucial question is whether the housing problems of such people were eased.

Housing and income
The relationship between housing poverty and income poverty in Bethnal Green was discussed in the previous chapter. The pattern for Britain as a whole in 1971 is shown in Table 7.1. The poorest were more often without a bath or their own WC and less often had central heating. But, as in Bethnal Green, the correlation was far from complete. A few families even with more than £40 a week had no bath or WC of their own, and over a quarter of them had no central heating, while nearly one family in five with £10 a week or less did have central heating.

Table 7.1 Housing amenities by gross weekly income of head of household, Great Britain 1971

	No bath or shower %	Shared WC or none %	Central heating %
Up to £10	18	7	17
Over £10–£20	11	4	22
Over £20–£40	5	2	36
Over £40	1	1	73

Source: Office of Population Censuses and Surveys 1973

One explanation for such divergence is the Supplementary Benefits Commission: as long as the rent paid by someone on supplementary benefit is not considered unreasonably high, the Commission will pay it, so that some of those who are poorest in income live in fairly comfortable and well-equipped homes. But the main explanation is more general: there is not one 'market' for housing but several — owner occupation, council housing and privately rented property, with the last being divided into furnished and unfurnished, and with housing associations and the like forming a further small sector somewhere between council and privately rented. These markets operate in different ways and bargaining power in each is achieved by different means. For owner occupation, one needs a loan from a building society or local authority; for council housing one normally needs to be on a housing waiting list or in a house due for demolition; private tenants, unless long established, take what they can find, and many of those in furnished private tenancies are the people who have found nothing better.

Some council tenants are in old property in need of modernising. Some owner occupiers likewise are in old houses that they cannot afford to improve even with the help of grants. Others, often immigrants, have to meet the high cost of buying a house (often on a short-term mortgage or one at an exceptionally high interest rate) and so they sublet much of it, and tenants too are overcrowded and without amenities. But these are exceptions. By and large the worst housing is concentrated into the privately rented sector. It has the most unfit housing, the most overcrowding, the most sharing, the highest proportion of households without baths or inside WCs. Although there are rural slums, the bulk of this bad privately rented housing — and of hardship for its tenants — is concentrated in Britain's industrial towns and in the inner districts of large cities such as London, Birmingham, Liverpool and Glasgow.

There are broadly three kinds of people living in rented property in such places. First, the elderly who have always lived in rented property, usually unfurnished, often with poor amenities and in poor repair, but who are settled and pay relatively low rents. Secondly, single people or newly-

married couples, who pay high rents for unsatisfactory
rooms, often furnished, but stay only for a short time and
then move on to buy a house or to become council tenants.
Thirdly, people in furnished or, if they have been luckier,
unfurnished places, who want better housing but unlike
those in the second category are unable to make their escape
(Adams 1973).

The elderly often have little desire to move. Young people
are only transitory members of the housing poor. Those in
the third category are the worst off. Who are they?
They include many of the chronically sick and disabled, and
many families without an adult male wage earner (for
whatever reason). They include many semi-skilled and unskilled workers. Because people who move to London from
other parts of the country — or from abroad — can less easily
get into council housing, many in the third category are
migrants from other parts of the country or immigrants to
Britain.

There are additional obstacles for people with black or
brown skins. They are discriminated against in getting
mortgages and in unfurnished privately-rented housing, as
well as in council housing (Deakin and Ungerson 1973). It is
therefore not surprising that in Greater London in 1966, 44%
of coloured immigrants were in private furnished property
(with all its disadvantages) as against 7% of English households. Though many of the immigrants also have low
incomes, they are not all that poor; they thus represent as a
group the people who are in poverty in housing but not
necessarily in income terms. At the same time the badly housed
certainly include many whose access to decent housing has
been restricted because of low or unstable income.

It seems that major changes in the structure of tenure in
Britain over recent decades have increased inequality in a
period of generally rising standards, making things more and
more difficult for the kinds of people who remain dependent
on privately rented housing. The change over ten years is
shown in Table 7.2. This decade merely continued the
long-term trend: in 1900 about 90% of all households were in
privately rented property, compared with 15% in 1971. The
switch, as Table 7.2 shows, has been to owner occupation

and council housing.

Table 7.2 Households by tenure, Great Britain
1961—1971

	1961 %	1971 %
Owner occupied	41	49
Rented from local councils and new towns	25	31
Rented privately, unfurnished	24 ⎫ 28	12 ⎫ 15
Rented privately, furnished	4 ⎭	3 ⎭
Other	6	5
Total	100	100

Source: Office of Population Censuses and Surveys 1973

The change has happened for a variety of reasons. Public authorities have deliberately set out to renew slum districts and also to ease the problems inside old towns and cities by building large estates on the periphery — or in new or expanding towns. With rising real incomes and official encouragement to owner occupation there has been a growing demand for old as well as new houses to buy. The consequences have been summed up thus:

There is likely to be a continuing demand for rented property, particularly by new households and in the areas where new households form — the inner cities and particularly London. However, it is now more profitable for a landlord to sell his property rather than to rent it and the private rental sector is declining everywhere, in some cases producing considerable hardship. I think of this as the rabbits in the cornfield syndrome — as the harvester cuts its way round the periphery of the field towards the ever-diminishing standing corn in the centre, the strongest rabbits make a dash from the centre across the cut corn to the field hedges. The rest are cut to pieces when the harvester reaches the centre. (Adams 1973).

There are several pieces of evidence which support this view.

First, there has in recent years been a growing number of eviction orders in inner city districts (Lomas 1973). Secondly, and partly in consequence, homelessness seems to have been increasing. (The official figures on this are not easy to interpret, because since the Greve Report [Greve, Page and Greve 1971] there have been changes in the way homelessness is dealt with by councils, in particular its transfer from social services to housing departments, and a greater readiness on the part of the housing departments to recognise families as 'homeless' and to accept responsibility for helping them. But reports in September 1973 from Shelter Housing Aid Centres in London, Manchester and Bristol showed large increases in the numbers of families seeking help during the preceding months.) Thirdly, a survey published in September 1973 of what had been done during the previous twelve months by 33 local authorities about the particular problem of the single homeless, showed that three-quarters of the councils had as yet no plans to provide accommodation for such people (Campaign for the Homeless and Rootless 1973). Fourthly, though no figures were available, there were reports towards the end of 1973 that in London and some other cities local authority waiting lists were growing and vacancies in council dwellings falling. All in all it seems unlikely that the trends of recent years were being reversed; in 1973 things probably went on deteriorating for those living in privately rented housing in inner city areas.

Council house building
As already explained, one of the problems has been that at a time when the private rental sector has been declining, council housing has remained relatively inaccessible to some categories of people in housing need — immigrants in particular and migrants to the cities in general, single people (including students) and newly-married couples. Several years ago the Cullingworth Committee (Cullingworth Report 1969) suggested that councils should take a broader view of their duties, and this policy was endorsed by the government in April 1973 in its White Paper, *Widening the choice: the next steps in housing* (1973). So far most councils have done little, but presumably they will gradually adopt a broader

brief and more people in housing hardship will become eligible for council tenancies. For this reason, as well as generally to improve the housing stock and housing standards, we need to continue to build more new houses and more new council houses in particular.

The general pattern over the past few years has, however, been one of decline in council housebuilding. In 1968 local authorities in Britain started building 170,948 new homes; in 1972, 99,585. Houses started by new towns fell proportionately less, from 11,610 to 10,546 (as did those built directly for government departments themselves, from 3,501 to 3,153), and those by housing associations increased a little, from 8,290 to 9,705. In the public sector as a whole (these four categories taken together) the number of houses started fell from 194,349 in 1968 to 122,989 in 1972. Housebuilding progress, in the private sector as well as the public, during the first three-quarters of 1973 compared with the same period in 1972, is shown in Table 7.3.

The Table shows that 8% less new homes of all kinds and 19% less new council houses were completed during the first nine months of 1973. Housing starts were also down, in total and in council housing in particular. The number of council houses under construction was about the same and of other houses somewhat higher than in 1972. This is mainly a reflection of the fact that past strikes in the construction industry, together with other delays, mean that it is now taking longer to build homes.

The most useful single measure is probably the housing starts. These show a decline in council building which is not being compensated by the increase in the (relatively small) remainder of the public sector or by private housebuilding. With the increasing difficulty of selling private homes, mentioned later, it seems likely that even private housebuilding was falling by the end of the year.

Table 7.3 does not take account of rehabilitation; this has been growing in importance. The number of grants for conversions and improvements – council property as well as private – increased threefold from 1969 to 1972, to over 350,000, and the trend continued into 1973; there were 342,000 grants in Britain in the first three-quarters of the

Table 7.3 Housebuilding in Great Britain 1972 and 1973

	Local authorities	Other public sector	Private sector	All
New houses started				
January—September 1972	76,767	17,190	170,937	264,894
January—September 1973	67,449	19,743	172,804	259,996
Percentage increase(+) or decrease (—)	—12%	+15%	+1%	—2%
Under construction				
At 30 September 1972	164,703	33,868	221,319	419,890
At 30 September 1973	165,746	40,499	258,114	464,359
Percentage increase(+) or decrease(—)	+1%	+20%	+17%	+10%
Completed				
January—September 1972	80,304	13,244	144,474	238,022
January—September 1973	64,977	14,294	140,721	219,992
Percentage increase(+) or decrease(—)	—19%	+8%	—3%	—8%

Source: Department of the Environment/Scottish Development Department/Welsh Office 1973

year compared with 263,000 in the first three-quarters of 1972. Such improvement work — representing as it does a deliberate switch of resources away from the bulldozer — ought to be brought into the reckoning. If the total building work — in new housebuilding and improvement combined — were computed for 1973 it might show that as much was done in housing as in 1972. But, as shown later, although some of the rehabilitation work obviously does help the poor, much of it does not. More public housing is anyway needed, particularly in and around the cities.

Why has it declined? There are several interpretations. On one analysis it reflects the decline in demand in some parts of the country. Some local councils now have virtually no housing list; they can offer council housing to new applicants almost immediately. But 'some of the worst falls have been experienced in the worst areas' (Eversley 1973). So this cannot be the sole explanation.

Another cause has been the difficulty in some areas of finding building land. In the ten years up to 1972 land costs increased by two and a half times in the country as a whole. In the second quarter of 1973, sites of new houses cost 65% more than in the same quarter of 1972 — £2,955 compared with £1,787. These are national averages: over the year the increase was 16% in Scotland and 23% in the north east; in London and the south east it was 31%; in the south west it was 67% and in the eastern region 82% (Nationwide Building Society 1973). Prices for housing land seemed to be easing, and in places actually falling, during the second half of the year. But if there was a fall it was from very high levels and it is unlikely that land prices will go down all that much.

The government announced in its April 1973 White Paper that it wanted to release more land for building, including some in green belts, and new guidelines on this were set out in an official circular at the beginning of October. The White Paper also promised a 'land hoarding charge' to discourage private developers from 'unjustifiable delay' in developing land for which planning permission for housing had been given. This proposal will have to wait on legislation. Obviously neither of these policies has yet had any effect. Shelter reported in September that it had been told by local authorities in ten cities in England and Wales that land shortage was restricting new housebuilding.

Another obstacle has been the cost of construction itself, where inflation has been even more marked than in the economy as a whole. In the second quarter of 1973 house-building — wages and materials — cost 29% more than in the same quarter of 1972. Councils have suffered particularly as a result. This is partly because, though they have understandably preferred fixed-price contracts and have been encouraged in this by the government in an effort to keep costs down, contractors have found it increasingly difficult to put in realistic tenders and have been increasingly reluctant to tender at all in a period of accelerating costs. In September

1973 the government announced that in certain tightly-controlled circumstances ex-gratia payments could be made to builders on fixed-price contracts who found themselves in difficulties, but it is not clear how much difference this is likely to make.

The so-called 'cost yardstick' has contributed to the builders' lack of enthusiasm. Introduced in 1967 this was also intended to hold down costs. Under the scheme only contracts falling within the laid-down cost limits normally receive government loan approval. The limits have not been revised since April 1972, although there is a 'market condition allowance' (introduced in November 1972) which means that government approval can still be given for high-priced tenders if they are not grossly out of line with the standard levels.

Opinions differ about how important the yardstick is in discouraging council building. A number of professional bodies have criticised it, including the County Architects' Society in January 1973, the Association of Municipal Corporations in May, and the Royal Institution of Chartered Surveyors in July. Some local authorities have themselves complained. A Greater London Council deputation told the government in August that the yardstick might mean that it would build 2,000 less houses during the year than it otherwise would. The Council said that over a period it had approached 714 contractors for 58 competitive jobs but only 212 had bothered even to tender.

The problem has not been helped by the existence of the 'lump' — the arrangement under which builders, desperate for workers, employ 'labour-only sub-contractors'. Because this system is non-union, authorities, especially Labour ones, are increasingly unwilling to allow it. This in its turn reduces the number of contractors with enough of a labour force to take on council work.

In early October as part of its Phase III proposals the government announced a three-month halt in the awarding of public building contracts, except for housing and roads. It is thought that one purpose was to ease the pressure so that contractors would be keener to tender for council building. This, together with easier land prices, might help. But it looks as if the decline in council housebuilding will probably continue, and those who might otherwise move into new council housing will suffer.

Rents

1973 was the first full year of the government's new policy on housing subsidies, expressed in the Housing Finance Act 1972. The main question is how this affected the rents paid by council and private tenants and in particular the poorer ones. Chapter 3 brought in rents as part of a general review of the consequences for the standard of living of various changes in 1973. This chapter tries to sketch in the background to one of the most important changes of the year — a culmination of many years of debate — and to make some assessment of the new policy. It is obviously too early to make any final judgment about how the new arrangements are working or what their long-term effects will be. But some sort of interim view can be formed.

The central purpose was to relate the subsidy to the family and its needs rather than to the dwelling and as a corollary to make the rents for different kinds of property more 'consistent with each other', which meant increasing most. The government took over and extended the system of 'fair rents' introduced by its predecessor in the 1965 Rent Act. The argument, set out in the White Paper *Fair deal for housing* (1971), was that those who could afford to pay this fair rent would then do so; those who could not, whether council or private tenants, would be subsidised. The biggest break with the past was in giving subsidies to private ('rent allowances') as well as to council tenants ('rent rebates').

An important point is about the cost of this package of proposals. In the 1971 White Paper the government argued that if continued the former system would impose a 'staggering addition to the nation's tax burden'. To start with, the new scheme is expected to cost much the same as the old. But since the costs of the new arrangements are not expected to rise like those of the old, the saving is likely to be about £50 million in 1973–74 and £150 million or more by 1975–76. Because of the complexity of the system, with nine different subsidies, three of them temporary, it is not easy to calculate with any confidence to what extent this difference will be met by the higher rents of the council tenants who do pay them, and to what extent local authorities — or which local authorities — will be worse off. The government has argued that those with heavy slum clearance responsibilities will actually be better off. Meanwhile, the fact has to be borne in mind that the new policy is intended to cost the taxpayer less than its predecessor.

The scheme started for council tenants on 1 October 1972. The rent allowance scheme started for unfurnished private tenants on 1 January 1973, and for some but not all furnished tenants on 1 April 1973. Councils, which previously had themselves decided on the rents of their tenants, had the responsibility of setting fair rents for all their dwellings by 1 October 1972 — taking into account the age, character, locality and state of repair — and publishing the provisional fair rents by 9 February 1973. As is well known, some councils have refused to implement the new Act or to increase their rents, notably Clay Cross Urban District Council in Derbyshire, whose councillors have had a £7,000 'surcharge' levelled against them by the district auditor acting for the government, and have been deposed by a government-appointed Housing Commissioner who will try to implement the Act in their stead.

Between 9 April and 9 June 1973, councils had to submit their provisional rents to area Rent Scrutiny Boards (appointed by the government) which have power to revise the figures. In the first stage of moving to the (higher) fair rents, council rents were increased by an average of up to £1 per week on 1 October 1972, by 50p on 1 October 1973, and will be increased by another 50p each year until the fair rent levels are reached. In any case the fair rent levels have to be reviewed every three years.

Because the idea of a fair rent is a vague one, nobody knows how high the council fair rents will be. One of the first local authorities to hear from a Rent Scrutiny Board was Lees Urban District Council, Lancashire, in mid-1973. The rent of a two-bedroomed house in Lees was increased in

October 1972 to £2.02 (before the Act it had been £1.07).
The council's proposal for a fair rent was £2.50. The
rejoinder from the Scrutiny Board was that it should instead
be £3.25. Another Board increased the suggested fair rent of
£6 for a four-bedroom council house (in Ilkley, Yorkshire) to
£8.40. If these examples are any guide to what might happen
elsewhere, council rents generally may rise substantially.

With privately rented housing, the idea was to move from
rent control to fair rents — alternatively expressed as from
rent control to rent regulation or from controlled tenancies
to regulated tenancies — in steps over three years, with the
new rents being fixed by agreement between landlord and
tenant, by the local Rent Officer or, if there was a dispute,
by a Rent Assessment Committee. The point at which
controlled tenancies move over to regulation depends on the
rateable value, the higher-rated properties going first. The
first step was to have been on 1 January 1973 but this was
postponed for three months because of the government's
wage and prices freeze. During the first year the rent could go
up by 50p per week or a third of the difference between the
old rent and the new, whichever was the greater. Then, as
with council rents, it increases in stages until the new rent is
reached. These private rents also can be reviewed after three
years.

Thus in 1973 council tenants had, on top of their rent
increase in 1972, an average increase of 50p per week (under
the Act no individual tenant could have an increase of over
75p per week). As for private tenants, it is not clear how
many had their rents increased during 1973 under the Act,
but rough calculations based on rateable values suggest that it
might have been as many as half. Furnished tenants are not
covered by the fair rents scheme — as before, they can appeal
to Rent Tribunals — but rents are hardly likely to have fallen
or remained stable. All this means that it is impossible to
calculate an average increase in the rents of private tenants
generally during 1973. Some had increases of 50p; others had
larger increases; others, still outside the fair rents scheme, had

none. It seems reasonable, however, to assume overall an average increase in private rents, as in council rents, of 50p during the year.

The increases in rents have to be set against the average increases in wages (between 1 November 1972 and 31 October 1973) given in Chapter 3: £3 for a low-paid, £5 for an average, and £7 for an affluent worker. But the rents are of course only half of the government's new deal for housing. The rebates and allowances are intended to compensate the poor, though people are of course eligible for them whether or not their rent has actually gone up. In January 1973 the government estimated that about two million council tenants in England and Wales (about 40% of all council tenants) would be eligible for rent rebates and about 750,000 private tenants (about 30%) for rent allowances. Furnished tenants are eligible in certain circumstances, and the latter figure includes an estimated 120,000.

There are national scales to determine whether families are eligible for a rebate or allowance and if so how much. (Local councils have powers to operate somewhat more generous schemes). As explained in Chapter 4, there are three elements in the calculation − the rent, the income of the tenant and his wife, and the family's needs allowance (based on such things as the number of children, and whether the tenant or his wife is blind or disabled). The needs allowances were increased twice during 1973 − in April and October. The idea of the changes was that they would offset the rent increases during the year of those eligible for help. The effect of these rebates and allowances has been taken into account in Chapters 3 and 4. Table 7.4 gives more detail: it shows the rebates to which people would be entitled: (a) at three different rent levels, (b) with different family circumstances, and (c) at the three levels of gross income used in Chapter 3. Also shown is the rent they would pay if they claimed their rebate or allowance.

The Table shows that if he claimed, the low-paid worker with children would benefit a good deal from the scheme,

Table 7.4 Rent rebates and allowances
(after 1 October 1973

	Net rent of £3		Net rent of £6		Net rent of £9	
	Rebate	Rent to pay	Rebate	Rent to pay	Rebate	Rent to pay
Low-paid worker *(£25 per week)*						
Single	£0.18	£2.82	£1.98	£4.02	£3.78	£5.22
Couple	£1.08	£1.92	£2.88	£3.12	£4.68	£4.32
Couple with 1 child	£1.59	£1.41	£3.39	£2.61	£5.19	£3.81
Couple with 2 children	£2.24	£0.76	£4.04	£1.96	£5.84	£3.16
Couple with 4 children	£3.00	None	£5.54	£0.46	£7.34	£1.66
Average worker *(£38 per week)*						
Single	None	£3.00	None	£6.00	£1.57	£7.43
Couple	None	£3.00	£0.67	£5.33	£2.47	£6.53
Couple with 1 child	None	£3.00	£1.18	£4.82	£2.98	£6.02
Couple with 2 children	None	£3.00	£1.69	£4.31	£3.49	£5.51
Couple with 4 children	£0.91	£2.09	£2.71	£3.29	£4.51	£4.49
Affluent worker *(£57 per week)*						
Single	None	£3.00	None	£6.00	None	£9.00
Couple	None	£3.00	None	£6.00	None	£9.00
Couple with 1 child	None	£3.00	None	£6.00	None	£9.00
Couple with 2 children	None	£3.00	None	£6.00	£0.26	£8.74
Couple with 4 children	None	£3.00	None	£6.00	£1.27	£7.72

NOTE 'Net rent' means excluding rates and charges for things like heating or a garage.

while the average married worker would benefit at the
two higher rent levels, and the affluent worker with two
children would get a rebate or allowance at a rent of £9 per
week. For the low-paid worker with children, and even for
some of the others, the rebate or allowance would more than
offset an increase of 50p in weekly rent. The gain would be
particularly marked for private tenants who before 1973
were not eligible for a rent allowance at all, and they
included, as shown earlier, many of the worst off.

It seems as if the so-called 'wage-stop' families on
supplementary benefit (noted by Syson and Young in Chapter
6) are one particular group who have benefited from the new
scheme. Since they can now receive rebates or allowances
(and family income supplement) in work as well as out of it,
their supplementary benefit payments are less likely to be
held down to the level of their wages. The numbers of
families that were 'wage-stopped' fell during 1973 from
about 20,000 earlier in the year to about 6,000 towards the
end, and the new rent scheme is thought to be the main
explanation for this change.

But a crucial question is how many people in general take
advantage of the scheme. We have some evidence from the
1973 Bethnal Green survey reported in the previous chapter.
There, 96% of council tenants and 68% of private tenants
knew about the rebate/allowance scheme. We made a series
of detailed calculations to discover which households were
eligible, on the basis of income, family circumstances and
rent. Of the tenants who seemed eligible, 60% in council
property and 23% in private were actually getting the rebate
or allowance.

There are as yet no authoritative national figures, but the
government has given estimates of the proportions of those
eligible who in May 1973 were receiving rebates or allowances. These were 85% of council tenants and 50% of
unfurnished private tenants. If the estimates prove accurate,
then take-up generally is not as low as in Bethnal Green, but
there is still a sharp difference between the two sectors.

The higher take-up by council tenants is presumably
explained partly by the fact that, unlike most private tenants,
they were told about the scheme by their landlord, and at a

time when with rent increases the incentive was strong. The low take-up among private tenants is presumably mainly due to ignorance, together with some reluctance to apply.

The new policy raises some fundamental questions about the distribution both of incomes and of housing tenures. On incomes, it is clear that a transfer is taking place specifically from better-off council tenants to poor tenants, public and private. It can also be argued, as it has been for instance by the National Association of Local Government Officers (1973), that, since the total subsidy to council housing is being held down while the tax relief to owner occupiers is not, the policy represents a redistribution in favour of the latter.

On tenure, some critics have suggested that the policy will lead to very high fair rents in 'desirable' areas, drive out poorer tenants (since they will find such rents too high even with rebate) and thus lead to social polarisation. Others have said that, by pressing better-off tenants into owner occupation, it will turn council housing into the preserve of the poor. It is clearly too early to say much about both these criticisms. There are also more immediate doubts about the detailed administration of the scheme (see Nevitt 1973) and there are criticisms of the arrangements for furnished tenants, which are framed much less generously than those for unfurnished tenants.

All these are important questions. But in general the new scheme seems admirable from the point of view of the poor, apart from the problem of take-up. As long as only a small proportion, of private tenants especially, get the rent allowances to which they are entitled the scheme can hardly be judged a success.

Owner occupation and mortgages

For owner occupiers, as distinct from tenants, two important developments in 1973 were in prices and in mortgage rates.

House prices have been rising sharply in recent years, particularly in 1972. The average price of new dwellings mortgaged with building societies by private owners nearly doubled from 1966 to 1972, though the increases (like the prices themselves) varied widely from one part of the country to another, being highest in southern England and lowest in Scotland. During the first half of 1973 prices were still rising. In the second quarter of 1973, the average price of a new house mortgaged by a large building society had gone up 35% compared with the same quarter of 1972; that of a modern existing house by 30%; and that of an older house by 27% (Nationwide Building Society 1973). But these increases represented a slowing down compared with what had been happening, and towards the end of the year it looked as though prices were stabilising or even falling. They had, however, risen so much previously — particularly in regions like London and the south east, where in mid-1973 the average price of an old house was £11,700 and of a modern one £13,300 — that they were clearly still well beyond the reach of most people.

High interest rates did not help (they were probably part of the explanation for the falling demand for houses). At the beginning of the year, the normal rate of mortgage interest was 8½%. The building societies wanted to increase this to 10% in April but the government intervened, lending the societies £15 million over three months in an effort to hold the rate down to 9½%. When the three months were over, the rate went up too — it rose to 10% in August and 11% in September.

The government had tried to avert these higher rates with the £15 million subsidy and with the limit it imposed in September on the rates of interest that banks could pay to borrowers. Towards the end of 1973 it was also trying to work out with the building societies a scheme which would allow new purchasers to pay a lower rate of interest to start with. The idea was that the buyer would pay at 8½% in the first year and ½% more each successive year until the sixth, when he would pay the normal rate. This arrangement, though initially cheaper, would actually cost the borrower more in the long run if, as was assumed would happen, the differences between the normal rate of interest and the lower rate were simply added to his outstanding debt.

The consequence of the increases during the year, for an owner occupier who was buying his house on a variable interest-rate mortgage and was unable to extend the period of the loan, was that his monthly interest payments went up from January to September by as much as a quarter or even a third. According to the *Evening Standard* (25 September 1973) one housebuyer with a mortgage of £4,500 had to pay £43 a month in September compared with £36.80 earlier in the year. Few such people were likely to be poor, though there may have been some with relatively modest means who felt the pinch, particularly during a period when increases in pay were restrained and other prices were rising.

Despite high interest rates, the 'running costs of home ownership remain exceptionally cheap', as *The Times* put it after the rise to 10% mortgages in August. Even 11% is reduced by tax relief to 7.7%, and for the richest people — those paying tax at the higher rates of 50%, 60% and 75% — the rate of interest is correspondingly further reduced. This tax relief is in effect a subsidy to house-purchasers, costing almost as much in total as the straight subsidies (Central Statistical Office 1972), and likely to overtake them in future years.

Owner occupied houses, unlike other forms of investment, are exempt from capital gains tax and are thus attractive on this score also. The inequity as between owning and renting has been noted by several writers (for example, Nevitt 1966 and Evans 1973) and two particular 'undesirable features' of the present system were recently pointed out:

> First, an important part of real income is effectively untaxed and the subsidy is regressive in that it gives most to those who already earn most. Second, it encourages housing demand by the rich as against the poor and it drives building resources to the rich end of the market as against the poor end, by encouraging building for owner-occupation, building resources have been channelled away from areas of greatest need. (National Association of Local Government Officers, 1973).

In a period of inflation — in the long run, and as long as it continues, houses will continue to be worth more and more — house-purchase is the most obvious economic sense, for those who can afford it. The distinction between owner occupiers, who are hedged against inflation, and tenants, who are not, is a major division in British society.

This is related to what was said earlier about the Housing Finance Act; it will do nothing to reduce that division and may well deepen it, since it deliberately sets out to hold down the future cost of subsidies and ignores mortgage relief.

It is not entirely clear what the long-term consequences are for the distribution of income and wealth. Day (1973) has argued, on the basis of Inland Revenue data, that rises in house prices increase the wealth held by those in the middle of the income and wealth distribution, at the expense of the poor and the very rich. Clearly the poor have little or no wealth anyway. The Inland Revenue statistics show that estates in the middling wealth range have a high proportion of house property, and high wealth estates have a high proportion of shares. In a period when house prices have risen more sharply than share prices — as has happened over the last few years — there must have been a redistribution of capital towards the middle range. This process is reinforced by the tax relief on mortgages already mentioned. It is also reinforced by improvement grants, through which the government meets part of the cost of home improvements. Those that go to owner occupiers — about one-third of the total — are a subsidy in the form of capital appreciation to those families who already have capital or are, with the help of a mortgage, acquiring it. The conclusion is that, although the rich are of course still much richer than the rest, the relative share of wealth held by middle-range owner occupiers has increased. As their numbers increase — from about a quarter of households in the late thirties to about half now — such people have, increasingly, a stake in capital wealth not shared by those who are tenants.

New policies for the housing poor

If fewer council houses are being built and the homes built for sale are well beyond the reach of most of the housing poor, it does not seem so far that they benefited much from what happened in 1973. But there were during the year some developments (as well as rent rebates) intended specifically to improve their chances of access to better housing. The starting point was the fact already noted that, although there are families with housing problems in all forms of tenure and in almost all kinds of district, the housing poor are concentrated in privately rented housing in the inner areas of Britain's towns and cities.

Some new policies were announced in a White Paper, *Better homes: the next priorities*, published in June 1973. Again it is too early to evaluate the proposals (some of them depend on legislation) but some sort of assessment can be made of the likely effects.

There are two main approaches. The first is a set of proposals to restrain property speculators, restrict the allocation of improvement grants and generally give less encouragement to the process described as 'gentrification'. On improvement grants, the government, while arguing that the system had generally worked well, acknowledged that there had been some abuse — 'some owners have sought to make unjustifiably high profits by abusing the improvement grant system'. The grants have if anything made the problem worse for the housing poor in stress areas. By encouraging higher house prices for older houses, they have made it more profitable for developers or owners to evict or by other means 'winkle out' existing tenants. Some evidence from the London Borough of Hammersmith was given by the Borough's house improvement officer, speaking at the Public Health Inspectors' conference in October 1973. He said that an examination of 500 recent complaints of alleged harassment showed that 21% (probably an understatement, since many families would not complain) involved properties on which applications for improvement grants had been made or granted.

The White Paper proposed the following: limits (though fairly high ones) on the maximum rateable values at which grants could be given; no grants for second homes; powers for local authorities to impose conditions, in particular to stop grants to speculators. These proposals were implemented in a government circular (99/73) (Department of the Environment) sent to local authorities at the beginning of September. Another measure to encourage the full use of property and to discourage speculators is that local authorities will have greater powers to impose rates, rising to 100% on empty property. These various proposals are likely to help, though not drastically.

The second main approach in the White Paper is to 'redirect priorities' to those districts where the worst housing problems are concentrated, not only the inner city areas where bad housing goes with high demand, but also areas in the older industrial towns where poor housing and environment go with falling population and low demand. Such districts are to be treated as 'Housing Action Areas', an idea obviously stemming from a proposal originally made by the Milner Holland Committee (Report of the Committee on Housing in Greater London 1965).

These areas would usually be fairly small — 400 or 500 dwellings. In such areas the management of tenanted properties is expected to pass increasingly from private landlords to a strengthened housing association movement. The local council would also have extra powers to compel owners to repair and improve their houses (or do it themselves instead); to insist that landlords selling rented property offered first refusal to a housing association or to the council itself; to nominate tenants for houses deliberately left empty; to give larger improvement grants and grants for repairs only. The local councils would also have a duty to rehouse tenants in these areas temporarily or permanently displaced by redevelopment or rehabilitation.

Are these proposals likely to be effective? The strong impression is that though they are well-intentioned and may do something to help they are unlikely to make much difference. *The Times* (13 June 1973) commented: 'What is missing is any strengthening of the agencies by which the policies will be executed. Local authorities are to carry on . . . Unfortunately . . . housing in the conurbations (which in this context are the places that matter) remains primarily in the hands of the metropolitan districts. In many cases they have not the resources, the administrative muscle, or the land to see the job through.' A review of what the proposals would mean in practice in a fairly characteristic inner London area of housing stress (the Alexander Road area in Islington) concluded that the proposed scheme: '. . . would not halt the impending obsolescence of much older housing in the area; it would not ensure the provision of self-contained accommodation for the majority of tenants; it would not enable tenants in the furnished sector to obtain security of tenure, with all the rights and benefits that flow from that; it would not ensure that improved accommodation was let at rents which low income families can afford' (Holmes 1973).

Scepticism about the impact of the White Paper's proposals will be all the greater as long as there is uncertainty about the resources that will actually be made available. In the spring of 1973 the government announced that, despite some other cuts in spending, it was going to allocate another £35 million to housing. So far it has not explained exactly what this money is to be used for, or how it is to be paid out, and the sum is anyway not very large. Without a major commitment of resources, these new schemes may promise strong action without actually leading to it.

Conclusion

In judging housing progress during the year, a distinction has to be made between action to improve the housing of the worst off and action affecting its cost.

On the first, the record is not good. There was less new council housing, with the prospect even of less private housing, and house purchase as a possibility remained remote. The new White Paper proposals may do something to help in the worst districts, but not much and not very quickly.

On the financial side, the Housing Finance Act does do something to help the poor, particularly those in privately rented housing. But, quite apart from other doubts about its long-term consequences, as long as the take-up of rent allowances remains low, particularly among private tenants, the help will obviously not get through to most eligible families. One of the crucial housing questions about 1974 will be whether or not take-up does materially increase.

References
B. Adams, (1973) 'Some social problems of housing', unpublished

paper, Department of the Environment.

Better homes: the next priorities, (1973) cmnd. 5339, HMSO.

Campaign for the Homeless and Rootless, (1973) *Thirty-three local authorities one year after.*

Central Statistical Office, (1972) *Social Trends*, no. 3, HMSO.

Cullingworth Report, (1969) *Council housing: purposes, procedures and priorities*, HMSO.

A. Day, (1973) 'Poor thinking about the rich', *Observer*, 22 April 1973.

N. Deakin and C. Ungerson, (1973) 'Beyond the ghetto: the illusion of choice', in D. Eversley and D.V. Donnison (eds.), *London: urban patterns, problems and policies*, Heinemann.

Department of the Environment/Scottish Development Department/ Welsh Office, (1973) *Housing and Construction Statistics*, no. 6, HMSO.

A. Evans, (1973) 'Suggestions for the reform of housing finance', paper to Centre for Environmental Studies Urban Economic Conference.

D. Eversley, (1973) 'Priorities in housing', *Municipal and Public Services Journal*, vol. 81, no. 41.

Fair deal for housing, (1971) cmnd. 4728, HMSO.

J. Greve, D. Page and S. Greve, (1971) *Homelessness in London*, Scottish Academic Press.

C. Holmes, (1973) *Better homes — the next priorities: a critical review*, North Islington Housing Rights Project.

G. Lomas, (1973) 'Current problems and prospects' in *London's housing needs*, London Council of Social Service.

National Association of Local Government Officers, (1973) *Housing: the way ahead*, Report of the NALGO Housing Working Party.

Nationwide Building Society, (1973) *Occasional Bulletin 116*.

A. Nevitt, (1966) *Housing, taxation and subsidies*, Nelson.

          (1973) *Thamesmead rents*, Greater London Council.

Office of Population Censuses and Surveys, (1973) *The general household survey: introductory report*, HMSO.

Report of the Committee on Housing in Greater London, (1965) cmnd. 2605, HMSO.

P. Townsend, (1973) 'Everyone his own home, inequality in housing and the creation of a national service', *RIBA Journal*, vol. 80, no. 1.

Widening the choice: the next steps in housing, (1973) cmnd. 5280, HMSO.

Poor housing is a little easier to identify
than poor education. But that does not mean
there are not large gaps in the quality of
education received by members of different
classes and racial groups living in different
parts of the country. By and large children
with poorer parents have had the worst deal.
But there are signs of a change: 1973 was
notable for the long-awaited introduction of
nursery schools, for further support for
Educational Priority Areas, and in other ways
as well.

8   Education

STELLA DUNCAN, MICHAEL YOUNG and MARION KIRKWOOD

The relationship between poverty and inequality has been
raised repeatedly throughout the book. With education, the
difference is that one cannot sensibly discuss it without also
discussing the positive notion of equality. This is because the
framework of ideas within which the educational system
operates is unlike that shoring up any other of the social
services except health. The concern of the Supplementary
Benefits Commission, or the welfare services, or housing
authorities – to mention just three examples – is not with
the whole population but with the minority of adults who
cannot fend for themselves. The education service is in
principle concerned with everybody, defined not by income
or wealth, but according to the single universalist yardstick of
age.

By the same criterion, at the other end of life, the claims
of the old are as generally accepted as those of the young. All
people who have retired from work and contributed to
national insurance are entitled to a pension. But although this

is paid to them whether they are rich or poor it is not intended to do much to lessen the gap between them. Some rich old people are driven, or drive themselves in Jaguars to get their state pension; others totter along on foot or at best travel free by bus. For children the aspiration is more ambitious — that they should have actual equality of a particular kind. The education system does not, of course, have a formally expressed ideology like the American declaration — 'all men are created equal', or anything of that sort — but running through the many other strands of faith and hope which influence it is a dominant belief in equality of opportunity. Although this means many different things to many different people there is also a common thread: that all children, irrespective of the means of their families, should have the same opportunity to benefit from education. Rich parents can buy a privileged education for their children, and practice does not therefore square with the principle. All the same it would hardly any longer be possible to find anyone who declares that the children of poor parents should just because of their birth have a poor education.

A number of ideas have joined together to buttress this general proposition — the long-lived Christian belief that all men are the children of God, and in that way equal, has had special force when applied to those who are literally children. The virtues of throwing careers open to the talents have been part of a bourgeois ethic espoused by many who would not countenance any other sort of equality except that of opportunity. Whether people believe in original sin or not they can hardly think that children who are handicapped by the family circumstances into which they are born are themselves responsible for their fate. They are innocent of the blame which poor adults have not been wholly allowed to escape from (even in their own eyes blame may become shame) by the formal extinction of the Poor Law. Education occupies a realm governed by higher ideals than the rest of a society in which self-interest is given such large scope. The one belongs with the other. But there is some looseness of fit between them — education being not just more sensitive to ideology than the occupational system but also to an altruistic ideology.

Now or hereafter

Education has had special appeal because many of its proponents have taken the opposite point of view to the one expressed in 1973 by the National Association of Schoolmasters (National Association of Schoolmasters 1973).

> We do not think it to be any part of a teacher's professional role to determine the nature of society.

So much reforming zeal has gone into education — partly because zealots have thought that they might thereby shape the nature of society, and that success could be doubly egalitarian. Education is not only life, it is a preparation for life. If therefore the difference between the most and the least favoured children could be lessened then so would the difference between the most and the least favoured adults. The more equal child would be father to the more equal man. This meant continually pushing up standards at the bottom, so that as education was allied to talent and skill to hand and brain, Alfred Marshall's forecast made exactly a century ago would be borne out and 'by occupation at least every man would be a gentleman'. (Marshall 1873).

This has obviously not happened. Educational opportunity has expanded, yet the distribution of incomes has remained much as before. This is partly because the general expansion in education has not removed the gap between top and bottom. As in so many other spheres, the top has been pushed up along with the bottom. Each time the minimum leaving age is raised for everyone more children stay on voluntarily well beyond that point. It looks as though continued inequality amongst adults may also coexist with rather greater equality amongst children, because schooling has less long-term effect than it was once credited with. The debate has continued to be transatlantic. The Coleman Report published in the USA in 1966 showed that it made much less difference to attainment which school a child went to than which home he came from or who the other children were he mixed with (Coleman 1966). The Plowden Report a year later in Britain concluded much the same from its survey; at any rate it stressed that the family seemed to matter a great deal more than the school, even to academic

achievement. Halsey in his report published shortly before
the beginning of our year said that 'the major determinants
of educational attainment were not schoolmasters but social
situations, not curriculum but motivation, not formal access
to the school but support in the family and the community'
(Halsey 1972). It only remained for Jencks to draw the
conclusion, supported by a wealth of statistics, that if the
character of a school did not have all that much influence
upon academic progress neither did it upon the incomes
which people earned in later life. 'We cannot blame economic
inequality on differences between schools, since differences
between schools seem to have very little effect on any
measurable attribute of those who attend them' (Jencks
1973).

But if equalising opportunity is not a means of equalising
results in schools hereafter, it is a more realistic ambition for
the here and now. Seen in this way one can only be pleased
that one of the kindest research findings from a large
international study was that 'England was one of the few
countries where, on average, children like school more than
they dislike it (National Foundation for Educational Research 1973; Comber and Keeves 1973). Insofar as education
is a benefit, and even one that is actually enjoyed, it can be
shared more, or less, equally. If education is not quite the
preparation for life it was once thought to be, it is still life; if
an end in itself rather than a means to an end it still matters a
great deal whether access to it is equal or not. The same
issues of equity arise whether the focus is on the short or the
long-term effects of education. The difference between
education and the other social services is, as we have said,
that with the former there is much more agreement that
equality is at any rate in many respects something that
should be sought.

To be more specific: it is widely held that no children
should be deprived of educational opportunity on grounds of
wealth, or lack of it, territory, or where they live, ability,
colour, or sex. It follows that education should set itself
against (1) inequalities of class, (2) territorial inequalities, (3)
inequalities of ability, (4) racial inequalities, and selective as
it is bound to be, we are going to discuss in turn the,

application in the year we are considering, 1973, of these four principles, leaving out the fifth that could have been added — sex discrimination. This is not, needless to say, because it is unimportant. It is perhaps more so because sex discrimination works both ways. In the earlier years of school, unlike the later, the pattern is reversed. At the age of seven boys more often have speech difficulties, tics, head banging or 'rocking', hernias and delayed bowel control as well as being more backward in the classroom (Davie 1973). It is just that nothing of great moment was done to reduce discrimination for either sex, unless the raising of the leaving age is counted a measure of sexual justice because of the lower leaving age of girls in the past.

Inequalities of class

The initial class inequality between children was as obvious in 1973 as in any other year. A report on the National Child Development Study which has been following up seventeen thousand children born in March 1958 said that

One of the most striking and disturbing findings from the first follow-up was the marked and consistent relationship between the occupational status ('social class') of the children's fathers and most aspects of the children's behaviour, development and ability. For example, over half of the children whose fathers had unskilled occupations (social class V) were judged by their teachers to have below average general knowledge ('awareness of the world around'). This compared with less than one in twenty of the children from higher professional families. Social class differences in the same direction were also found in relation to all other measured abilities and attainments in school as well as to social adjustment in school, speech difficulties, dental health, height, bowel and bladder control and also physical coordination. At home the children in lower social class groups were more likely to be over-crowded, to lack or to share household amenities and to come from a large family. They were less likely to be living with both natural parents; and their parents were less likely to show an overt interest in their children's educational progress. Finally, despite the greater need of services which was often apparent amongst children from the lower social class groups, they were in general less likely to be receiving such services. Fewer of them had attended a dentist or dental clinic. They were less likely to have been immunised against diphtheria, smallpox or poliomyelitis and no more likely to have received speech therapy. (Davie 1973).

If the deficit suffered by some children is so great, education is hardly likely to make it good. But compensation can at least be attempted by the application of egalitarian principle. 1973 was chiefly notable for the effort made to do so by the extension of the period of education, backwards into the pre-school years and forward into adolescence. The central argument for doing so was in each case the same. If some children, largely because their parents are better off, have what is regarded as the advantage of staying on at school longer, this advantage should be more widely shared amongst poorer children both by raising the school leaving age and by an earlier start to school.

On behalf of each extension the appeal to the first of the four principles of equality for children — that between the classes — has been reinforced by the appeal to the second, for territorial equality. At the secondary level the trend over a long period has been for children to stay longer at school. But regional disparities, though reduced, have remained. In 1972, in the north, nearly half the children left school as soon as they legally could as compared with a third in the south east. This was not only an affair of relative wealth; attitudes to education varied too. The east Midlands, despite its greater prosperity, came out no better than the north, the north west and Scotland (Taylor and Ayres 1969; Department of Education and Science 1973a; Scottish Education Department 1973). But degrees of wealth were critical. The income that the children could earn if they went to work could less easily be spared. It was not obvious that they would do better if they stayed on at school. The schools that they would stay on at were also on the whole less good than those in places that had more money to spend. Compulsion — forcing children to keep off the labour market whether they wanted to or their parents wanted them to or not — could in these circumstances be presented as a measure of rough, if real, justice.

The rise in the leaving age by one year to 16 took effect between September 1972 and September 1973. An extra 226,000 boys and girls who would otherwise have been in jobs stayed on instead for a fifth year at secondary school. No one could complain that the event had not been planned for. In this 1973 was not at all like 1947 when the age had last been raised, when another women (Ellen Wilkinson) was Minister of Education. Almost the only preparation then had been the commissioning by the Ministry of Works of more than 6,000 hutted classrooms. Most arrived months after the pupils. On the most recent occasion the 1970 date was chosen in 1964, so that there was ample time to erect new buildings, to train extra teachers and for the newly founded Schools Council and others to work up a great variety of Raising of the School Leaving Age (ROSLA) schemes designed to hold the interest of children allergic to orthodox teaching. Even so, many teachers were thankful for the bonus time given for preparation when in 1968 the date for raising the age was put off by two years as part of the package of economies following devaluation. School building plans made by the Labour government were also postponed and taken over by their successors in 1970–73. The capital building programme of £144 million at 1972 values naturally benefited most the regions and districts where there had been fewest children staying on voluntarily. Proportionately more went to the north than to the south of the country, and to the east than to the west of London, a city where the contrasts are 'as great as those between a declining northern town and an expanding one in the south' (Taylor and Ayres 1969). The fortunate areas were doubly fortunate: the buildings were new in concept as well as in materials. In accord with the advice given in DES Building Bulletins there was more accommodation for informal purposes – group rooms, common rooms and coffee bars – which made school a little bit less like school and a little bit more like a club or even a disco (Department of Education and Science 1966). The general effect was to level up if only by a little the least well-favoured districts.

It was not quite so easy to plan for the increased

recruitment of teachers. With roughly speaking 20,000 additional ones a year, it was far easier in 1973 than it would have been in 1971. But unlike buildings, people will not necessarily go where they are told to go. There were long-standing difficulties too in getting enough teachers in subjects such as mathematics, craft and home economics (teachers in home economics are notoriously quick to marry). But on the whole, considering the great scale of the operation, there was remarkably little friction. Teacher shortages, leading to short time for pupils, were reported in Essex, Norfolk, ILEA, Bootle, Croydon and Liverpool. 22 schools and 15,833 pupils were affected; about four-fifths of the pupils were in the ILEA (*Hansard* 18 October 1973). Teachers wanting to settle down or marry were likely to be deterred from coming to London even when helped by the ILEA's relatively generous allowances for teachers moving residence. But some of the trouble was due to the bitter dispute with the National Union of Teachers (NUT) earlier in the year about the London Allowance, the addition to pay to meet the higher cost of living. The basic pupil-teacher ratio at 17:1 remained more favourable in London than in many other areas where there were fewer difficulties reported, suggesting that in London some teachers were as it were working to rule in order to draw attention to the shortages, and hence to the need for an increase (in our view certainly well deserved) in their pay.

Whether the use of the law to compel children to remain pupils till 16 will be accompanied by more non-violent and violent resistance within schools and by more truancy without, cannot yet be predicted. Surveys show that the 226,000 will be a little shorter, a little lighter and a little more delicate than the general run of boys and girls. Will they also acquiesce a little less in schools? This despite the vast number of projects designed to entice them, including some with work experience thrown in, others in which schools and further education are linked (thought not quite as thoroughly as might have been), yet others with an element of boarding to them. There are not many facts about school aversion. But in October 1973 the Secretary of the National Association of Education Welfare Officers said that 10% of children were

absent from school at least once a week and only half had a
genuine reason (*Times Educational Supplement* 12 October
1973). That meant that 500,000 children were playing truant
or staying away with their parents' connivance each week,
not counting those who skipped away after the registers were
marked. At the time of going to press the Department of
Education and Science (DES) was reviewing the information
available on truancy to see whether — and what — research
was needed. Several authorities were planning specially
favourable and informal environments — 'sanctuary' groups
within schools — for small groups of children who might
otherwise play truant or be disruptive. If these measures fail,
and if truancy appears to grow, that will strengthen the hand
of those, in and out of the new type of Free Schools, who
want to withdraw some or all of the compulsion from
attendance. Rhodes Boyson was one headmaster who, in the
same month that schools first felt the full impact of the
conscripts, proposed that boys and girls should 'leave at the
age of 14 or 15, provided they pass a test in literacy,
numeracy and general knowledge . . . have attended 95% over
their last three years . . . and have a job to go to' (Boyson
1973).

The careful planning for ROSLA inside the schools has
unfortunately not been matched by anything being done, or
even conceived, to meet more generously the financial needs
of some of the poorer parents who will have to go for
another year without the support of a member of the family
who, but for ROSLA, would already have become a wage
earner. The allowances which can be given for individual
children by local education authorities are almost as much a
sad ragbag as ever they were. Maintenance allowances were
first introduced to meet the cost of keeping at grammar
school children who won scholarships. But they have never
been at all fully used, for this or any other purpose, and the
differences in local practice have been immense. In 1971 the
average annual allowance ranged from £18 in Burton-on-
Trent to £123 in East Sussex and as the extremes illustrate
there was little obvious connection between the amount and
the neighbourhood (*Hansard* 16 June 1972). Differences
were due to variations in maximum awards, in the net income

scales entitling people to awards, and in the deductions allowable from gross income in order to arrive at the net income. Some authorities publicised their schemes, others kept them dark. In 1973 the Conference of Education Officers of London and the Home Counties agreed a carefully thought-out scheme with income scales linked to those for school meals and subject therefore to regular revision. There are some other local agreements. But these piecemeal arrangements do not go far enough. Throughout Scotland there is a uniform scale of allowances known as higher school bursaries. They are regulated by the Secretary of State for Scotland but administered by local authorities. The award and income scale is on balance more generous than that adopted for the south east (Statutory Instrument 844 (S.63) 1972). An extension of some such scheme to the whole of the United Kingdom is very much overdue.

There are similar anomalies about grants for school uniform and clothing. Here there might be some justification for local discretion if the grants bore any relationship to the uniforms actually required by schools. But often the amount provided is far less than the cost of the uniform. Clothing grants often relate to items which were thought essential a decade ago. The vagaries of the grants stand out in contrast to the improved arrangements made in 1973 for help provided nationally. In September 1973 it was announced that the schedule of incomes on which eligibility for school meals was based would be reviewed annually. The scale was somewhat more generous for meals than for supplementary benefit and family income supplement. It was further settled in April 1973 that save in short term emergencies free meals and milk were to be provided on a twelve-month period even though parents' incomes rose. On this basis it may be a little easier to protect children from being known as entitled to free meals.

Had this Report been published much more than a year ago there would have been recognition of the 20,000 nursery places provided under the Home Office's Urban Programme between 1968 and 1972 in downtown areas, but nothing otherwise to say about national policy. The Butler Act of 1944 promised that nursery schools would become part of the maintained system, and the promise remained. Its redemption was in 1960 officially and explicitly postponed by the Ministry of Education's *Circular No 8/60* which forbade local education authorities to provide more nursery school places and except for the children of teachers they were not provided. In the decade that followed priority for spending went to higher education. Butler had to wait.

Thirteen years after the ban and thirty years after the Act came another Circular, *No 2/73*, from the Department of Education and Science (*No 39/73* from the Welsh Office; *No 861 (1)* from the Scottish Education Department). This put some flesh on the main new proposals for the expansion of nursery education contained in White Papers published in the previous month (*Education: a framework for expansion* and *Education in Scotland: a statement of policy*). The government accepted the objective as being 'to make nursery education available for children who want it from the beginning of the term after their third birthday, until the term after their fifth birthday'. Thus in the same year in which the school *leaving* age was raised to 16, the case for reducing the *entry* age to 3 was expressed, not by the Nursery Schools Association, the Pre-School Playgroups Association or the Plowden Report, but by another Conservative Minister.

'Nursery education for all' did not perhaps have quite the same crusading ring as 'secondary education for all' had once had. A book that predicted what would happen did not succeed in making out quite as stirring a case as had been made earlier (Blackstone 1972). Instead it paraded the Bertrand Russell of 1926:

> The nursery school, if it became universal, could, in one generation, remove the profound differences in education which at present divide the classes, could produce a population all enjoying the mental and physical development which is now confined to the most fortunate, and could remove the terrible deadweight of disease and stupidity and malevolence which now makes progress so difficult.

But the change announced by Mrs Thatcher was a substantial

one all the same, even if the hopes were not quite as dizzily high as once they would have been.

This was perhaps partly because the hunters, not having found their quarry elsewhere, were no longer quite so confident — as we mentioned earlier in the chapter. The expansion of primary, secondary and tertiary education had by no means achieved Marshall's goal. Could this be because preschool (to use a term which will before long have narrowed its meaning) had not been attended to? Bloom, in a much-quoted report, had argued that much of people's intelligence is acquired before 5, thus attributing to the early years the same crucial part in cognitive development that Freud had in emotional development (Bloom 1964). The Plowden Report assembled other evidence to the same effect. If the basis for later inequality were laid before 5, then it seemed to many people to follow that education should again try at that crucial stage to offset the injustice of heredity and early environment. It did not greatly matter that the evidence, such as it was, was not all that encouraging. Douglas and Ross had followed Nisbet and a score of American researchers (before and after the massive Headstart programme of nursery education in USA) in showing that comparative gains in IQ and attainment achieved by children who had been to such schools had disappeared by adolescence. Fortunately for the campaign, the test results of the Douglas and Ross children who had enjoyed nursery education were not just the same by the time they were 15; they were actually lower than those of children who had first entered school at 5. This, and the details recorded about their homes, suggested that it was because they were unusually badly off that they had been accepted at school so early (Douglas and Ross 1964). If the antis could not draw all that comfort from this sort of evidence neither could the pros. The main claim, in effect was that all children (whose parents agreed — this first stage of education was to be no more compulsory than the last beyond 16) had a right to this new service. Children at least were to be more equal, that is as children, whether or not they became as a result more equal 20 years on.

The intent was universalist, that is in so far as universalism can rest upon the voluntary. The White Paper and the Circular accepted the Plowden estimates of demand, even though these in their turn had been based upon rather shaky evidence, by then out of date. It was expected that the parents of 15% of 3 and 4-year-olds would opt for full-time education; and of 35% of 3-year-olds and of 75% of 4-year-olds for part-time, making the equivalent of 250,000 additional places by 1982. But the implementation was to be to some extent selective — that is guided by the new principles of class geography also enunciated by the Plowden Report in inventing the term, Educational Priority Area. The policy proposed was of inequality to scotch inequality (Plowden Report 1967).

Because this is the most signal example in 1973 of an idea about positive discrimination which could well be applied in other welfare services, and in urban planning more generally, on this point it is worth quoting in full from the Circular (2/73).

> Nursery education is particularly valuable as a means of reducing the educational and social disadvantages suffered by children from homes which are culturally and economically deprived. It is for this reason that the Secretaries of State have *concentrated* the resources available for nursery education in areas of social deprivation eligible for the Urban Programme. Recent research findings confirm that such children are greatly helped in two ways. The first is through increasing the interest of the parents, particularly mothers, in such a way that they understand more of their children's development, are able to assist them at home and co-operate with the teachers at school. The second is through educational programmes which enrich the children's experience and thereby directly offset their environmental handicaps. In making plans for providing nursery education throughout their areas authorities are accordingly asked, in consultation with social service departments and voluntary bodies, to give priority to meeting the needs of these children, while ensuring that in any one class a balance between them and other children is maintained.

'Class' in that last sentence referred to the sort which is still common in schools.

The year began more gloriously than it did or could continue. When the deadline prescribed by *Circular 2/73* was reached, only 51 out of 163 Authorities had submitted their bids for the first phase of expansion. Gradually the score mounted until it included every authority in the country and their estimates overran by one-third the £34 million set aside for building. 'Over half' the nursery places proposed were for places of social need. (Department of Education and Science 1973b). Priority for the disadvantaged, the sole criterion in the Urban Programme, had evidently taken on a rather weaker meaning even in the first phase of expansion.

The speed of planning, at least in contrast to the long years of inaction, almost inevitably favoured the authorities which had already made some progress with nursery schools and therefore had committee members, administrators, and advisers able to put forward a convincing programme quickly. But this does not fully explain anomalies in the allocations. The ILEA's case for £1,915,000 (all it asked for) was evident; likewise Glasgow's share — more than £1 million — of the Scottish programme. (*Hansard* 15 June, 1973). But are Oxford and Bootle equally served by an allocation of £60,000? The social contrasts between them are sharp. Bootle has more than one-seventh more children than Oxford; though Bootle has had some help from the Urban Programme, in 1965 it had only about one-eighth of the nursery places of Oxford (Blackstone 1971). The identical allocations are probably based on the formula by which two-thirds of the money available for 1974-76 was to be distributed by degree of disadvantage, and one-third by the gap between existing provisions and the White Paper target. If so, they emphasise the need for more subtle assessment, identifying for example areas where full-time nursery education for more than 15% is essential.

The need for haste and for economy, as well as the suggestions in the Circular, led most authorities to concentrate on adding nursery classes to primary schools rather than building nursery schools. The arrangement has advantages. There will be fewer schools for mothers to get to know and to take their children to. Children will have no break in education between 3 or 4 and 7 and 11. Primary heads can supervise nursery classes. But it also means that where sites are crowded no provision can be made. (That helps to explain why only five out of the eleven projects in the Brent 1974—76 programme will be in a 'deprived' area.) No provision, that is, unless children are already being taken in full-time to the infant schools at 4. When that has been done, often with the best of intentions but in conditions which may be unsuitable for such young children, parents and teachers may need a good deal of persuading to accept part-time nurseries for 4-year-olds even when there are no compelling reasons for full-time. There is a real danger that part-time pre-school will be provided for the 3-year-olds and full-time conventional school, with far too few adults for the children, will begin at 4.

Most of the real innovation in the last few years has been associated with projects in the Urban Programme. Many mothers, like the ones in the fatherless families featured in Chapter 6, need for their children the longer hours and short holidays of the day nursery. Yet these same children could be helped by the emphasis given to education rather than childminding in 'the nursery class. By September 1973, 11 nursery centres had been built, combining day nursery and nursery class and sometimes including clinics as well. A few more were planned or being built. A few nursery schools have begun to work extended hours.

Several education authorities have also taken the advice of the White Paper and followed the pioneers who gave support to playgroups. Accommodation free or at peppercorn rents, grants or loan of equipment, guidance from nursery advisers — all have become fairly common. Rural counties, such as Oxfordshire and Devon, have been working out how they can help playgroups to provide for the under 5s in villages without schools. An example of what can be done is the exceptionally thoroughgoing support, but of a kind that will not erode the responsibility of mothers, that has been given to a playgroup in Norwich. The group had been meeting in the community centre on a working-class estate before the White Paper came out. The authority has now taken over most of the cost. Rent and heating are free and there is a grant for equipment. Grant is also paid to the

parents' committee for the salary of the supervisor — not a
teacher — and the other staff. Mothers are heavily involved in
the day-to-day running of the group as well as being on the
committee. The head of the infant school next door has
joined it as a non-voting member.

The Secretary of State has asked local authorities for
information about their plans for cooperating with the social
services and for involving parents. Whether this mild stimulus
will counterbalance the reinforcement of traditional attitudes
by the generally conventional pattern so far shown in the
first phase of expansion has yet to be seen. Much will
depend on the freshness of mind of the nursery teachers and
their trainers and on their readiness to accept, indeed to seek
out and cultivate, a relationship with mothers as well as
children. But will the teachers with this or any other state of
mind be available? In 1972, 47 colleges of education had
planned courses for 1973 to prepare students for nursery
teaching. Following the White Paper, 7 more colleges joined
them and another 7 will do so in 1974 (Association of
Teachers in Colleges and Department of Education 1972,
1973ab). But it is the numbers on the various courses that
matter most. In 1974 admissions to colleges are to be cut by
10%, because, for the first time since the war, the prospective
supply of teachers is beginning to outrun the likely demand.
Cuts will not apply to those training for nurseries and some
other kinds of work where shortages are marked. Nursery
courses will become more popular as a result and the
qualifications — formal at least — of those applying will be
raised. Informal enquiries to some of the colleges running
postgraduate courses for teaching young children suggested
that some of these students were turning to nursery schools.
This is the more important since it is intended that the
numbers in postgraduate courses in colleges of education
should grow substantially both absolutely and in proportion
to the total numbers in training.

Yet a teaching force heavily weighted with young women
will naturally need constant renewal. That will not necessarily be conducive to new ways of involving mothers. It is at
least as important to provide in-service training. For 1974—75
there are to be 15 new one-term 'conversion' courses and 4

more are waiting approval. 4 new courses lasting a year will lead to a diploma qualifying holders for work as advisers or college lecturers. Expansion in other types of courses, national and local, is to be on a similar scale.

Nursery classes are to have a ratio of thirteen children to one adult (26:1 teacher). That will call for a big increase of nursery nurses. A plan has been put forward to reduce the time that nursery students spend on practical work in their training – there are simply not enough nurseries to receive them on the old scale – and to lower the bars to mature women entering a shortened one-year course. Unfortunately it hung fire and will not now come into force before 1974. When it does, there is little doubt that students will come forward, even though salaries, recently raised in proportion to rises for nurses, are little more than a pittance. But despite all the reservations it has in this sphere been a year of hope and of positive achievement.

Territorial inequalities
We have not been able to avoid mention of this form of inequality before, even though to do so cuts across the structure of the chapter; social class and geography go together too closely to allow any clear division. But at least the first of the changes that we have discussed so far was not intended primarily to reduce territorial inequalities, even though the extension of the period of education at the top end might do a little towards it. Insofar as the aim was egalitarian at all, it was to reduce the inequalities between classes, whatever their geographical location. Although the policy for nursery schools is to have a strong territorial bias at the start, the aim is 'that nursery education should be widely available within ten years for children of three and four' *(Education: A framework for expansion)*, 'widely' meaning in rich as well as poor areas. With the policy for Educational Priority Areas the emphasis is definitely the other way on. The observation on which it is based is that much disadvantage is geographically clustered – parents in low-paid jobs, unstable families, rundown houses, mean streets, poor schools, all hang together. A study, based on an ILEA Literacy Survey made in 1969 and published in 1973

(Little and Mabey 1973), showed that poor attainment in reading was much more closely associated with this kind of multiple disadvantage than simply with the mixture of social class in a school. It seems to follow that a new kind of attack can be made on poverty, at least insofar as it affects children, by concentrating attention on schools in such areas and by trying to make them not just as good as but better than schools in more favoured districts.

The proposal for Educational Priority Areas, or 'positive discrimination', to use the American term, was first made in an official document in the Plowden Report in 1967. From that stable came two horses — one which has been running (or at any rate walking) in the DES and one which we have already mentioned several times in the Home Office.

The Labour government, through its Education Ministers, treated the proposal gingerly. The first thing, announced in 1967 but taking effect in 1968—70, was to make a special allocation of £16 million for building schools in priority areas. In the same year, the Burnham Committee on teachers' pay awarded a flat-rate allowance of £75 a year to schools recognised by the Secretary of State as 'of exceptional difficulty' (another term less compelling to do duty for educational priority). The idea was to give these schools a better chance of attracting, and even more important of holding, good teachers. But the negotiated settlement included a ceiling of £400,000 a year to cover the cost of the allowances and that limited severely the number of schools that could be included. They contained about 2½% of all children instead of the 10% that the Plowden members had hoped would benefit. For 1968, the year the allowance came into force, education authorities were also invited to apply for teachers additional to their quota. An extra 2,700 teachers were allocated in this way for the needs of EPAs and immigrants. At the same time, the Social Science Research Council, supported by the DES, set going a series of five experimental projects in Dundee, the West Riding of Yorkshire, Liverpool, Birmingham and London. These were described in the Halsey Report which has already been referred to. In 1969 the government returned to the attack on nineteenth-century school buildings concentrated in poor districts. An additional £18 million, operative in 1971–2, was set aside for the replacement of pre-1903 schools in districts with severe social difficulties.

Whether because of the impact of the Halsey Report, whether it was finally accepted by a Conservative Minister that geographical selectivity fitted well with the more general selectivity in the social services that her party had espoused, whatever the cause, 1973 saw an acceleration in help for EPAs. The geographical priorities set for the introduction of nursery classes, even if only a first step towards generalisation, were in accord with the policy. An important change to do with teachers' salaries was also made. There had for a long time been argument about whether the best way to strengthen staffing in EPA schools was to make a flat-rate payment to all teachers in them or to improve the chances of promotion. Teacher turnover was stepping up in some areas and to have more teachers on higher scales might help to reduce it. In 1973 the Burnham Committee gave local authorities discretion to raise by 20% the 'points score' of schools of exceptional difficulty. This score, based on numbers and the age of the children, determines how many teachers can be paid above basic scales and by how much. The criteria for schools of exceptional difficulty are the same as in the earlier scheme but the decisions are now left to authorities. Some guidance is given by a costing estimate of £800,000 a year – just twice as much as in the earlier scheme. The flat-rate allowance, raised in 1972 to £105 pa, continues for those schools recognised on the earlier basis. Whether either allowance is adequate to its purpose remains very doubtful.

The present government has had the responsibility of carrying out the already mentioned £18 million building programme for the replacement of obsolete schools in EPAs, mainly in the north, the midlands and Greater London. This programme has become the starting point for a more wholesale rebuilding of pre-1903 primary schools in 1972–76. In that period nearly 2,000 primary schools will be improved or replaced, at a cost of £239.7 million (1973 prices). A substantial part of the 1972–73 programme is again being devoted to districts with social handicaps. Some of these projects are likely to be postponed under *Circular 12/73*, which in October 1973 announced the rephasing of educational building programmes as part of the more general rephasing of public sector construction. Improvement schemes are easy victims.

The rebuilding of so many schools in rundown areas is likely to bring fresh hope and stimulus to pupils and teachers. But inflated building costs are taking a toll of standards. For the first time since cost limits were fixed schools are having to be built to minimum standards, which were meant only as a minimum which would always be exceeded. Space indoors, covered outdoor working space, the extras in design and finish which make a school more domestic and flexible — neither a row of boxes nor one large box — all are in jeopardy. School playing space which is sub-standard in size or barren, is particularly sad when provided in inner cities where, because of the cost of land, alternatives are hard to find.

Positive discrimination depends at least as much on the policy of local education authorities and on attitudes within the schools as on action by the central government. Even before the Plowden recommendations, there were many authorities whose dealings with priority schools were exceptionally sympathetic. Staffing and equipment were generous and probationer teachers of exceptional quality were appointed. There is little doubt that after Plowden this kind of help became greater in scope, more systematic and more widespread. What seemed to be a second wave of local authority intervention on behalf of EPAs in 1972—73 may have been due to anxiety about the raising of the school leaving age, to tension between central and local government, or be yet another effect of the Halsey Report. The ILEA, for example, devised a graduated index to assess the severity of secondary school handicap, similar to the one they had made earlier for primary schools. These indices are ways of adjusting resources to the degree of need. All London schools are now able to use flexibly resources above those needed for establishing basic standards. The power given to individual heads to choose according to their ideas of urgency between extra teachers, non-teaching staff, equipment, residential accommodation and so on is particularly valuable to priority schools. They need even more flexibility than others.

Many local initiatives have aimed at making EPA schools something like 'community schools' which 'take education into the home and bring parents into the school', and which seek 'almost to obliterate the boundary between school and community'. (Halsey 1973). Though there are common principles and devices, each community school is by definition unique, a response to a particular environment. Belfield Primary School, Rochdale, officially opened in November 1973, is one of the more revolutionary examples. The school is being run by a council on which 20 residents, all elected (one for every 100 houses) sit side by side with teachers and administrators. Everyone who lives near by can use the amenities of the school. In the evening it is available for adult groups and for children who need a quiet place to do their homework. Rochdale is also planning advice for parents, which could be seen to be impartial. The call was for an advice centre 'to provide in a High Street shop information which the general public might be reluctant to seek by climbing the Town Hall steps'. If several authorities would do the same, a national bank of educational information could be set up to back up the local service. It could also supplement the overworked information service of the DES and could be based on what is already done on a smaller scale by the Advisory Centre for Education in Cambridge (Holden 1973).

Belfield is not alone. The DES Building Bulletins and Design Notes illustrate different emphases on community use (Department of Education and Science 1969, 1970ab, 1973cd). Schools in line with their ideas are being built up and down the country, in and out of EPAs. A growing number of authorities — 30 in May 1973 — were including, if not twenty, at least one parent on governing and managing bodies (*Education* 18 May 1973). Though the turnout for the first batch of these elections in the ILEA was disappointing, a hundred parents were present to choose the governor for Morpeth Secondary School in the same Bethnal Green that has already had a chapter to itself. When one school can achieve this, others may follow. The last phase of the Urban

Aid Programme has added parents' rooms to a number of established schools, and has increased the number of teachers and other workers specially charged with linking home and school, notably in the north east. The ILEA asked parents, teachers and the public to comment on its reorganisation plans. Even more important, it has accepted their advice for retaining some small schools, particularly in EPAs and seems to be modifying its general policy on size of school.

Tutor wardens are being appointed in many secondary schools to combine work in the day and the evening. Ten years after the Newsom Report agreement has been reached to experiment with the extended day in Manchester. It could even be promising that teachers' unions, dissatisfied with bargaining only about salaries, are beginning to think about conditions of service. There was idealism in the belief that a teacher should fulfil outside ordinary working hours and quite voluntarily all the extra duties that his work in school involved him in. But the burdens were always unequally shared. A closer definition of hours and duties could make the community school easier to run. There will still be plenty of room for altruism well beyond what the unions negotiate.

Whether or not arrangements are made which enable some teachers to work round the clock they are bound to need the help of social workers, especially in EPAs. Over the years the one-time School Board men or Truancy Officers have changed their name to Education Welfare Officers (EWOs) and broadened their work. They now have a general concern with any circumstances outside school which prevent children from profiting inside school. The Seebohm Committee recommended that social work in school should become an integral part of the responsibilities of general purpose social workers. The Local Government Social Services Act 1970, which excluded educational welfare from the social services, allowed authorities to transfer responsibility for it if they wished. Eight authorities did so; in many other places everything went on much as before. Education Welfare Officers continued to carry a heavy load of work, including routine administration, for low pay and low status. Not surprisingly, the minority of trained younger officers tended to leave their posts for better jobs in the new Social

Services Departments. In 1973 a working party of the Local Government Training Board reporting on the strong element of social work in an educational setting in the Education Welfare Officer's role, made recommendations, as many had done before, on the need for training and affirmed the need for a national policy on the future of an 'under-valued and under-developed service' (Ralphs 1973).

The reorganisation of welfare services which bases officers on groups of related schools rather than on education offices is still awaited. Without this change EPA schools will be without an essential link with some of the most needy homes and with the social services.

The geographical inequalities discussed so far have been tied up with each other. It has been because areas are declining and unattractive that few save the poor live there, schools have been big enough for falling populations and have therefore not been replaced, and teachers have often preferred to go elsewhere. Other inequalities between authorities are quite arbitrary, like those in the health services discussed by Phyllis Willmott in the next chapter, though they can bear particularly harshly on the school in a poor neighbourhood. The most striking example is the range of capitation allowances — the amount allowed for each child on the roll for the purchase of equipment, materials and books. It is difficult to be exact. Authorities vary greatly in the way they categorise the allowances they provide, in the frequency of ad hoc grants and, as has been implied, in the flexibility permitted. But some notion of the differences can be sensed in the contrast between 59p a head for books in Swansea primary schools and £2.98 in Brecon. Allowances for books in secondary schools can vary between £1.83 and £6.52 (Educational Publishing Company (EPC), 1973). The suburban school can often make good any deficiencies there are. The school in a poor district is bound to use up resources more quickly, and to find more difficulty in tapping help from parents.

Inequalities of ability
Class and territory are the first of the two criteria by which resources have been rationed. The third is 'ability'. The word

has, after a quarter of a century's campaign, been forced to retreat behind inverted commas; but in many areas ability, at least as it is tested by the 11+ examinations, still remains the arbiter for deciding which kind of school a child goes to — secondary modern, grammar, comprehensive or hybrid. It has by and large been true that children who fail the 11+ have had less spent on them in each year of their schooling and, even more markedly, over the whole of its span. They have in purely educational terms been 'poor', and, so labelled, they have been more likely to end up justifying the adjective in income as adults than other children who have jumped through the looking-glass at 11. This familiar case against the 11+ has if anything been strengthened by what has been published so far of a massive international research project for the evaluation of educational achievement. This has shown that unselective systems produce as high levels of attainment in the top 5% as selective. The more selective a system, the greater the social bias (Postlethwaite 1967; Comber and Keeves 1973). But the most encouraging finding of the year about comprehensive schools in Britain comes from a study by G. Neave, summarised in *Comprehensive Education* for Summer 1973. The percentage of working-class students at universities has long remained steady at 28%. An analysis was made of the social class of one in five of all comprehensive school pupils entering universities in October 1968, and was related to the length of time the schools had been comprehensive. The following table shows the result:

Table 8.1 Entrants by social class to universities from comprehensive schools

	Overall entrants to universities	*Date school became comprehensive*		
		Up to September 1961	*September 1961–65*	*After September 1965 (control)*
Middle-class	72%	62%	53%	69%
Working-class	28%	38%	47%	31%
Number		585	171	212

The schools which have most recently become comprehensive were used as a control since the changeover could hardly have affected those entering the sixth form then or later. It looks as though the comprehensive organisation may have brought a breakthrough in the number of working-class pupils going to universities.

The comprehensive school is the corollary to the abolition of the 11+, and has been since the 1940s when the first such schools were planned and built. 'A comprehensive school is one that accepts all children from a defined district, whatever their social class or ability, just like a local primary school'. (Ross and Chanan 1972). That has remained the definition with different variations since this new kind of secondary school was first mooted. Between then and now there has been considerable growth. This was particularly marked after 1965 when Mr Crosland, who was then Minister of Education, issued a Circular (*10/65*) which said: 'It is the Government's declared objective to end selection at 11+ and to eliminate separation in secondary education'. The increase in tempo is shown in Table 8.2.

Table 8.2 Growth of comprehensive schools in England and Wales

	1960	1965	1970	1971	1972
Middle schools			136	265	323
Pupils			46,241	91,561	121,509
Comprehensive schools	130	262	1,145	1,373	1,591
Pupils	128,835	239,619	937,152	1,128,417	1,337,242
Percentage of pupils aged 13+, in comprehensive schools, for whom LEAs are financially responsible	4.7%	8.5%	31.0%	38.0%	41.3%

Source Department of Education & Science 1971, 1972, 1973a *and Hansard* 15 May 1969

All figures 1970—72 include pupils in middle schools

The main debate in 1973 has been whether this long-term growth has been checked under another Government by Mrs Thatcher's use of the powers she enjoys under Section 13 of the 1944 Education Act to refuse sanction for a new school or a change in status of an old school. It would inevitably take some years before a new policy was evidenced in the numbers of new comprehensive schools created. It certainly looks as though there has been a sharp rise in 1973 in the number of proposals for comprehensive schools that have been rejected, with the figure as high as 29% during the six-month period ending July 1973. Without knowing a great deal more than anyone outside (or perhaps inside) the DES it is not possible to pin down the part played by politics. Whether a particular scheme put up by a local authority is considered educationally sound or not is inevitably a matter of opinion, and politics and opinions are liable to go together. If all new comprehensive schools were purpose-built there would be less reason to turn them down. But this has certainly not been true, nor ever will be. The need for comprehensives has had to compete with the need for more accommodation for the ROSLA children, that is wherever the ROSLA money was not used to ease the way for a comprehensive reorganisation. Capital being so scarce, old school buildings cannot ordinarily be pulled down. When there is a change of policy they have to be converted if possible and used for new purposes. The buildings occupied by a secondary modern have to be paired with those of a grammar school and the whole called a comprehensive; the secondary modern or the grammar has to be picked out as the nucleus of an expanded school; the secondary modern has to become one tier and the grammar another tier of a two-tier system, with the break at age 13, 14 or 16 — the variations are numerous, and so are the objections which can be raised against any new composite. One Minister can easily think that the demerits of a proposal — and none are without them — are far outweighed by the advantages of ending the 11+, and amongst other things relieving the primary schools of the pressure it places on them; another Minister may go the other way. It appears that Mrs Thatcher has gone the other way, which makes it as difficult for local education authorities to plan sensibly as it was for the steel industry when it was caught between the political parties.

The figures in Table 8.2 may in one important respect be misleading. The schools included in it are called comprehensive even though they do not conform with the definition we have just given. Many of them do not in practice take in all the children whatever their ability from a defined district, because some grammar or independent schools still take many of the cleverest children – this without implying that all schools should have just the same ratios of ability according to some Procrustean formula. The fullest survey there has yet been of the growth of comprehensive schools highlighted the extent to which this coexistence of selective and non-selective schools continues.

> Many of our findings reveal the harmful and undermining effects that a policy of systematic 'coexistence' of selective schools has upon comprehensive schools. This effect is the same whether the 'coexisting' sector schools are maintained, direct grant or voluntary-aided grammar schools, selective 'interim' comprehensive schools, or fee-paying schools with selective places paid for by an authority. (Benn and Simon 1972).

At a conference in September 1973 (*Guardian* 12 September 1973) Caroline Benn returned to the same point. She had made a new survey of heads of comprehensive schools. A large majority said that coexistence deprived them of high ability children, made their schools seem like second choice places, added to the difficulty of getting good teachers, and made the teaching groups in the upper forms uneconomically small. The critics believed that the government was much readier to allow a secondary modern to be called a comprehensive than for a grammar school to change its role. It was this which made 'coexistence' more and more noticeable.

The same fact was stressed in a study by the National Foundation of Educational Research (NFER) on the effectiveness of comprehensive schools. The sample of 12 comprehensive schools – all of which had the advantage of having been comprehensive since 1966 – suffered from a shortage of able pupils. 'Only 12 per cent of pupils were in the more able category, whereas 20 per cent would have been expected if there were a fair spread' (Ross and Chanan 1972). At the sixth form level they did less well than the national average but that was to be expected since they were less able.

How damaging is a systematic coexistence which seems to be as near to a comprehensive system as many authorities will get during the span of office of the present Secretary of State? Though some schools will certainly be more equal than others in the number of children of above average ability they admit, there is a little evidence of working-class parents preferring the comprehensive to the grammar school even for children (particularly girls) of high ability (Reid and Franklin 1973). Increasingly and above all in local authorities whose committees are in conflict with national policy, parity in resources which was a bad joke after 1944 is nearer achievement for all secondary schools. That is good not only for the secondary sector but also for the primary schools since acceptable alternatives to grammar schools at least reduce the unfortunate effects of the 11+. Grammar schools certainly have a pull in getting highly qualified teachers of subjects where there is the greatest shortage and they are likely to have large sixth forms and to be able to run a big range of courses. But it is easy to overstate the necessary size of fifth and sixth forms and to underestimate the number of options that can be provided with some cooperation between schools (Halsall 1973). There are bound to be — ought to be — some differences between schools unless an arithmetical equality is forced upon them which reduces parental choice and the capacity of response to particular community needs. Coexistence artificially enlarges those differences. But it would be too pessimistic to suppose it to be no better than the tripartite system it is replacing.

Advocates of comprehensive schools have often pointed out that the goals of the reorganisation will only be half achieved unless the mixing of children of different abilities in the same schools is complemented in the class. If there is streaming or banding according to ability, the more clever children may see no more of the less able than they would if they were at separate schools. Information about this is scanty. The best is in the book by Benn and Simon. They believe that the trend is towards non-streaming. But all they could claim was that by 1971 one-third of the comprehensive schools had reached the point where they were using 'predominantly mixed ability methods of grouping in the first year' — in the first year alone it might have been added (Benn and Simon 1972). It has been shown by research (Lunn 1970) that even when mixed ability groups are introduced, little good results unless teachers are in sympathy with the change and adapt to it. Just how subtle the adaptation needs to be has been well brought out by a small-scale close study of teacher's perception and pupil's performance published in 1973 (Nash 1973).

There is clearly a long way still to go before the reform started in the 1940s is anywhere near complete. The changeover has been made in the places where it is easiest, such as the counties with mainly Conservative authorities which have not had to contend with nearly as many entrenched grammar schools as in the big boroughs. The going is likely to get harder especially if time itself erodes some of the initial enthusiasm. 1973 was, if anything, a year of setback.

For many years, the most able, the most fortunate as many would think, have also been the most privileged. More has been spent on them at school and they have had support from taxes paid by the rest in going forward to higher education. But compassion and expediency have also combined to give some priority to those who are least well placed both mentally and physically. Hence the development of 'special educational treatment' and special schools where the cost per pupil has been about twice that for ordinary pupils. 1973 has not brought the enquiry into special education which many of those most knowledgeable have been asking for. But there were advances. First, the need for quite specific improvements in the special schools was accepted. In 1971 the Education (Handicapped Children) Act 1970, came into force, so ending the harsh exclusion of 'severely mentally handicapped' children from the educational system. Superficially, the immediate effect was small. Some children continued to go to training centres, now renamed schools; others were in hospitals, in institutions or at home. Yet some authorities appointed teachers even where there was nowhere to work and they began to add to the quality of the lives of some children. The White Paper (*Education: a framework for expansion*) recognised the need for much more to be done to turn a legal change into a reality. From 1972—73 the special school programme was to rise yearly, reaching £19 million by 1976—77.

Staffing for the children now covered by special educational treatment was another problem. It was not only that children who were severely handicapped mentally had to have more help to deal with their physical needs or that there was now the hope that training might be replaced by education. Medical care was also saving the lives of children with grave and often multiple handicaps. *Circular 4/73* gave guidance to local authorities on staffing special schools and classes. The needs of the children in them are so variable that guidance had to be flexible. In general the objective is to bring all practice up towards the best. It was estimated that the new staffing policy would require an additional 2,000 teachers above what might be needed from growth in numbers. The build-up was to be gradual — a target of 1,000 by March 1975. Suggestions were also made for heavy recruitment of ancillary helpers, rising for the severely subnormal to a number equivalent to the teachers. In 1974, when the intake to colleges is to be cut, an exception will be made for those who intend to work in special schools. A substantial programme of in-service training has also been planned.

While much was being done to improve the lot of those in special schools, a more radical view has been gaining ground that schools for the community should include also the handicapped. Assessment of handicap has been based on 10 statutory categories, and the special schools provided correspond to some extent to these. Longstanding dissatisfaction with these groupings has now come to a head. During 1973 five authorities began experimentally and with the guidance of the DES to substitute a profile of educational need as a means of deciding what kind of school would be right for individual children. As the emphasis changed from medical to educational need there was a better chance that the long-hoped-for collaboration between doctors, educational psychologists and teachers would become more of a reality.

One of the most disturbing aspects of special schooling, especially when provided for the rarer disabilities, has been the way children in boarding schools were cut off from their families. Following the reorganisation of local government, there are to be a series of regional conferences involving both the local authorities and the voluntary bodies responsible for many schools for the handicapped. One hope is that special schools can be reorganised in such a way that children will be near enough to home to go there at least at weekends. Another objective will be to bring the non-maintained schools into closer contact with the others (Department of Education and Science 1973e).

The DES has long taken the view that whenever possible children should be educated in ordinary schools, either in special units or in normal classes. Half the physically handicapped are in ordinary schools. Recent research in a small number of them showed that the great majority were happy and socially well integrated though some of their teachers needed more specialised help than they were getting. (Anderson 1973). With the cooperation of the DES, Sheffield embarked in 1973 on a plan to incorporate all its physically handicapped in ordinary schools; its experience will be a guide for others. The Burnham Committee in 1973 recognised the growing tendency for children to have special help in ordinary schools in the arrangements made to pay teachers above the basic scale. There was also unusually generous treatment of special schools where teachers' hopes of reaching higher scales have often been limited by the small size of the school they work in. Progress towards integrating the handicapped in ordinary schools has certainly not gone as fast as many would wish. Apart from those children whom the sheer difficulty of survival necessarily separates out, the problem is to decide how fast planning can and should run ahead of the attitudes of the average teacher and the public. For children to be in a school but not of it is the worst solution. The public too have to learn to accept the handicapped.

Inequalities of colour

No one contests that many immigrant children are among the worst off in educational terms as well as in many others, and in many ways their disadvantages are the same as the poor whites whom they often live near to and go to school with. Without referring to them specifically we have in effect been talking about them in each of the previous three main sections of the chapter. The question now is whether they have any special needs requiring special attention.

This is not the live issue it once was. The answer has become more and more obvious. The first reason is that immigrants are very much more territorially concentrated even than other poor people. According to admittedly unreliable DES statistics which are still all that we have to go on, 'there were about 280,000 immigrant children in this country in January 1972. 40% were from the West Indies, 20% from India, 10% from Pakistan, 10% from Africa, 10% from elsewhere in the Commonwealth and 10% from non-Commonwealth countries'. (Select Committee on Race Relations and Immigration 1973). Such a relatively small number — some 3% or 4% of all the children — might hardly be noticed if they were spread evenly throughout the country. In fact the 'London area, inner and outer London, accounts for slightly more than half followed by south Lancashire and the west Midlands'. (Community Relations Commission 1973). In Haringey, just to mention one of the London boroughs with a very high density, the proportion was said to be 28%. In some schools the proportions are a great deal higher than that.

Immigrant children would have special difficulties anyway. The greatest difficulty is over English. This is comparatively straightforward with children for whom it is not a first language. It is clear that they need special teaching from people trained to teach English as a second language, either (or both) in special centres or in special classes within the school. It is not so easy with West Indian children who have no other language than English.

How does one persuade young West Indians, who already speak acceptable English in the home and the playground, to realise they need help? The answer probably lies in the ambition of West Indian parents for their children. If the advantages of standard English (and the corresponding disadvantages of not having it) are stressed to them they may encourage the children to seek the help they need. By no means all West Indian children are affected, but local education authorities when it is applicable should consider how best to approach, with tact and discretion, the convincing of West Indian parents that some of their children may need special English teaching, without implying that their children, because they lack standard English, are basically inferior. (Select Committee on Race Relations and Immigration 1973).

West Indian parents might well prefer their children to have some skilled English teaching early if they knew that otherwise they might end up in classes for slow learners. That was the solution adopted for children with language difficulties in a quarter of the secondary schools reviewed in a recent research study (Townsend and Brittan 1972). Some immigrant children found themselves already relegated to low streams at 5. There was ability grouping in a quarter to a fifth of the infant schools, nearly half the junior schools and a little more than a half of the first year classes in secondary schools. In all these instances, coloured children tended to cluster in the lower streams. There are likely to be many reasons for these placings. But it seems certain that some young immigrants start in a lowly position because of language difficulties and that subsequently transfers are few. This partly explains the small number of immigrants selected for grammar schools. It also helps to explain why though immigrants are enthusiastic for schooling and a high proportion have stayed on after 15, they often pass the same examinations about a year or more after English children in the same schools.

At the other extreme some of the same circumstances must account for the high proportion of West Indians in schools for the educationally subnormal in some parts of the country. In November 1973 the DES sent some advice to Chief Education Officers about immigrant children who may need special education. It suggested the need for supplementing standardised tests with 'systematic observation' of children's 'responses to an educational environment'. 'Consultation with parents . . . as an essential part of the assessment procedure' was recommended, as were regular reviews to see whether transfers from special schools were desirable. Sadly, though it asked for language facilities in ordinary schools for immigrants (more widely interpreted than in DES statistics), it did not refer to the dangers of streaming.

On this subject 1973 gives ground (like any other year) for both hope and gloom. The most recent survey showed that the great majority of schools believed in changing the curriculum to fit a multi-racial school society -- and an irrelevant curriculum can be almost as big a barrier to immigrants as poor command of standard English (Townsend 1973). Many schools had already made changes, rather fewer had them ready to make. Ironically Religious Education, the only 'agreed' syllabus in the curriculum, appeared to have been among the most malleable, perhaps because it was less often subject to examination, and the absurdity of teaching nothing but Christianity to Muslims and Hindus was obvious. But there was also disturbing confirmation of earlier findings that only a tiny minority of teachers in schools with large numbers of immigrants have learned either in their initial training or later about the problems facing such children.

For 1973—74 the DES allocated 3,121 additional teachers to the quotas of 39 authorities to help them to provide a more generous number of teachers for immigrant children. They are of course already counted once in the general roll that is the basis of the quota. It does not follow that authorities can or do necessarily recruit all these teachers but they are more likely to do so. In addition, part-time and other off-quota teachers can be employed. Substantial help in paying for teachers, ancillaries and other helpers such as welfare and liaison officers whose duty is to make contact with parents, has been made available by the Home Office under the Local Government Act 1966. The Home Office pay 75% of local education authority expenditure. Expenditure of between £3 and £4 million in 1969—70 rose to a figure of nearly £9 million in 1972—73. It was also difficult for local authorities to provide buildings specially needed for immigrant children. A centre for language teaching might have to compete with the long overdue improvements of a primary or secondary school. The Urban Aid Programme has also helped here. Between 1968 and 1972 grants were made for centres where non-English speaking immigrant children could be received when they first arrived, and for language centres where specialised help could be given to children and teachers. There have been many small-scale imaginative projects, notably language schools and camps for immigrant children in the holidays. But in 1973 there was much less in the list of approvals relating to immigrants.

Conclusion

If anyone, almost whatever his politics, had been told in 1953, even 1963, that the school-leaving age would be raised; nursery schools set forth by the government as part of the regular system of education; that the most deprived districts would get rather more resources allocated to them of some kinds than the districts more fortunate in other respects; that more determined attempts would be made to help handicapped children and to establish community schools, all in a single year, he would probably not have thought such a catalogue of change even plausible. Or if he had, he would almost certainly have thought that it would be a wonderful year indeed that could boast of such multiple achievement. Now that it has come and gone, and can be seen close to, it does not, as often happens, seem quite so remarkable. There has been something of a go-slow on the further reform of secondary schools which has marred the record; many immigrant children are still having to put up with the second rate and in every sphere, as always, the outstanding — authority, school, head, teacher — seems to inhabit almost a different planet, a different country, from the mediocre. Close to, we are as bound as ever to be as aware of all that still needs to be done in any year. Aware too of the growing rumours of cuts which could threaten much that has been achieved. But that is no reason for not rejoicing a little in the solid gains that have been made in pushing up the level of the basement in education, and perhaps even more than that, holding out some hope of yet more tangible gains to come.

References

E.M. Anderson, (1973) *The disabled school child – a study of integration in primary schools*, Methuen.

Association of Teachers in Colleges and Departments of Education (ATCDE), (1972) *Summary of teacher-training courses at colleges and departments of education 1973.*
(1973a) *Summary of teaching-training courses at colleges and departments of education 1974.*
(1973b) *Further information leaflets.*

C. Benn and B. Simon, (1972) *Halfway there*, Penguin Education.

T. Blackstone, (1971) *A fair start: the provision of pre-school education*, Allen Lane.

H. Bloom, (1964) *Stability and change in human characteristics*, Wiley.

R. Boyson, (1973) 'Truancy: open the school gates at 14', *Observer*, 23 September 1973.

J.S. Coleman (et al.), (1966) *Equality of educational opportunity*, US Government Printing Office.

J.C. Comber and J.P. Keeves, (1973) *Science education in nineteen countries. An empirical study*, John Wiley.

Community Relations Commission, (1973) *Evidence to the Select Committee on Race Relations and Immigration.*

R. Davie, (1973) 'Eleven years of childhood', in *Statistical News: Developments in British official statistics*, HMSO.

Department of Education and Science,
(1966) 'Additions for the fifth form', *Building Bulletin 32*, HMSO.
(1969) 'Henry Fanshawe School, Derbyshire', *Design Note 2*, DES.
(1970a) 'School and the community', *Design Note 5*, DES.
(1970b) 'Sedgefield School, Durham', *Design Note 6*, DES.
(1971) 'Schools 1970', *Statistics of Education*, vol. 1, HMSO.
(1972) 'Schools 1971', *Statistics of Education*, vol. 1, HMSO.
(1973a) 'Schools 1972', *Statistics of Education*, vol. 1, HMSO.
(1973b) 'Nursery building allocations 1974–6', *Press Notice*, DES.
(1973c) 'Maiden Erlegh secondary school', *Building Bulletin 48*, HMSO.
(1973d) 'Abraham Moss Centre, Manchester', *Building Bulletin 49*, HMSO.
(1973e) *Report on Education 77*, DES.

Education: a framework for expansion, (1972) cmnd. 5174, HMSO.

Education in Scotland: a statement of policy, (1972) Scottish Education Department.

Educational Publishing Company (EPC), (1973) *Books in school.*

E. Halsall, (1973) *The comprehensive school*, Pergamon.

A.H. Halsey (ed.), (1973) *Educational priority vol. 1: EPA problems and policies*, HMSO.

Hansard 16 June 1972 vol. 838, col. 257
15 June 1973 vol. 857; cols. 399–402
18 October 1973 vol. 861, col. 32

A. Holden, (1973) 'A lesson from Lancashire', *Sunday Times*, 14 October 1973.

C. Jencks (et al.), (1973) *Inequality, a reassessment of the effect of family and schooling in America*, Allen Lane.

J.C. Barker Lunn, (1970) *Streaming in the primary school*, National Foundation for Educational Research.

A. Little and C. Mabey, (1973) 'Reading attainment and social and ethnic mix of London primary schools', in D. Donnison and D. Eversley, (1973) *London: urban patterns, problems and policies*, Heinemann.

Alfred Marshall, (1925) 'The future of the working class' in A.C. Pigou (ed.), (1973) *Memorials of Alfred Marshall*, Macmillan.

R. Nash, (1973) *Classrooms observed*, Routledge & Kegan Paul.

National Association of Schoolmasters, (1973) *Evidence to the Select Committee on Race Relations and Immigration*.

National Foundation for Educational Research (NFER), (1973) *Press Release* of the IEA publication of international studies in evaluation in science, reading, comprehension and literature.

G. Neave, (1973) *Comprehensive Education*, summer 1973, Campaign for Comprehensive Education.

N. Postlethwaite, (1967) *School organisation and student achievement*, Almqvist and Wiksell, Stockholm.

Plowden Report, (1967) *Children and their primary schools*, HMSO.

Lincoln Ralphs, (1973) *Summary of the report of the Working Party on the role and the training of Education Welfare Officers* (to be incorporated into a training recommendation and published after submission to the Local Government Training Board in 1974).

I. Reid and M. Franklin, (1973) 'Comprehensive parents', *New Society*, 31 May 1973, vol. 24, no. 556.

J.M. Ross and G. Chanan, (1972) *Comprehensive schools in focus*, National Foundation for Educational Research (NFER). A summary of research carried out on comprehensive schools between 1965 and 1971, reported most recently in J.M. Ross, W.J. Bunton, P. Evison and T.S. Robertson, (1972) *A critical appraisal of comprehensive education*, NFER.

Select Committee on Race Relations and Immigration, (1973) *Session 1972/3, Education*.

Scottish Education Department, (1972) *Scottish Education Statistics 1973*.

G. Taylor and N. Ayres, (1969) *Born and bred unequal*, Longman.

H.E.R. Townsend, (1973) 'Multiracial education: need and innovation' *Schools Council Working Paper 50*, Schools Council.

H.E.R. Townsend and E.M. Brittan, (1972) *Organisation in multiracial schools*, National Foundation for Educational Research.

*The National Health Service is perhaps the
most securely grounded of all in the ethics
of society. Hardly anyone questions the
belief that the sick should be cared for, not
in ratio to their means but to their needs.
Practice still falls short of precept,
although some worthwhile advances were made
in 1973. Phyllis Willmott examines local
welfare services along with health, the two
in many ways being linked.*

9   Health and Welfare
PHYLLIS WILLMOTT

In 1969 the sum spent on both national health and welfare
services in the United Kingdom was close to £2,000 million.
In 1970 it had easily passed that mark and in 1972 it had
climbed again to around two and three quarter millions.
Against the £500 million odd for the early years of these
services, or the £1,000 million of the early sixties, the
increases are great. In real terms we have more than doubled
expenditure since the post-war years. Most of the cost of
these services is met out of exchequer funds (71.5%) or local
rates (15%). A small amount (9%) comes from indirect
taxation by means of the NHS contribution included in
national insurance, and a smaller amount still (4.5%) comes
from health charges for such things as prescriptions, dental
treatment, or, for welfare, charges for such things as home
helps or residential care outside hospitals (Department of
Health and Social Security 1972a).

Health and welfare are both the responsibility of the
Department of Health and Social Security. The hospital
services are run by hospital regional authorities directly
answerable to the central government department, but the

so-called 'community health services' are run by major local authority health departments, and the welfare services by major local authority social services departments. In April 1974 this will change. The community health services will become the responsibility of the Area and Regional Health Authorities which are to replace the present Regional Hospital Boards and hospital committees. (General practitioners will also then lose a little of their former autonomy and be drawn closer into the more centralised system.) The welfare services (which in April 1971 were officially retitled the 'personal social services') will remain apart from the health services and remain the responsibility of the major local authorities. Whether or not this administrative division between health and welfare services makes sense is the subject of current debate – for example, whereas some believe that both should be unified at local as well as central level, others believe that welfare services would be better combined with those of social security. The fact remains that apart from statistics (such as those with which this chapter began) and although under the same central government department, the health and welfare services are administratively separate, and for this reason in this chapter we shall look first at health and, secondly, at welfare services.

Geographical inequalities in health
By almost any measurement it is true to say that bad as it is to be ill anywhere, if you have to be ill it is better in England and Wales to be south of a line from the Severn to the Wash (with some exceptions mentioned below) and better still to be in or around London or the Home Counties. In the first place patients going into hospital there are more likely to find themselves in reasonable surroundings because current and capital expenditure per head are way above average, whereas apart from the Liverpool region (which is somewhat above average) the rest of England and Wales are in greater or lesser degree below average. There are substantially more doctors to be found at work in hospitals in London and the Home Counties (68:100,000) than in other areas, where ratios vary from 39:100,000 in the Sheffield region to 56:100,000 in the Liverpool region. There are also more

administrative and clerical staff in the favoured areas, and more professional and technical staff. It is the same with nursing staff and ancillary workers, except that Liverpool again comes out with a slight advantage over the London Metropolitan Region (Department of Health and Social Security 1972a).

For medical care outside hospitals the official statistics show similar inequalities. The average list for general practitioners in England and Wales is 2,444, whereas in Wales, East Anglia, the south east and south west, practices are smaller; in the north and the Midlands they are larger. In the south-east and south-west of England dentists are not doing too badly with 3,280 and 4,007 (1971) patients per dentist, as against the average of 4,431, and extremes of 6,248 (in Wales), 6,152 (in the east Midlands) and 6,128 (in the north).

Although the main regional differences are between the older industrial areas of the country and the rest, one must not overlook the inequalities existing within regions as well. Again 'poor' people tend to live in 'poor' areas, and these in turn tend either to have 'poor' health services or to under-use those available. For example, it is in the centre of cities like London where most of the famous teaching hospitals are to be found, and so are many of the city's poorest families. There is some evidence that, in proportion to their need, fewer go to such hospitals than people in better circumstances.

Active medical treatment for ill health has been the main responsibility of general practitioners and hospitals, whereas *maintaining* health (or preventing ill health) has been largely the work of the local (or 'community') health services. As I said, this is to change in April 1974. Meanwhile, variations between local authorities are if anything even more remarkable. As these services are controlled at local level, there are amazing differences in expenditure and staffing ratios across administrative boundaries. At one extreme this shows up most clearly in London, where borough boundaries inevitably cut through streets and where a different health service can therefore be found on one side (or at one end) of a street from the other! In 1971—72, for example, whereas Bromley spent £1.31 on clinics and centres for each child under 5, its neighbour Lewisham spent £9.61. Similarly, while Ealing gave 17,860 chiropody treatments in the course of the year, nearby Wandsworth, with a population of virtually identical size, gave 42,390 (Institute of Municipal Treasurers and Accountants 1973). Similar differences exist between towns and between counties throughout England and Wales.

Inequalities within different parts of the health service
Regional variations in standards of services broadly reflect the general unequal division between the 'rich' south and the 'poor' north (Taylor and Ayres 1969). There are other well known but none the less disturbing inequalities to be found within different parts of the health service. The most outstanding example is undoubtedly 'mental disorders' (this legal term includes both the mentally ill and the mentally handicapped). The cost per in-patient week in a London teaching hospital is five times that in a non-teaching hospital for the mentally handicapped, and four times that in a non-teaching hospital for the mentally ill. Then again, although 45% of NHS patients are in hospitals for the mentally ill or handicapped, they receive less than one-fifth of current expenditure on hospitals. What is more, the mentally handicapped have less than 1% of the total National Health Service (NHS) hospital medical staff, and the mentally ill a mere 8%. In other words, 45% of hospital patients have to make do with 9% of the NHS's total of medical staff. Of the 10,000 top medical men – the *consultants* employed by the NHS – only 122 (1%) in 1971 were in the field of mental handicap, and 1,020 (10%) in that of mental illness. In these Cinderella hospitals similar outstanding discrepancies exist in the amount spent on food, in their size and out of date buildings, and in the extent of overcrowded wards (see Department of Health and Social Security 1971a, 1972b, 1973a and Morris 1969). Even pocket money for patients in mental hospitals is provided on a different, and more cheeseparing basis. Mental patients are dependent on the goodwill of the hospital staff, and have no right to – and do not get – pocket money at a standard rate (at present £1.55 per week) from the Supplementary Benefits Commission, as

other hospital patients in need of pocket money do.

Social class
Marked as the geographical and internal differences are,
another of even greater importance is in social class. North or
south, 'good' or 'bad' authority, social class divides everywhere. That 'free' health services are an advantage to the
poorer, and in some sense an 'egalitarian service' of great
benefit to them, cannot be denied. What can be questioned
— and in recent years has been — is how far the poor benefit
more or *less* than the rich. In 1968 Titmuss concluded:

> We have learnt from fifteen years' experience that the
> higher income groups know how to make better use of the
> service; they tend to receive more specialist attention;
> occupy more of the beds in better equipped and staffed
> hospitals; receive more elective surgery; have better
> maternity care, and are more likely to get psychiatric help
> and psychotherapy than low income groups — particularly
> the unskilled. (Titmuss 1968).

The argument is not simply that the rich invariably make
greater demands on the services. Managers and professional
men of working age are, for example, likely to see their GP
slightly less often (Office of Population Censuses and Surveys
1973) but in general they aim for — and tend to get — more
out of the health services in proportion to their need.

By contrast, those at the bottom need more care from the
health services. But although they suffer more ill health (and
die younger) what they do not get is either the best or the
most appropriate service. There is an increasing body of
evidence that shows that they use preventive services less
often, that they accept lower standards of care, and that they
often demand care for serious health conditions at a later
stage of ill health. There is what one medical man (Hart
1971) describes as an 'inverse care law':

> In areas with most sickness and death, general practition-
> ers have more work, larger lists, less hospital support, and
> inherit more clinically ineffective traditions of consul-
> tations than in the healthiest areas; and hospital doctors
> shoulder heavier case loads with less staff and equipment,

more obsolete buildings, and suffer recurrent crises in the availability of beds and replacement staff. These trends can be summed up as the inverse care law: that the availability of good medical care tends to vary inversely with the need of the population served.

Class inequalities in health chances begin before birth (more stillborn babies in the lower classes), continue after birth (higher infant mortality rate) and go on throughout life (the unskilled die earlier than others). The most recent evidence from the General Household Survey confirms that not only do mortality statistics show an inverse relationship with social class, so also does ill health. Unskilled men of working age, says the Report are three times as likely to say that they suffer from chronic sickness as professional men of the same age group. Furthermore, *younger unskilled men are more often than professional men sufferers at middle age.* The unskilled are three times as likely as the professional class to suffer from mental disorders (and thus end up in one of the poorest parts of the NHS — see above); twice as likely to suffer from arthritis and rheumatism; and even that condition most associated with an 'executive' style of life — heart disease — is still *more often* a cause of long-standing illness for the unskilled.

The same survey shows that the lower classes are therefore more often off work sick, and more often call upon their doctors. But the professional classes still appear to get more care, need for need, than the unskilled (see Table 9.1). Whereas the latter are off work sick more than four times as much, they do not see their GPs much more often than the professional class.

What is true for unskilled men seems also to be true for their families. For example, both mothers and their young children in these families, although likely to be in less good health and in need of more care, make less use of child welfare and medical services (Davie and others 1972). By school age the children of unskilled men are more often ill and accident prone (Wedge and Prosser 1973). Another recent report (Office of Health Economics 1973) adds to this sorry list the fact that for the children of the unskilled manual worker the incidence of mild mental handicap is

Table 9.1 Socio-economic group by average number of consultations per person per year with GP (NHS) and average number of days off work sick per year

Socio-economic group	All males 15 or over (GP consultations)	Working males 15 or over (days off sick)
Professional)		3.9
Employers & managers)	3.7	7.2
Other non-manual	3.6	6.7
Skilled manual	4.0	9.3
Semi-skilled manual)		11.5
Unskilled)	4.2	18.4
Rate for all	3.8	9.1

Source: Office of Population Censuses and Surveys 1973

roughly nine times greater, and that such handicap more usually stems, not from inherited low intelligence, but from 'undetected physical defects or abnormalities combined with poor nutrition for both children and their mothers, and inadequate education and stimulation both at home and in school'. The resulting cycle of health deprivation is summed up neatly thus:

> The prospects of good health are significantly worse for children of unskilled manual background throughout their lives. They have a higher rate of death in infancy. They are shorter at school age. When they enter work they have more and longer spells of sickness. They are more likely to be admitted to mental hospitals. As they grow old they are more likely to suffer from chronic bronchitis or to become disabled. They will die younger. (*Health care* 1973).

Enough has already been said to make it clear that changes in health services are seldom of a kind to be able to reveal measurable differences over short periods, such as one year, or even over five or ten years. We must therefore be content in the next section to look briefly at recent changes largely with a view to their *likely* effects on the 'health poor' (such as the mentally disordered) and the low-income poor.

Ironing out geographical inequalities

One of the gains hoped for from the proposed administrative reorganisation of the NHS which comes into force in April 1974 (together with the reform of local government), is that there will be a levelling up of all health services in different places. Efforts to do this in the past have not been a resounding success. However, in 1971—72 a new method of allocating revenue to the regions was introduced more in accord with their respective needs. This new method 'is designed to reduce inequalities of financial provision between Regions progressively over a period of about 10 years' (Department of Health and Social Security 1972c). Present inequalities between community health services should also be reduced when local authority health services become the responsibility of the area health authorities, along with hospitals and general practitioners.

What might prove to be a further aid in redistributing key staff more equally is the Central Manpower Committee established in 1972 at the DHSS. One of the objectives of this new body is to secure 'greater regional equality in the proportion of (medical and dental) staff to population served' (Department of Health and Social Security 1972c). It is still too early to judge how effective the Committee will be. More to one means less to another. A cry of anguish in October 1973 from one of the teaching hospitals (which traditionally are favoured above all others for almost every resource) suggested that 'This decision will adversely affect both the quality and the quantity of medical education' and that it is, furthermore, 'a short-sighted and short-term expedient'. (First of a series of letters to *The Times*, from the Chairman of the *Association of University Clinical Academic Staff*.)

Levelling up within different sectors

As with regional differences, efforts made to distribute doctors, specialists and money to those parts of the health service which need more but get less have not been markedly successful. In 1963 47% of all in-patients on any day were in mental hospitals but only 10% of all medical staff; by 1971 the figures were 45% and 9%. Partly as a result of increasing

pressure from voluntary organisations concerned with the
mentally ill and mentally handicapped, partly because of
increased public awareness of the tragic consequences arising
from existing conditions in certain mental hospitals, as
revealed in a series of official enquiries (Ely Hospital in 1969,
Farleigh in 1972, Coldharbour in 1972, South Ockendon in
1973) stronger efforts are being made to redress this
longstanding imbalance between mental hospitals and others.
These have included:

(a) The setting up of the Hospital Advisory Service (this
followed the publication of the enquiry on Ely
Hospital) to ensure a regular system of visiting and
inspection, initially 'concentrating on hospitals for
the mentally handicapped, the mentally ill, the
elderly and long-stay hospitals generally' (Department
of Health and Social Security 1969).

(b) Interim measures to introduce 'minimum acceptable
standards' for hospital care by 1975, backed by
additional sums to hospital authorities for both
current and capital expenditure (Department of
Health and Social Security, 1971b and 1972c).

(c) Long-term plans to integrate the treatment for mental
illness with the general hospital service, involving
increased capital expenditure for small 'units'
attached to general hospitals for the mentally ill, and
the building of smaller hospitals for the mentally
handicapped likely to need long-term care (Department of Health and Social Security, 1972c).

(d) A long-term plan to improve the quality of community care services for the benefit of both mentally
handicapped and mentally ill. For this about £250
million will go to health and personal social services
over the five year period up to 1975—76 over and
above the annual average increase of £80 million.
Most of it will go to improving services for the
mentally ill, the mentally handicapped and the
elderly in both hospitals and the community
(Department of Health and Social Security, 1971b).

Important and welcome as these developments are there is
no prospect, unfortunately, that they will swiftly or sub-

stantially improve the lives of mentally ill or handicapped people and their families. The White Paper, *Better services for the mentally handicapped* (1971c), suggests 'we must think in terms of development programmes for local authority and hospital services lasting 15—20 years over the country as a whole. The rate of progress will vary from one area to another. In some areas it may be possible to complete the service we want in about 20 years, other are less well advanced now and will need longer to complete'. The DHSS memorandum, *Hospital services for the mentally ill* (Department of Health and Social Security 1971d) speaks of 'the ultimate aim of replacing large mental hospitals' as taking place 'in phases over several years'.

Improving health care
Inequalities of health care arising from class differences are entangled with other inequalities — of education, income, housing and work — and two quotations from medical journals must serve to illustrate how it may only partly be a question of getting appropriate health care to the patient:

> It was found that children with less favourable social backgrounds had a poorer experience of medical supervision [for acute ear infections] and poorer end results following treatment. (Paterson and MacLean 1970.)

> Mothers who lost a baby in the perinatal period were more likely, when compared with the central group, to have a poor attitude to ante-natal care, to have a poor diet, to have serious family problems. (Vaughan 1968.)

The depressing fact is that action on health alone cannot 'solve' the problem of the ill health and inferior life expectation of the poor. The recent 'opposition green paper' (*Health care* 1973) suggests that there is a need for 'priority areas' for health services as there are for education (EPAs) and social problems (Community Development Projects). How helpful this would be may depend on the effective geographical alignment of any health priority areas with the others.

In the long term some developments which we might reasonably hope to lead to some better services for those most in need of them, include the more than tenfold

increase, since 1959, of health centres, the rapid expansion of
family planning facilities and the reform of the abortion laws.
Unfortunately, the extent and distribution of these services
varies tremendously from place to place. There are 365
health centres in England, and 438 more are planned, but
whereas a few local authorities have over 20 most have only 1
or 2 and many none at all. Local authorities provide family
planning services either directly at their own clinics or
through voluntary bodies, but in 1972 only 97 authorities
had a domiciliary service, and even for those who have, the
service did not always cover their whole area. The number of
abortions also varies regionally, and only a third take place in
NHS hospitals. The Chief Medical Officer of the DHSS
comments (1973b) 'where the standard is strict' (that is in
regions where gynaecologists are reluctant to undertake
abortion) 'a large number of women simply go to the private
sector locally or elsewhere'. One might add 'if they have the
money and live in the right place' (British Pregnancy
Advisory Service 1973). Another point about the value of
these services to the poor is that, being broadly 'preventive',
they are likely to be used disproportionately more by higher
classes. As the Chief Medical Officer, summing up recent
evidence, bluntly states 'Family planning services are used
more by well-to-do women than by those with lower
incomes'.

Three changes more certain, more immediate, and possibly
also having a long-term effect on the poor, are the charges for
prescriptions, dental care and welfare foods. From April
1971 NHS prescription charges were raised from 12½p to
20p per item (and 25p or 50p for each piece of elastic
hosiery). Under a new system of dental charges half the cost
of treatment falls on the patient, with a maximum charge of
£10. At the same time the longstanding cheap welfare milk
scheme was ended. (Under this scheme expectant mothers
and all children under five were each able to get one pint of
fresh milk a day at a subsidised price — 2½p a pint in
1970 — by handing tokens to their milkmen.) The changes
made, so the government announced, were intended to
enable more help to be given to those whose need was
greatest. To this end the government launched an expensive

advertisement campaign and also extended entitlement benefits to more low-income families by raising income limits of eligibility.

At first sight the government appears to have had some success. There has not been any drop in the total number of prescriptions or dental treatments, or the total consumption of milk, although the DHSS annual report (1971b) suggested that a decrease of nine million in the number of *paid for* prescriptions might be due not only to a rise in the number of *free* prescriptions but to a 'moderation in demand following the increase in the charge'. It seems unlikely that this 'moderation' comes from the richer section of society for whom a rise of 7½p per item is not likely to be much of a deterrent. It seems very probable, on the other hand, that the increased charges do deter some poorer people and that charges for dental treatment will do so too. The DHSS (1971b) point out that those going for regular dental attention could in fact often pay less under the new system than before, but again this is obviously more likely to help middle-class people – who make the fullest use of this service – particularly in more affluent places where there are more dentists anyway.

The claims procedure for getting the above benefits free is complex – there are six qualifying categories for prescriptions, each with a different claim procedure; there are five qualifying categories for welfare milk (each with several different procedures for claiming), but only two for dental treatment. With such complexity it is hardly surprising that most of those who should be getting these free benefits, and maybe in most need of them, continue to go without (Child Poverty Action Group 1971; and Meacher 1973).

By July 1973 the government had spent £200,000 on advertising free welfare milk and free dental treatment and prescriptions. It was particularly concerned to reach low-income families other than those receiving regular supplementary benefits or family income supplement (FIS) (these, by using their order books as 'passports', qualify automatically as do certain other categories, such as the elderly who need only fill in a declaration on the back of the prescription form). The effect on take-up of free pre-

scriptions for those on low incomes (as defined in the last
sentence) was at first dramatic: in 1970 these totalled
15,000; during 1971 they climbed to 69,000, but in 1972
they had fallen again drastically to 38,000. A similar picture
emerges of the numbers in the same low-income category
who were claiming free welfare milk — a dramatic rise in the
'advertising' year (from the 1970 figure of 1,500 families to
the 1971 figure of around 61,000 families) with a drastic
drop in 1972 to around 33,000.

Adding on the money spent on publicising FIS, the
government spent, between June 1970 and July 1973, a total
of close on a million pounds (£970,000) on advertising these
benefits for low-income families, yet take-up remains persis-
tently low. By 1973 take-up nationally for FIS was estimated
as 52% and such limited evidence as exists suggests even
lower for the other benefits. In contrast, during the same
period, the government also advertised widely a new benefit
without means test — the attendance allowance for disabled
people. The result was striking: by June 1973 instead of the
estimated 50,000 expected over 100,000 awards had been
made.

The conclusion is that, for means-tested benefits,
occasional advertising campaigns, however massive and
costly, are likely at best to improve things only partially and
temporarily. In contrast, at relatively little expense (£92,000
was spent on advertising the attendance allowance) advertising a valuable benefit not based on a means test can be highly
successful.

To do without medicine, dental care and welfare milk may
be more serious in the long term than the short term.
Following the alteration in the welfare milk scheme (and also
for school milk and meals in the same year) so much concern
was aroused that the government undertook to take steps to
monitor for adverse effects. A Sub-Committee on Nutritional
Surveillance was set up. For its first report (Department of
Health and Social Security 1973c) it had no evidence of any
effects from changes so recently made. The sub-committee,
however, did express some anxiety over possible long-term
effects. It pointed out that even with subsidised welfare milk
(that is, as before 1971) survey evidence suggested that

pregnant women were on average taking *less* than the medically recommended daily amount of milk. They also commented that the continued fall in the peri-natal mortality rate may have resulted from the 'better condition of present-day mothers who benefited from welfare foods in their youth'. Thirdly, and perhaps even more ominous, the sub-committee pointed out:

> Some of the possible consequences of any reduction (if this occurs) in the milk consumption of pregnant women are potentially more serious than those that might occur in schoolchildren. Furthermore, if any diminution in growth rate occurred in pre-school children the effects might be more difficult to reverse than those of any diminution observed in schoolchildren.

Bearing in mind the class differences in health mentioned earlier (and the class differences in actual physical height of schoolchildren), it is hard to escape the conclusion that both in the short and long term the changes in policy for prescriptions, dental charges and welfare milk are likely to reinforce, and increase, the disadvantages of the poor. The changes have saved the Exchequer about £36 million a year (Department of Health and Social Security 1971b and 1972c). Ironically, Mr Barber's Budget hand-out on sweets, ice-cream and crisps — exempting them from VAT — will cost three times the amount saved. To this £110m per year in cash must be added the as yet unknown price of increased dental decay and possibly, in time, more serious consequences to health.

Social and welfare services
In April 1971, as a result of the Local Authority Social Services Act 1970, a reorganisation of services took place within the major local authorities having responsibilities for social and welfare services. The purpose of this reorganisation, closely following the recommendations of the Seebohm Committee (1968) was to draw together into one local authority department the functions formerly spread between three. As a result, each authority set up, under a new statutory committee, a social services department to administer the wide range of social and welfare services

(renamed 'personal social services') for deprived children, the mentally ill and handicapped, the disabled, the elderly and the homeless. One of the most important aims of the reorganisation was to ensure that in future effective help should be offered to any family or any individual in need.

At the same time as they had to remake their social and welfare services, local authorities also had to fulfil new duties and obligations placed on them by various Acts. The Children and Young Persons Act 1969 much increased their responsibilities for deprived and delinquent children; sections of an earlier Act (Health Services and Public Act 1968) were brought into force and extended responsibilities for providing home helps and other services for the elderly, disabled and mentally disordered; the Chronically Sick and Disabled Persons Act 1970 extended old obligations and introduced new ones.

It is too early for a proper assessment of such an upheaval. It is at least clear that more money has gone to social services — £337 million in 1972—73, as against £237 million in 1970—71 (Department of Health and Social Security 1972c). What is equally clear is that the increase in resources is no more than a drop in the bucket. Evidence of the gap between demand and resources has accumulated rapidly since the publication in the 1960s of the plans for health and welfare services of the local authorities (Department of Health and Social Security 1963 and 1966) provided both a catalogue of the extensive deficiencies and a blueprint for progress. To find out in detail what progress has been made, and the extent of remaining deficiencies, we must await the publication of the *Local authority social services ten year development plans 1973—1983* which the DHSS began to prepare in 1972.

Meanwhile, a circular has offered guidance to local authorities. It points out, for example, that in 1968 there was an average of about 15 field social workers per 100,000 population, and that by 1971 this had risen to an average of 25 (including trainees and assistants). Some progress thus appears to have been made. But the DHSS suggests that 50 to 60 workers are the *average* to aim at, with some places, such as inner city areas, needing many more. Doubling or trebling of staff is recommended for home helps and residential workers. And a similar degree of expansion is demanded for virtually every other service for which local authorities are responsible — meals on wheels, day centres and day nurseries, residential homes and staff. What the circular offers (Department of Health and Social Security 1972d) is little more than a list of present inadequacies — as no doubt the plans will too when they appear.

The aim of the 1971 reorganisation was to provide an effective family service. It clearly cannot be achieved if such gross shortages persist. Help will continue to be subject to severe rationing. With rare exceptions, such as some of the disabled or elderly people who seek fairly limited practical help or advice, most of the clientcle of social services departments are, and will continue to be, poor or in some other way disadvantaged people — the single-parent family, the low-income family, the homeless and the mentally ill — amongst whom the inadequate services will have to be spread either equally and desperately thinly, or unevenly and leaving some in great need unaided.

The euphoric hopes raised by Seebohm amongst social workers have, therefore, shown signs in the past year of collapsing into disillusion. In one or two places this has exploded into social workers joining with their clients in public demonstrations. Juggling with the inadequate resources, unable in any fundamental way to improve the lot of their clients who need better housing, higher incomes, good schools and so on, is being seen more and more for what it is — an impossible task; especially in a situation when more, not less, help has been promised and public expectations of a better service have been aroused.

In 1972 the British Association of Social Workers formed a 'poverty special interest group' to mobilise professional concern over the 'problems of low means and poor provision in our society'. Their first national lobbying of Parliament was held in 1973 to press for the payment of tax credits direct to all mothers, as with present family allowances, to increase benefits, and to include the first child.

It is against this background that some limited, but real, progress in the past year or so must be seen.

Expansion of home help and meals services

The survey. *A home help service in England and Wales.*
(Government Social Survey 1967) suggested that a two-to
threefold increase was necessary to meet then existing needs.
At the time there were 5 home helps per 1,000 elderly
people. By 1971 this had risen to 5.5 per 1,000. Since then
there have been further 'encouraging signs of continued
growth' (Department of Health and Social Security 1972c)
but at the same time demand has increased. What is more,
because of the different degree of priority given by different
local authorities there are still enormous variations between
areas. The home help service has largely been used to help the
elderly, although it can also be given to maternity cases,
mothers with young children, or because of illness in a
family. From April 1971 it could also be used for families
containing a young disabled person. Whether under present
circumstances this new call on the services can be met
without sacrifice to the old remains to be seen. In 1972 the
figures for elderly and disabled had both slightly increased.
This is more probably a result of the decline in the maternity
load (and also the decline in home confinements) than of the
slight expansion in the service. Annual expenditure in
England rose from £18.8 million in 1967–68 to £32.9
million in 1971–72. The home help service is one for which,
at the discretion of local authorities, a charge *can* be made on
the basis of an income assessment but does not need to be. In
1972 twelve local authorities had abandoned charges wholly;
this meant one less unnecessary means test for the fortunate
people in their areas.

The meals service is another which largely benefits old
people. It is one which is of both practical and financial
benefit to them, ensuring a cooked meal, which they might
not otherwise go to the trouble and expense of preparing,
and a subsidised one. Charges vary from about 5p to 15p per
meal; it is generally assumed that old people prefer to pay
something. Again there has been a steady overall expansion,
both for meals on wheels and of meals served at clubs, but
most old people served still receive in their homes only one
or two meals per week. Weekend meals are rare and once

again enormous local variations in the meals service remain. (See Table 9.2.).

Table 9.2 *Meals served in year 1971—72 by ten local authorities per 1,000 population over 65*

Lewisham (LB)	18,777
Manchester (CB)	10,900
Bootle (CB)	6,157
Lancashire (CC)	5,266
Bournemouth (CB)	3,858
Buckingham (CC)	3,194
Brent (LB)	3,141
Sussex, East (CC)	2,724
Eastbourne (CB)	1,319
Brighton (CB)	1,001

Source: Institute of Municipal Treasurers and Accountants 1973

Help for the disabled
In 1970, backed by the many organisations involved in the welfare of the disabled, and many members on all sides of the House, Alfred Morris, MP, managed to get his private member's Bill on to the statute book. Known popularly as the 'Charter for the Disabled', the Chronically Sick and Disabled Persons Act 1970 held out great promise. Under the Act social services departments were obliged to find the disabled people in their areas and to tell them about the help available. The departments' obligations to provide services, such as adaptations to the home, domestic help, telephones and so on for those in need of them, were also more strictly defined. The Act also puts pressure on local authorities and others to make life easier for the disabled in many other ways — by improving access to public buildings and lava-

tories, parking facilities, educational opportunities and so on. Since the Act came into force the pressure groups for the disabled have kept a rigorous watch on progress. They have, in the main, been disappointed both in the slowness of action and in the variations in the level and type of services provided by different authorities (see for example the report of the National Fund for Research into Crippling Diseases (NFRCD) (National Fund for Research into Crippling Diseases 1973).

As an official survey (Office of Population Censuses and Surveys 1971) found, there is a great deal of overlap between the elderly and the disabled. The services discussed above are likely to help the disabled too. But the other way on there is always the danger of competition *between* groups in different but equal need. When there is not enough for everyone, a gain for one group can be a loss for another. More visiting of the chronically sick can mean less for the blind (or so the latter clearly thought when they protested in one area against a deterioration in their services). The fact that more telephones for the disabled may mean a less rapid extension of meals or home helps service for the elderly may be one genuine reason for the different extent to which this power has been used by local authorities. The NFRCP survey found that some authorities were providing ten times as many as others. Manchester, which has installed 2,000 telephones since the Act came into force, is thought to hold the record (*Health and Social Services Journal* 1973).

The nightmare of priorities is always there. All the same it is clear that for the disabled some limited progress has again been made. In 1963 the total number of people on local authority registers for the disabled totalled 121,000. The numbers increased by about 14% a year before the Act came into force. By March 1973 the total had reached 352,246 – an increase of 30% over the previous year. This is still only about one in four of the numbers estimated as eligible to register, and although registration is not a condition of benefiting from social services, research has shown that only a minority of those not registered are likely to have had any help. Although for most services in most areas charges are made, both the amounts charged and the methods of assessment vary from place to place (National

Fund for Research into Crippling Disease 1973).

Unusually, one London borough makes no charge up to the first £100. The help given under the Act can sometimes be substantial. For example, where extensive adaptations of the homes of severely disabled people are carried out, sums of £500 to £1,000 or more are involved. Help with minor improvements and aids are, of course, less expensive and perhaps more common. Figures of actual assistance given are promised by the DHSS and will make possible further illuminating comparisons between the performance of different authorities. Meanwhile, although so much remains to be done, we can conclude that the recent changes (especially taking into account others such as the introduction of the attendance allowance and invalidity benefit discussed by Tony Lynes in Chapter 5) have been of real help to some of the disabled. The most urgent task now is to even out the excessive disparities between different authorities.

Families with children

There is the same need for levelling up another service. Social services departments have powers to give money and material help to families with children. Such help can be given for the payment of debts, underwriting of rent, play group fees, and so on — these can sometimes be a means of avoiding families under stress being broken up and children being taken into care. Table 9.3 shows how variably this power is used. The following facts are relevant:

In the year March 1971 to March 1972 (latest available figures) 3,575 children in England were taken into care because of homelessness, which represents 7% of children taken into care for all reasons in the year.

In the quarter ending September 1972, 2,004 families who lost their homes because of being in rent arrears applied to local authorities for temporary accommodation.

Of the 2,004 families, 1,569 (78%) were council tenants evicted by local authorities.

One unusual innovation likely to be of real benefit to some families with disabled children began in August 1973. This is the Family Fund, established by the government with a sum of £3 million but run by the Joseph Rowntree Memorial

*Table 9.3 Expenditure per 1,000 population under 18 years
on preventing children being taken into care, 1971—72*

County boroughs

Spending nothing	Tynemouth	–
	Preston	–
	York	–
	Oldham	–
	Birkenhead	–
Lowest three	Merthyr Tydfil	£4
	Sunderland	£3
	Kingston-upon-Hull	£1
Highest three	Bath	£215
	Rochdale	£512
	Oxford	£572

Average for CBs   £54

London boroughs

Spending nothing	Bexley	–
	Wandsworth	–
Lowest three	Hillingdon	£6
	Harrow	£15
	Redbridge	£23
Highest three	Lambeth	£2,294
	Islington	£1,383
	Westminster	£1,010

Average for LBS   £296

County councils

Spending nothing	Montgomery (Wales)	–
	Cardigan (Wales)	–
Lowest three	York E. Riding	£1.68
	Stafford	£4.07
	Essex	£2.69
Highest three	Kent	£216
	Wiltshire	£171
	Huntingdonshire	£91.29

Average (England & Wales counties)   £41.91

Source: Institute of Municipal Treasurers and Accountants 1973

Trust. The aim is to help those with a very severely *congenitally handicapped* child between the ages of 10 and 16 who are in need of money, goods or services to relieve stress in the family. The kind of help given includes transport (sometimes even the cost of buying a car), holidays, and laundry equipment (such as washing machines). Although economic and social circumstances are taken into account there is no formal means test. The Family Fund usually calls on local social services departments to visit the family on their behalf to discuss the application, but any family can apply direct to the Fund in the first instance. By the end of July 1973, 1,000 applications had been received, but only 8 had been refused.

Conclusion

The aim in this chapter is the same as in every other — to discuss how what has been happening in the past year or two has influenced the incidence of poverty. The health and welfare services are guided by different philosophies. The Health Service has one very great merit. It is in intention even more universalist than education. Anyone, equally — that is without any reference whatsoever to his or her income — is supposed to be able to get good care and good treatment. The poor are therefore a great deal better off in this respect than in many other industrial countries. But it is not yet by any means true that the poor get the same quality of service as the rich in our society. Furthermore, where services are not entirely free — as with dental and prescription charges — the poor are most affected. This matters especially because they do not need just the same quality; they often need better quality because their health is worse by reason of their poverty. We are still far away from that goal.

One important change — or should I say beginning of a change — is in what is being done to improve the lot of mental patients. Many of them are poor in income: that almost goes without saying; they have also in the past been pushed down into the cellars of the Health Service. It would be too early to say they have been lifted out; but there is a new concern.

The personal social services are in one vital way quite

different. They are not used by everyone, that is by rich and poor alike, but mostly by the poor. As one Area Director of social services commented:

> In a recent analysis of new referrals to my own office it appeared that something like 80 per cent of all applicants sought a material service — domestic help, aids, adaptations, housing, money, day and residential care. Judging by the comments of social workers from all over the country, and from recent literature, this is a fairly typical situation. (Barter 1973.)

The clients of the new social service departments are, it is true, usually not only poor but needy in some other way as well, which means that they, like the sick who are also poor, have a double claim. Even for the elderly and disabled for whom the period under review has been one of slight progress, against the background of needs still unmet — on a scale for which the word colossal is not extravagant — there is still more cause for alarm than complacency.

References

J. Barter, (1973) *Social Work Today*, 6 September 1973, vol. 4 no. 12, British Association of Social Workers.

British Pregnancy Advisory Service (1973), *Client statistics for 1971.*

Child Poverty Action Group, (1971) *Poverty*, no. 20 Winter 1971.

R. Davie, N. Butler, H. Goldstein, (1972) *From birth to seven*, The Second Report of the National Child Development Study, Longmans.

Department of Health and Social Security, (1963, 1966) *Health and welfare*, The development of community-care plans for health and welfare services of the local authorities, cmnd. 1973 and cmnd. 3022, HMSO.

(1969) *Annual Report*, HMSO.

(1971a) *National Health Service Hospital Advisory Service Annual Report*, HMSO.

(1971b) *Annual Report*, HMSO.

(1971c) *Better services for the mentally handicapped*, cmnd. 4683, HMSO.

(1971d) 'Hospital services for the mentally ill' *Memorandum HM(71)97*, Department of Health and Social Security.

(1972a) *Health and personal social services statistics*, HMSO.

(1972b) *National Health Service Hospital Advisory Service Annual Report*, HMSO.

(1972c) *Annual Report*, HMSO.

(1972d) *Circular 35/72*, Department of Health and Social Security.

(1973a) *National Health Service Hospital Advisory Service Annual Report*, HMSO.

(1973b) *On the state of the public health*, Annual report of the Chief Medical Officer for 1972, HMSO.

(1973c) *First report by the sub-committee on nutritional surveillance*, HMSO.

Government Social Survey, (1967) *A home-help service in England and Wales*, HMSO.

J.H. Hart, (1971) 'The inverse care law', *The Lancet*, 26 February 1971 vol. 1.

Health and Social Service Journal, 3 November 1973.

Health care, (1973) Report of a Working Party, The Labour Party.

Institute of Municipal Treasurers and Accountants, (1973) *Local health and social services statistics*.

Molly Meacher, (1973) *Rate rebates*, Child Poverty Action Group.

P. Morris, (1969) *Put away*, Routledge and Kegan Paul.

National Fund for Research into Crippling Diseases, (1973) *The implementation of the Chronically Sick and Disabled Persons Act*, Report by Social Policy Research.

Office of Health Economics, (1973) *Mental handicap*.

Office of Population Censuses and Surveys, (1973) *The general household survey: introductory report*, HMSO.

Office of Population Censuses and Surveys, (1971) *Handicapped and impaired in Great Britain*, Part I, HMSO.

J. Paterson and D.W. MacLean, (1970) 'Acute otitis media in children', *Scottish Medical Journal*, 15.289.

Seebohm Committee, (1968) *Report of the committee on local authority and allied personal social services*, cmnd. 3703, HMSO.

G. Taylor and N. Ayres, (1969) *Born and bred unequal*, Longmans.

R. Titmuss, (1968) *Commitment to welfare*, Allen & Unwin.

D.H. Vaughan, (1968) 'Some social factors in perinatal mortality', *British Journal of Preventive and Social Medicine*, vol. 22, no. 3.

P. Wedge and H. Prosser, (1973) *Born to fail?* Arrow.

Geographical contrasts have been mentioned in the last three chapters. The great variations there are in a small compass between different parts of the United Kingdom are one of its assets — but this certainly doesn't apply to variations in the standard of living. Vivian Woodward pulls together in this chapter some of the available facts about the many regional differences there are in poverty, and what goes with it.

10 The Regional Dimension
VIVIAN WOODWARD

Facts about poverty at the regional level
Nearly all regional statistics produced regularly relate to the ten new standard regions of Great Britain. In recent years it .has been recognised that the existence of considerable intra-regional variations justifies the development of sub-regional statistics and there is now a limited amount of information for 61 sub-regions in Great Britain. The way of subdividing regions was influenced by the balance between urban and rural areas; the extent of urbanisation is an important factor in both inter-regional and intra-regional variations in economic activity. Both regional and sub-regional statistics have been developed to serve requirements for regional economic policy as it is worked out at national level. The major concern is with variations in unemployment rates which themselves have a major bearing on the incidence of poverty at the regional level.

Also relevant is the extent to which public services, which are of greater importance to poor households than others, vary in standard between regions and sub-regions. An attempt can be made to assess this at regional level, but not at the sub-regional. The data are not there, which is a pity because intra-regional differences are certainly not trivial. Sub-regions generally comprise several local authorities. Much information exists for each of them — there are over 1,400 in the country as a whole — but resources were not available to aggregate them. Most of the discussion that follows is about the position of the regions *relative* to Great Britain.

A survey of current regional variations
Unfortunately the publication of regional statistics for a particular year is generally subject to even more delay than those at national level and so it proved impossible to discuss systematically figures for 1973. In fact the only important regional statistics available for 1973 are those for unemployment, but they are the most significant of all. The absence of other statistics for this particular year is not really a handicap: regional variations have been fairly constant, at least over the last ten years. Unless changes in trend are referred to it can be assumed that the regional variations described are fairly persistent. A discussion of the most important regional trends is reserved for the concluding section.

The survey is at two levels. First, there is a discussion of indicators of poverty in the ten economic planning regions of Great Britain. This starts by comparing the proportion of households with low incomes in the different places. Regional variations in housing and health statistics are then discussed and, finally, conclusions are reached about the combined effects of income and services in kind. Then on to sub-regional variations. While some regions may appear much better off than others when taken as a whole, within them there may be pockets of inequality deserving special mention.

Income poverty
So how do the regions vary in the proportion of households with low incomes? The available information falls far short of the ideal requirements. The Family Expenditure Survey (FES) has data on household composition by range of income but at the regional level the sample size is too small to give more about the distribution of household income

Table 10.1 Indicators of income poverty at the regional level
Great Britain = 100

	N	YH	EM	EA	SE	SW	WM	NW	W	S
1 Average household income per person	94	94	94	92	116	92	100	98	89	91
2 Proportion of households with household income half national average or less	111	107	101	112	82	105	100	111	118	105
3 Proportion of population over retirement age	96	99	95	107	103	117	87	100	104	95
4 Number of payments of supplementary benefit per head of total population	137	116	87	87	81	89	96	117	127	115
5 Male unemployment rates	185	109	82	67	58	94	85	142	133	173
6 Female employee activity rates	93	97	99	88	108	81	107	104	77	102
7 Proportion of employment in low-paid occupations	118	103	94	154	79	115	91	98	130	126
8 Average earnings of male manual workers	98	94	96	92	105	95	106	100	100	98
9 Median earnings: adult males	97	95	96	91	106	94	105	100	100	96
10 Ratio of lowest decile to Great Britain median male earnings	97	97	98	94	104	97	106	100	100	95

N	North	SW	South west
YH	Yorkshire and Humberside	WM	West Midlands
EM	East Midlands	NW	North west
EA	East Anglia	W	Wales
SE	South East	S	Scotland

Sources: See Appendix on data sources at end of chapter

than the number of households by range of household income, not even distinguishing (in the range of household income table) between the number of persons per household, occupation or age. But I have to make do with what is available, and so, starting with the FES figures, I will supplement them with other sources of information about regional income distribution and population. It is not possible to state with precision the reasons for the low incomes, but only to infer the reasons from data relating to all households in the various regions. The small sample size of the FES precludes more detailed study of poverty at the regional level. The other data sources used were various earnings surveys and the Censuses of Population. The relevant tables of the 1971 Census were not available at the time of writing.

Table 10.1 shows various indicators of income poverty with figures for the various regions being expressed as relatives to the average for Great Britain. Data sources are given in detail in the Appendix at the end of the chapter. Line 1 of the table shows regional variations in average household income, adjusted for the number of persons per household, as they were derived from the FES. The south east is 16% better off than the national average and only the west Midlands and north west stand near it. The favourable position of the south east compared with the west Midlands is explained primarily by the concentration of persons with unearned income in the former region. All other regions are at least 6% below average, Wales and Scotland being the worst off − 10% below. The small sample size means that these figures are all very approximate. A comparison with Census of Population data, for example, shows some substantial differences between the composition of households in the FES sample and the generality. This suggests that the advantage of the south west is understated because retired people, who probably have more investment income than others, are under-represented in the FES.

Averages do not tell us much about poverty. Line 2 shows regional variations in the proportion of households with incomes half, or less than half, the national average, also derived from the FES. For the country as a whole, 27% of households come into this category. Again, the south east stands out above all other regions, having 18% less than the average number of low-income households. Wales is worst off with 18% more low-income households. The north, East Anglia and the north west follow with over 10% more low income households, while Scotland, Yorkshire and Humberside and the south west have 5% more than average. Apart from the south east only the east and west Midlands are about average.

Why should regions vary in their proportions of low-income households? There are many reasons. One is the proportion of retired persons in the regional populations. Line 3 shows that East Anglia is 7% above average, the south west 17% above and the west Midlands 13% below in this respect. In East Anglia and west Midlands this does seem to contribute to low incomes. In the south west the high proportion of persons over retirement age is made up in part of retired persons with above average investment incomes who have migrated from other regions. Another important fact is that there are regional variations in job opportunities for persons of pensionable age. This is shown by a comparison of employment rates (ie the proportion of persons in employment or seeking employment) for male employees aged 65 and over as shown by the Census for 1966. While the national average rate was 20%, in the south east and west Midlands the rates were, respectively, 23% and 17% above this figure. Employment rates of males over 65 are on the whole inversely correlated with male unemployment rates. Scotland was the exception to this general tendency. Employment rates for males over 65 were higher than for nearly all other regions outside the south east and west Midlands, although only the north has a comparable high unemployment rate. It might be thought that employment rates are the mirror image of unemployment rates; this is not the case because the demand for labour affects each differently and because many females fail to register as unemployed. The employment rates for males over 65 were markedly lower in Wales and the north than elsewhere, as might be expected by their relative male unemployment rates which are shown in line 3 of the table. In Wales the proportion of population over retirement age was above average and this, combined with the low employment rate for males over 65 already mentioned, must contribute to the relatively high proportion of low-income households. The same regional variations are evident in the number of payments of supplementary benefit per head of total population compared with the national average, as shown in line 4. At the end of 1972 retirement pensioners accounted for 65% of the number of payments of supplementary benefit, the sick and unemployed for a further 24%. The north and Wales have the highest number of payments relative to the national average, followed by the north west, which might be expected from that region's high male unemployment rate. Next comes Yorkshire and Humberside and then Scotland; although the latter has the second highest unemployment rate it ranks fifth in terms of the number of payments of supplementary benefit, presumably due to the relatively favourable employment opportunities for the retired.

The variations in male unemployment rates shown in line 5 are generally correlated with variations in the proportion of low-income households, the main exception being East Anglia, which has a relatively low unemployment rate but a high proportion of low-income households. Part of the explanation here is the relatively low female employment rate in East Anglia, in line 6 of the Table. The variations in these employment rates are also inversely correlated in general with the proportion of low-income households. The south east and west Midlands with the lowest proportion of low-income households have the highest female employment rates. The north west, however, has a relatively high female employment rate yet a high proportion of low-income households. This region also has a relatively high male unemployment rate. To anticipate what comes later, the proposition is that regional variations in male unemployment and employment rates and female employment rates are the most important facts of all from the policy point of view.

Regional variations in low-income households are also influenced by differences in average earnings. The latter is dependent partly on the occupational composition of

employment and partly on variations in average earnings in
the same occupation. The former seems to be the more
important. The proportion of employment in low-paid
occupations in each region relative to Great Britain is shown
in line 7 of Table 10.1. This proportion, 10% of the national
labour force in 1966, was 54% above average in East Anglia,
30% above average in Wales, 26% above average in Scotland
and 18% above average in the north. *Unskilled* manual
workers, agricultural workers and farmers without employees
are the ones assumed to be low paid. The number of
agricultural workers as a proportion of the labour force is the
main reason for regional variations. In 1971 male agricultural
workers earned on average only two-thirds of male average
weekly earnings.

Regional variations in average earnings in unskilled manual
occupations appear to be small, generally not more than +5%
of the national average. Ministry of Agriculture statistics
show this to be so for agricultural workers. Variations in
average earnings of male manual workers in industry are
shown in line 8 of the Table. In 1971 manual workers (as
defined here) accounted for two-thirds of the national labour
force and earned 75% of non-manual average earnings.
Earnings of manual workers were about 5% above average in
the south east and west Midlands. Only East Anglia was
outside this range of variation, being 8% below average. These
regional variations in average earnings for manual workers in
fact reflect those for all male employees. This is shown by a
comparison of regional variations in male manual worker
earnings in line 8 with median earnings for all male
employees shown in line 9, based on the New Earnings
Survey for 1971. Line 10 shows the ratio of average earnings
of the lowest decile in each region to median earnings in the
country as a whole.

There is in fact little difference between the regional
distribution of median male earnings and earnings of the
lowest decile, and both are fairly similar to the regional
variations in the earnings of male manual workers. This
suggests that regional variations in *average* earnings in fact
represent fairly well the regional variations in earnings by
range of earned income. This is confirmed by evidence from

another data source, the Inland Revenue Survey of Personal Incomes for 1969—70. The conclusion from this is that regional variations in average earnings are not primarily explained by above average employment in one or two low-paid occupations, although the latter does contribute, particularly in East Anglia. Since variations in the proportion of households with low incomes are much greater than the variations in average earnings it must follow that they are explained primarily by variations in the number of persons in employment.

Housing

While there is a good deal of recent information about housing standards in the different regions, no sources at the same time reveal the financial state of the households. The General Household Survey gives recent information about the lack of facilities and extent of overcrowding. Table 10.2, line 1, shows the proportions of households without a bath. Wales stands out below all other regions, followed by the north west, East Anglia and Yorkshire and Humberside. Perhaps an even more important indicator of poverty is the extent of overcrowding (line 2). In this instance, Scotland comes out remarkably badly, while the south east is the opposite. The commentary in the General Household Survey states that there was a considerable improvement in the percentage of overcrowded households living in Scotland in recent years; it was 15% in 1971, compared with 21% in 1965. Another source of data, the Census, shows that in terms of the number of persons per room in 1961 Scotland was 37% above average, indicating no improvement over its relative position ten years earlier, so this improvement is to be welcomed.

Regional variations in tenure are shown in Table 10.2, lines 3 and 4. Outstanding is the large proportion in Scotland of households renting from local authorities rather than private landlords. The same thing goes for the west Midlands (although to a lesser extent), which is surprising because this region stands next to the south east for average household income. There is no general tendency for regions with more than the average number of poor households to have a higher

Table 10.2 Indicators of regional variations in housing and
health. Great Britain = 100

Housing	N	YH	EM	EA	SE	SW	WM	NW	W	S
1 Lack of amenities	97	116	67	127	76	83	101	133	200	83
2 Overcrowding	103	81	82	57	89	70	104	95	70	216
3 Proportion rented from local authority	97	102	104	108	73	81	120	90	91	186
4 Proportion rented privately	106	107	79	72	130	72	79	119	74	53
5 Average rent charged by local authorities	87	89	85	102	131	103	101	99	102	78
6 Average rent paid by all households	83	77	86	86	133	102	97	92	85	76
7 Proportion of expenditure on housing	92	89	87	91	115	102	94	93	94	87
Health										
8 Infant mortality rate	107	112	106	85	90	88	100	112	104	112
9 Sickness rate	147	122	90	76	65	98	88	126	188	125
10 Death rate	102	107	96	96	96	109	90	107	110	101
11 Patients per doctor	104	105	107	96	100	93	106	106	91	89
12 Patients per dentist	136	125	137	121	73	89	133	117	139	115

Sources: See Appendix on data sources at end of chapter.

than average number of households in local authority
accommodation. Regional variations in average rents charged
by local authorities and by all landlords are generally similar
(lines 5 and 6 of Table 10.2). At the extreme, average rents
ranged from 30% above the national average in the south east
to 25% below in Scotland. These extremes are partly
accounted for by differences in the quality of accommodation but partly also by population density and differences in
real income. Line 7 of Table 10.2 shows regional variations in
the proportion of household expenditure on housing. The

most interesting fact is that the proportion of household expenditure on housing in the south east is about 15% above average. Apart from the south west, where the proportion is about average, variations between all other regions are small.

These figures on regional variations in rents and in the proportion of expenditure on housing relate to the position in 1971, and although they probably represent the position over the last decade, it is not clear how far they will be influenced by the workings of the Housing Finance Act 1972. It seems likely that regional variations in the proportion of expenditure on housing (excluding variations due to quality differences) may be considerably reduced because of rent rebates. Nevertheless, it still seems probable that low-paid workers in the south east will spend a higher proportion of their income on rents than in other regions, even after rent rebates, since their earnings are on average only about 5% above the national average; taking rents in this region as 30% above the national average and applying the national rates of rebate (see Table 7.4 in Chapter 7), their rent payments after rebates might still be 10% above average. It is not clear, however, how far rebates paid by local authorities will vary from the national average. Another factor is that the proportion of households renting privately is about 30% above the national average in the south east. It was pointed out in Chapter 7 that the take-up rate for rent rebates is much lower for people renting privately than for council tenants.

Health

To add to the last chapter on Health, it only needs to be said that there are again contrasts between regions. Relevant statistics are shown in lines 10–14, Table 10.2. Infant mortality rates show wide variations. Worst off are Yorkshire and Humberside, the north west and Scotland, with rates 12% above average. In marked contrast are East Anglia, the south east and south west, with rates at least 10% better than average. Sickness rates for males show even wider regional variations. In this respect Yorkshire and Humberside, the north west and Scotland again fare badly, being about 25% worse than average, but in the north the rate was 47% worse

than average and in Wales 88%. These variations are partly
due to climate, but are likely to be explained primarily by
differences in regional industrial structure, particularly the
contrast between the heavy industrial areas of northern
England and Wales and the office employment of the south
east. One might expect these variations in sickness rates to be
reflected in death rates, ie the number of deaths per 1,000
population, and this is in fact generally so, the south west
region being an exception because of the high proportion of
retired people who have migrated from other regions.
Variations in death rates, however, are much smaller than
variations in sickness rates.

Do facilities also vary and are regions with the worst health
at a double disadvantage? Hospital statistics yield data on the
number of available beds, occupancy rates, etc, but they
cannot be interpreted easily because treatment varies
markedly according to the type of hospital. Another indicator is the number of patients per doctor. Table 10.2 line
13, shows that regions with relatively large rural areas,
Scotland, Wales, East Anglia and the south west were best
off, having on average about 7% fewer patients per doctor.
But generally regional variations were not very large. Variations in the number of patients per dentist were much more
extreme. In 1971 the south west and particularly the south
east had such an advantage that all other regions had at least
15% more patients per dentist than the national average. In
the north, east Midlands, west Midlands and Wales there were
about 35% more patients per dentist. Except for the north,
where the ratio markedly deteriorated, these regions
generally showed an improvement compared with 1963. On
the other hand, while the superiority of the south east
remained about the same in 1963—71, the south west
improved still further. As might be expected, the average
number of courses of treatment per patient was inversely
correlated with the number of patients per dentist. In the
south east and south west, where the preponderance of
dentists is presumably related to the greater opportunities for
private practice resulting from the higher than average
proportion of wealthy retired persons, the number of courses
of treatment per patient was 20% above average.

Cash and kind together

Any conclusions drawn from the rather sketchy analysis above, based on very imperfect information, must necessarily be tentative. One broad conclusion is that regional variations in the proportion of poor households are positively correlated with variations in regional housing and health standards. Housing conditions in the north, north west, Wales and particularly Scotland, are worse than average; in terms of health standards these regions are also worse than average. The converse is true for the south east and west Midlands. But these inter-regional variations should not be over-emphasised because there are probably large intra-regional variations.

It has been suggested that variations in the proportion of low-income households to the total number in each region are, apart from demographic factors, primarily explained by differences in employment opportunities at the regional level. The policy implications are clear: the reduction of regional variations in the proportion of low-income households requires, so far as possible, more equalisation of regional economic activity rates. But incomes are not the only factor. Apart from housing, regional variations in prices are small (Woodward 1970). But housing matters a lot. While the south east region has a much smaller proportion of low-income households than other regions, housing costs are in comparison with all other regions extremely high. The journey to work also costs more. While the average earnings of male manual workers are higher than in nearly all other regions their real standard of living may be lower because the proportion of income spent on housing is, on average, much higher. Low-income households in the south east may in particular be relatively worse off than elsewhere. The definition of low-income households as being those with less than half national average income may be inappropriate for the south east. Policies to equalise regional activity rates will therefore do less to cut down poverty in the south east than in other regions, particularly as activity rates in this region are higher than anywhere else. In the short run it may be fair to say that *income* poverty in the south east requires relatively more intervention by local authorities than in other regions, where the solution is one of implementing regional employment policies at national level.

Sub-regional variations

Regional variations in male unemployment rates in August 1973 have already been described briefly. Before considering sub-regional variations further comment is called for. About one-third of the number of wholly unemployed males had been on the register for less than eight weeks. Regional variations in the proportion of unemployed out of work for a longer period were neither very great nor generally showed a close correlation with overall unemployment rates. The extremes were, however, exceptional; in the south east the proportion of unemployed out of work for more than eight weeks was 7% less than average, but in Scotland the corresponding proportion was 7% greater than average. Moreover, the prospects for Scotland improving its relative position in the near future are bleak. In the country as a whole in August 1973 there were four unemployed males for every vacancy. In the south east this ratio was as low as 1:1 but in Scotland the corresponding ratio was 7:1, in the north 6:1, in the north west and Wales 5:1.

Statistics by employment exchange area generally suggest that the average unemployment rates for the different regions reflect regional variations in the level of demand for labour which, to some extent, affects all areas within them. Hence virtually all areas in the south east had an unemployment rate much less than the national average while almost all areas in Scotland had an unemployment rate higher than the national average. A notable exception was the unemployment rate in Liverpool, 6.8% in August 1973, much higher than any other area in the north west. This, of course, is a development area benefiting from specific regional policies. At the same time there is a considerable range of unemployment rates within regions despite the tendency for rates in depressed areas to be consistently above the national average. Take the north, for example: the unemployment rate in Darlington was only 2.9% whereas in Peterlee it was 7.3%. Both these areas, which are roughly the same size, receive similar assistance under present regional policies. There are similar extremes in Wales and Scotland.

There are, unfortunately, no sub-regional statistics for both unemployment and average earnings which cover the same areas. One would not expect a close correlation because the price of labour locally is determined less by local demand and supply than by nationally negotiated rates of pay. Areas with relatively high unemployment may, however, have an above-average proportion employed in relatively low-paid occupations.

Table 10.3 Trends in regional unemployment rates etc.
Great Britain = 100

	N	YH	EM	EA	SE	SW	WM	NW	W	S	Rate for Gt. Britain %
			Unemployment rates (annual averages)								
1955–59	140	74		68		114	68	116	181	200	1.5
1960–64	191	70		62		93	67	122	159	208	1.7
1965–69	187	94	74	88	65	111	72	103	177	170	2.0
1970	188	116	88	84	64	112	80	108	156	168	2.5
1971	173	115	88	94	61	103	88	118	142	176	3.3
1972	170	114	84	78	57	95	97	130	141	173	3.7
1973 (August)	188	112	80	68	52	92	88	136	144	176	2.5
			Female employment rates (annual averages)								
1955–59	82	102[1]	94[2]	105		79	111	112	70	98	37.4
1960–64	84	101[1]	95[2]	106		80	110	108	72	98	38.7
1965–69	87	98	99	106		81	107	106	75	100	40.1
1970	90	98	100	106		81	105	104	76	102	40.1
1971	93	97	99	106		81	107	104	77	102	39.9

[1] East and West Ridings of Yorkshire   [2] North Midlands

Sources:
Central Statistical Office, (1972) *Abstract of regional statistics HMSO*
Department of Employment, (1970) *Historical abstract of British labour statistics,* HMSO
(1973) *Department of Employment Gazette* vol.LXXXI no.9

Since 1970 statistics of average earnings have been published for the 61 sub-regions of Great Britain, covering males and females and manual and non-manual workers. The intra-regional variations in average earnings of male manual workers are relatively small, the poorest sub-regions deviating from the regional average by no more than 15%. These sub-regions are mostly rural areas and so the relatively low average earnings may be explained by the low rate of pay of agricultural workers. Such areas may not have high unemployment, although they probably have few jobs for women.

As already mentioned, statistics at sub-regional level do not exist to allow a proper examination of the extent to which there are variations in standards of housing, health and social services.

Concluding remarks

I have said that in my view the most important trends are to do with jobs. The top section of Table 10.3 shows regional variations in unemployment rates for three sub-periods 1955–69 and for the last four years. One fact stands out clearly: there is no systematic tendency towards equalisation of unemployment rates. Some trends can, however, be observed. The unemployment rate in the south east has fallen continuously compared to the national average, although this region already had the lowest unemployment in the 1950s. If we consider the three regions which by most criteria are the poorest, the north, Wales and Scotland, there is little evidence of a significant or systematic improvement in their unemployment in relation to the national average. During the period 1955–64 Scotland's unemployment rate was twice the national average. The period 1965–69 saw some improvement, the unemployment rate being 70% above the national average; but since 1969 the relative position of Scotland has shown a slight deterioration. During the 1960s unemployment in Wales fluctuated between 60–80% above the national average; in recent years it has shown an improvement, the current rate being 44% above average. The north is not only currently the worst off but, unlike Wales and Scotland, there is little evidence of any long-term improvement. Unemployment in the north became markedly worse during the 1960s, when it was almost twice the national average. It is true that unemployment in this region improved relative to the national average in 1970—72, when the unemployment rate in the country as a whole rose from 2.5% to 3.7%. But now that the national unemployment rate has returned to the 1970 figure the north has returned in relative terms to what it was in 1970. In comparison with 1970 the north west shows the most marked change, currently registering a rate 36% above average.

It should be remembered that many females fail to register themselves as unemployed when leaving the labour force. It is therefore relevant to consider trends in female employment. The lower half of Table 10.3 shows the trend in female employment rates in each region. In contrast with unemployment rates female employee activity rates show a tendency towards equalisation over time. If more women are employed, however, it does not follow that regional variations in the proportion of households with low incomes will be eliminated. This is because jobs for women may be at the expense of jobs for men. A comparison of trends in relative unemployment rates and relative female employee activity rates in Table 10.3 gives some support for this view, although very detailed analysis would be necessary to prove this conclusively.

Unless regional policies are specific, ie related to particular *areas* and to particular *types of employment*, there is no reason to suppose that the social policy objective of reducing regional variations in the proportion of low-income households will be achieved. Regional economic policies are designed to induce the growth of employment in development areas. Emphasis has always been placed on achieving the 'optimal' location of industry in terms of access to raw materials, markets, etc, and so there is no restriction on the choice of location in development areas. This raises the possibility of conflict between regional social and regional economic policies. The existence of substantial intra-regional variations in unemployment rates has been pointed out. Regional policy may result in new jobs being created in an area of relatively low male unemployment rates within a development area with the result that the jobs may go to women. Average household incomes will be raised in this locality but it was in any case relatively well off because it had a low male unemployment rate; the number of low-income households in the development area as a whole may remain unchanged.

There is another possible explanation why regional variations in male unemployment rates have persisted for a long time while female employment rates have shown a tendency to equalise. There is some evidence that the growth in demand for labour nationally has generally favoured industries which employ more women than men. Regional policies to divert jobs to development areas will therefore also encourage the growth of female employment relative to male. Even if the new jobs go to localities within development areas with a high proportion of low-income households the effect of the additional income on household earnings will be much smaller than for male employment because females in full time employment earn only 60% of the amount earned by males.

The existence of persistent regional variations in male unemployment rates therefore calls for more specific regional economic policies than exist at present on social policy grounds. This involves to some extent sacrificing the supposed economic benefits of allowing free choice of location and type of employment, particularly in development areas. There is, however, a further reason why some control should be exercised on the location of jobs generated by regional policy. This is so that housing and health facilities can be planned in conjunction with new jobs. In this way the development areas can become more attractive places to live in. The more pleasant environment of newly developed urban areas may then become a major factor influencing the location of industry rather than the much heralded economic benefits of access to markets, etc.

To achieve the implementation of more specific regional policies favouring the elimination of poverty there has first to be a recognition that social policy objectives should prevail where they conflict with economic policies on the location of industry. But there also has to be a harmonisation of regional economic policies on the one hand and the development of regional housing and health facilities on the other, which are now the responsibility of separate government departments.

Reference
V.H. Woodward, (1970) 'Regional social accounts for the United Kingdom', *NIESR regional papers 1*, Cambridge University Press.

Appendix on data sources

Table 10.1
1) Source: Department of Employment, (1972) *Family expenditure*
2) *survey 1969/70*, HMSO.
3 Males aged 65 and over, females aged 60 and over.
   Source: Office of Population Censuses and Surveys, (1973) *Census of population 1971*, preliminary report, HMSO.
4 Number of regular weekly payments, third quarter 1972.
   Source: Central Statistical Office, (1972) *Abstract of regional statistics*, HMSO.
5 Numbers unemployed excluding school leavers and adult students as a percentage of economically active males, 13 August 1973.
   Source: Department of Employment, (1973) *Department of Employment Gazette*, vol. LXXXI no. 9.
6 Number of female employees, mid-year (in employment and unemployed) aged 15 and over as a percentage of number of females aged 15 and over.
   Source: Central Statistical Office, (1972) *Annual abstract of statistics*, HMSO.
7 Numbers in the following socio-economic groups as a proportion of total economically active: semi-skilled manual workers, unskilled manual workers, farmers without employees, agricultural workers.
   Source: General Register Office, (1967) *Sample census 1966, Great Britain, summary tables*, HMSO.
8 Earnings of male manual workers in index of production industries, April 1971.
   Source: Central Statistical Office, (1972) *Abstract of regional statistics*, HMSO.
9) Source: Department of Employment, (1971) 'New earnings
10) survey', *Department of Employment Gazette*, vol. LXXIX no. 11.
   Inland Revenue, (1972) *Survey of personal incomes 1969/70*, HMSO.

Table 10.2
1 Proportion of total number of households without a bath, 1971.
   Source: Office of Population Censuses and Surveys, (1973) *General household survey*, HMSO.
2 Proportion of total number of households with below standard number of bedrooms, 1971. More than one bedroom below standard given double weighting.
   Source: as 1.
3) Proportion of total number of households renting accom-
4) modation privately or from local authorities, 1969–70.
   Source: Department of Employment, (1972) *Family expenditure survey 1969/70*, HMSO.

5)   Average rent paid by households living in accommodation rented
6)   from local authorities, 1969—70.
       Source: as 3,4.
7   Proportion of total household expenditure on rents, rates and
       water charges, 1969—70.
       Source: as 3,4.
8)   Infant mortality rate per 1,000 live births: under 1 year of age.
9)   Death rates per 1,000 population, 1971. (Averages for hospital
       board areas grouped into standard regions).
       Source: Department of Health and Social Security, (1972)
       Health and personal social services statistics, HMSO.
10   Sickness benefit: days of certified incapacity 1969—70 for males
       expressed as rate per man at risk.
       Source: Central Statistical Office, (1972) *Abstract of regional
       statistics*, HMSO.
11)   Number of patients per doctor and dentist 1971.
12)   Source: Department of Health and Social Security, (1972)
       Health and personal social services statistics, HMSO.

*The earlier part of the book has been about
poverty inside Britain. To end up Charles
Elliott widens the vision in order to discuss
the same now even more sombre subject on a
global scale. Not only are less-developed
countries poorer overall than Britain but
there are greater inequalities between rich
and poor within them. There are sharp
implications for British policy on aid.*

11 The International Context of British Poverty

CHARLES ELLIOTT

This chapter is in two parts. Part I examines selected data for
a number of other countries and compares them with Britain.
Particular attention is paid to the consumption by the
poorest people. Part II seeks to establish the contribution
Britain has made in the recent past to the relief of
international poverty. The undertaking is immense and
methodologically complex. In the short space available I shall
do no more than highlight a few of the facts and suggest
some changes in British policy that might be desirable.

Part I International comparisons of standards of living
I must start with a most important caveat. Cross-national
comparisons are notoriously treacherous, especially of
standards of living. Even comparisons of physical data — e.g.
the number of hospital beds per 1,000 people — ignore
qualitative differences. The data in Table 11.1 are no more
than indications of orders of magnitude, not precise calculations. The nutritional figures, based on rough estimates of
national production, imports, exports, wastage and changes
in stocks, are particularly suspect.

Comparing incomes raises a whole array of difficulties. Not the least, especially at a time of turbulence in foreign exchange markets, is to choose the rate of conversion into a common currency. Two other problems must also be mentioned. The first is the valuation of goods produced and also consumed by farmers themselves. In rich countries this item can safely be ignored, but in poor countries, where as many as 80% of the population are farmers of one kind or another and where farm *cash* incomes are very low, it cannot. National income accounts tend to underestimate the value of this 'subsistence income' and therefore to exaggerate the differences apparent in column 1.

This raises, however, a more profound conceptual problem. Of what is income a measure? Formally, we can say it is a measure of an individual's ability to command saleable resources. That is true and also unhelpful. It tells us nothing about the relationship between an individual's need and his ability to meet that need from his cash (and subsistence) income. Needs are socially and culturally determined, and despite the impact of modern communications, they vary greatly from, say, Colombo to Coventry, or even from Colombo to Calcutta. If we are primarily interested in the relationship of needs to resources, Table 11.1 can tell us very little. It does not measure the *adequacy* of income (Tabbarah 1972). It is only useful as a guide, and a very rough one at that, to the total quantum of goods and services available. At the lower levels of economic performance that may tell us something about physical deprivation; but at higher levels the data leave completely open the relationship between needs and their satisfaction.

Even with all these cautions in mind, Table 11.1 still provides a backcloth against which to see the problems of British poverty. It is immediately obvious, for example, that the average resources available per head in Britain are not only less than half those in the US, but also substantially less than in France and Sweden. If we take Sweden-Eire as the range of incomes in the richer countries of Western Europe, the UK lies much nearer to Eire than it does to Sweden.

But the startling contrast, of course, is between the developed countries and the so-called less developed

Table 11.1 Social indicators in rich and poor countries

	Average income per head £	School enrolment ratios (ages) 1st level	2nd level	Infant mortality rate per 1,000	Life expectancy at birth in years	Food consumption Protein: gms.	Calories
Botswana	40	78 (7-13)	7 (14-18)	—	43.5	—	—
Chile	212	106 (7-14)	34 (15-18)	91.6	63.6	65.4	2,516
Ghana	80	56 (6-15)	54 (16-21)	(87.5)	48.5	43.5	2,084
India	48	56 (6-12)	15 (13-17)	—	51.8	50.6	1,964
Indonesia	40	72 (7-12)	(11)[1] (13-18)	—	48.1	38.4	1,760
Kenya	60	60 (6-12)	8 (13-18)	—	50.0	67.9	2,243
UAR	72	70 (6-11)	31 (12-17)	(118.0)	52.9	76.6	2,639
W. Malaysia	149	89 (6-11)	35 (12-18)	42.2	60.7	49.4	2,200
Eire	517	104 (4-11)	52 (12-16)	19.2	73.0	91.5	3,455
England & Wales	} 851	106 (5-10)	71 (11-17)	} 18.6	} 72.4	} 88.6	} 3,233
Scotland		98 (5-11)	50 (12-19)				
France	1,160	120 (6-10)	70 (11-17)	15.1	73.5	98.2	3,108
Israel	696	94 (6-13)	56 (14-17)	23.6	73.1	86.6	2,827
Sweden	1,622	96 (7-12)	100 (13-18)	13.1	75.3	80.4	2,907
US	1,894	110 (6-12)	101 (13-17)	19.8	70.6	93.7	3,156

[1] from earlier source

Sources: Annual Report of the World Bank, 1972
UNESCO Statistical Yearbook, 1971
UN Statistical and Demographic Yearbooks, 1971
FAO Food Balance Sheets, 1964-6

countries (LDCs). Even relatively rich LDCs like Chile and
West Malaysia have income levels less than half those of Eire.
The huge populous countries like UAR, Indonesia and India,
with, between them, one-fifth of the world's population,
have a total income significantly less than that of the
UK – with a population of less than half Indonesia alone.
Whatever qualifications surround these figures, the contrasts
are staggering.

Furthermore, the disparities between LDCs are hardly less
marked than between LDCs as a whole and rich countries as a
whole. The contrast between West Malaysia and neighbouring
Indonesia, for example, is the same as that between the US
and neighbouring Mexico. The intra-European disparity
between Ireland and Sweden – a factor of around two –
compares with that between India and the Philippines. On
the other hand, average income in East Malaysia is probably
around one-tenth of that in West Malaysia.

Too much should not be made of these contrasts in
income for they beg a basketful of methodological questions.
They serve to show, however, not only that the scarcity of
resources in the LDCs varies greatly but also that, however
much poverty there may be in the UK, there is strong
circumstantial evidence to suggest that it is a whole quantum
more severe in the poor countries.

A glance at the remaining columns in Table 11.1 reveals
that the disparities in physical measures of welfare are
sometimes even greater than monetary disparities. If we allow
for qualitative differences, for instance in education and
health care, these disparities are greater still. Especially
significant in any discussion of poverty is the difference
between school enrolment ratios at the primary and
secondary levels. Given the acute scarcity of all resources in
the very poor countries, the primary enrolment ratios are
impressive – though naturally (given the political demand for
education) quality is often sacrificed for quantity. Nonethe-
less, since education is closely associated with adult income
levels, the relatively low enrolment ratios of Egypt, India and
Kenya presage a concentration of income and wealth to the
detriment of those thus excluded.

Primary enrolment may be expanded at the cost of

secondary enrolment, thus introducing a second element of selectivity and associated concentration of earning power. In the very rich countries — in USA and Sweden — virtually all children continue right through the secondary cycle. By contrast there is a marked fall in Britain (and especially in Scotland). This will be reduced somewhat with the recent extension of compulsory schooling but the contrast with the very rich countries is likely to endure.

When we look at the poor countries this 'fall out' or rather 'squeeze out' rises dramatically. Whereas in Eire roughly one child in two is enrolled in full-length secondary school, in India the rate is slightly more than one in eight, and in Kenya one in fourteen. From the perspective of relative poverty, it is not only the great selectivity of the secondary school system but also the associated exclusion of primary graduates that contributes to the perceived differences of status and welfare. 68% of the secondary school age group in Botswana who have attended school at all finish their education at the end of primary school. In Ghana, where primary education is nearly universal but secondary education is still highly selective, 86% of adolescents find that despite their graduation from primary school they are excluded from the great rewards bestowed by full-term secondary education. We shall pursue some of the effects on income distribution below.

As for some of the other indicators of living standards, although the nutritional data are inevitably approximate, they compare with a 'minimum' requirement of 60gms of protein a day and 2,500 calories. Granted that these minima are in fact highly elastic (since communities can adjust to lower nutritional levels) the high infant mortality rates and low life-expectancy figures of the chronic food deficit countries such as India and Indonesia indicate the scale of absolute poverty. In a country with an overall shortage of food its distribution within families and between social groups is critical. Unable to compete in the market place and still adhering to traditional habits of food sharing (mother and children after the male adults) the poor exist at nutritional levels far below the averages accorded in the Table. Clearly these various features — life expectancy; food supply and income — are closely interrelated, both in terms of aggregates and distribution. The relationships are more subtle than is sometimes assumed, particularly among those groups for which income is a poor measure of welfare. But at the national level, recent work has gone far to establish the catenae of relationships between income and other indicators of levels of living (McGranahan 1972; United Nations Research Institute for Social Development (UNRISD) 1970).

For our purposes it is important to know not only how the total stock of resources in Britain compares with that in other countries but also how that stock is shared in the community as a whole. Table 11.2 presents some recently published data on the income accruing to the bottom 20% and 40% in a number of countries. Again it is necessary to qualify the data. They come from different years; are assembled from different types of information (tax returns, income surveys, household budget enquiries) and have different biases. Further the tails have been extrapolated on the basis of mathematical forms. Before they are used for any purpose more rigorous than illustration of orders of magnitude, reference should be made to the source (Adelman and Morris 1971).

What do they show? As one would expect, great variations in the proportion of income going to the lowest 40% of the population. The nearest approach to equity — interestingly by very poor countries — is 23% of total income accruing to that group in Burma and Niger. At the other extreme is the 6–10% of income recorded for rather richer countries like Colombia, Peru, Lebanon and Iraq.

This should warn us against the assumption that growth will remove inequities. Although studies on changes in distribution over time are scarce and perverse, they do suggest, at the very least, that redistribution does not just happen. Thus in Sri Lanka a very modest rate of growth seems to have been accompanied by definite progress in switching resources from the rich to the poor. In Ghana, on the other hand, an uneven history of economic growth may have been attended by the reverse — the rich seem, according to one (methodologically questionable) study, to have been getting richer. In Uganda political independence was followed by the displacement of a white élite by a black élite, and also by the rapid

Table 11.2 The share of the poor in national income

	Lowest 20%	21-40%	
	% of national income	% of national income	% cumulative income
Brazil	3.50	9.00	12.50
Burma	10.00	13.00	23.00
Ceylon (Sri Lanka)	4.45	9.21	13.66
Chile	5.40	9.60	15.00
Colombia	2.21	4.70	6.91
Gabon	2.00	6.00	8.00
India	8.00	12.00	20.00
Iraq	2.00	6.00	8.00
Israel	6.80	13.40	20.20
Ivory Coast	8.00	10.00	18.00
Jamaica	2.20	6.00	8.20
Kenya	7.00	7.00	14.00
Niger	12.00	11.00	23.00
Nigeria	7.00	7.00	14.00
Pakistan	6.50	11.00	17.50
Philippines	4.30	8.40	12.70
Tanzania	9.75	9.75	19.50

Source: Adelman and Morris 1971

growth of an African urban middle-income group
(Rasaputram 1972; Ewusi 1972; Elliott 1973). Although
none of these studies is without serious heuristic problems, at
the very least they suggest that the poorest sections of the
community are not receiving a disproportionate share of the
benefits of economic growth. In relative terms the poor are
not automatically getting less poor — they may well be
getting relatively poorer.

The figures in Table 11.3 should also be treated with the
greatest caution. They are intended only to give an
impression of the cash income of the poorest groups in
countries on which recent findings are available. They should
be set against the average income for the same country and
not against what the cash sum would buy in England. Tastes
and comparative prices vary so much between countries that
cross-references become highly misleading.

Despite some unusual cases like Libya it appears that the
bottom 20% of income receivers get around a quarter of
average GNP per head and that the lowest 40% get around
one-third. However, since the first two columns refer to wage
receivers and the average to GNP *per head of the whole
population*, these ratios *understate* the gap between the poor
and the average. Very crudely we can assume that one
income supports 1½–2½ people (depending on family size,
labour participation and unemployment rates). In that case,
the bottom 20% get only around 12% of the average; and the
lowest 40% around 16%.

But are the *very* poor in Table 11.3 at all? In many
countries the very poor are not in receipt of a regular income
of any kind and are therefore frequently not included in
official statistics of income receivers. This is true not only of
subsistence farmers but also of the urban unemployed or
those who scrape together a livelihood in the so-called
informal sector. These are usually young men (though there
is evidence that larger numbers of young women are now
migrating to town in search of work), relatively undereducated, recently arrived from rural areas with little or no
technical competence that will give them a competitive
advantage in the job hunt.

The recent interest in unemployment, symbolised by the

Table 11.3 The incomes of the poor
Year 1970; unit £

	Average annual income per head		Overall average	col i / col iii %	col ii / col iii %
	Lowest 20% (i)	40% (ii)	(iii)	(iv)	(v)
Argentina	86.9	107.4	310.4	27.9	34.6
Bolivia	14.3	31.5	59.6	23.9	52.8
Brazil	18.0	32.1	92.4	19.5	34.7
Ceylon	13.0	19.9	68.0	19.1	29.3
Chile	19.8	58.4	173.2	11.4	33.7
Colombia	12.1	18.9	100.4	12.0	18.8
Costa Rica	48.9	54.3	169.2	28.9	32.1
India	9.4	11.8	38.0	24.7	31.1
Israel	189.2	281.1	541.6	34.9	51.9
Japan	133.7	217.6	487.2	27.4	44.7
Libya	3.5	7.0	487.6	0.7	1.4
Mexico	30.3	43.5	190.4	15.9	22.8
Morocco	27.6	28.2	76.8	35.9	36.7
Peru	25.9	28.5	118.8	21.8	23.9
Philippines	16.6	24.5	65.6	25.3	37.3
South Africa	26.8	42.5	236.0	11.4	18.0
Tunisia	20.6	22.2	80.8	25.5	27.5
Venezuela	76.1	115.9	336.8	22.6	34.4

Source: Calculated from Adelman & Morris 1971.

Employment Programme of the International Labour Office (ILO), has revealed its scale in many of the poor countries. Although some of the countries of South East Asia have achieved high rates of growth of employment by expanding the export of manufactured goods (often through 'foreign sourcing'), more usually the rate of employment creation has been only fractionally above population growth. This suggests a long wait for the disappearance of chronic unemployment. Indeed some recent work has focused attention on the tendency of employment in the modern sector to *fall* either absolutely (in certain non-agricultural sectors, and usually for limited periods) or, more frequently, in relation to the demand for employment associated with a rising population and increasing rates of migration (International Labour Office (ILO), 1970, 1972; Fry 1971; Rasaputram 1972; Elliott 1973). Where this has happened, it is highly likely that the number of unemployed has risen.

Some of those who have been unable to find work return to the rural areas. Their economic status then depends crucially on three factors: their access to land; their access to inputs required to make that land productive; and their access to markets in which they can sell that production at a profit. The landless are the most vulnerable group of all, and it is concern for them that has led to a thorough-going re-evaluation of the so-called Green Revolution.

For the introduction of new agricultural technologies — mainly high-yielding seeds, fertilisers and pesticides — in the rural areas can have a traumatic effect, for good *or* ill, on the local demand and supply of agricultural labour. At its best, the new technology can increase the demand for farm labour (as a result of double cropping) without simultaneously increasing its supply by forcing out of business the small producer who is unable to make use of the new technology. With an increase in income to both farmer and labourer the demand for local services and artefacts rises and therefore the demand for non-farm labour is also increased. That is the most optimistic view which probably holds for very limited areas of India, Pakistan, Sri Lanka, East Africa and perhaps the Philippines. But the new technologies can be accompanied by rapid mechanisation, the consolidation of holdings (by buying out smaller owners) and falling grain prices to the producer. This grim scenario fits the experience described in a number of case studies. But it should no more be taken as typical than should the other. Experience has been so diverse that no valid generalisation is possible. Early optimism that the Green Revolution would 'solve' the problems of rural poverty in the developing countries can at any rate now be seen to be wholly unfounded.

Apart from landless labourers, one other rural group needs emphasis — the subsistence or quasi-subsistence producers who have not yet fully entered the commercial economy. By the standards of cash income they are by definition poor and even a liberal allowance for the value of the food they produce and consume leaves them among the poorest groups — though perhaps better off than those without job or close kin in the town. But it is at best an open question whether and to what extent they see themselves as poor. At the limit they proudly maintain a culture and family system which gives them great (if non-material) satisfaction. While they would like to own some, even many, of the products of the modern economy, they are well aware of the social, cultural and economic costs of doing so. Although the rising demand for education and the subsequent migration of the young people may be evidence of a greater readiness to pay those costs, it would be false to regard at least some low-income communities as poor in the same sense that, for instance, an unemployed second generation urban labourer is. Not all communities identify riches with material assets.

There is one *economic* process of which they are all likely to be victim. That is the rise in prices of manufactured goods relative to the price of the goods and services they sell. Given current rates of international inflation and the cost-raising nature of the strategies of industrialisation adopted by many poor countries, domestic prices have been rising extremely fast — even in many of those countries in which 'orthodox' monetary policies have in the past ensured a low rate of inflation. In this situation some groups are better able to protect themselves than others. Perhaps most vulnerable of all are the rural poor.

Rural wages are not very responsive to inflationary

pressures and falling real living standards of farm employers
are unlikely to lead to a rapid rise of employment. Only if
inflation is accompanied by high export crop prices will
employment tend to rise. This may be happening on a
modest scale in countries producing cocoa, timber, oilseeds
and wheat. But in global terms the effect is marginal.

Hardly less exposed are the urban unemployed. Indeed, in
so far as they have to buy even their basic food (which the
rural poor can sometimes produce for themselves) they may
be harder hit. In that case they are likely to return to the rural
areas and compound the problems there.

Turning from income to the distribution of other social
goods there are fewer figures to go by. But in some areas at
least the main features and trends are clear enough to make
detailed statistical analysis unnecessary. Although there are
naturally variations between countries the broad picture is
that for education and health the lower income groups are
handicapped by three sets of factors — economic, social and
geographic.

The first, economic, may best be illustrated by reference to
education. The extent to which parents are required to pay for
education varies greatly. Some poor countries like Sri Lanka
provide it free right through university, others, like Uganda,
introduce fee paying at the primary level and subsidise
proportionately more heavily higher levels of schooling. Still
others offer free primary schooling and require parents to
meet progressively higher proportions of total cost. The
economic impact on low-income families varies accordingly.

It should not be assumed, however, that even where
education is said to be free throughout the system there are
no economic constraints on poor parents. First, there is a
variety of hidden costs. These include uniforms, books, food,
transport, boarding expenses. Even if the child lives with a
relative, a gift or some other reciprocal acknowledgement will
be expected. Second and more important, a child in school is
a child not earning — or a child not seeking to earn. It is hard
to over-emphasise the significance of this opportunity cost to
those unfamiliar with the finances of poor families in poor
countries. Faced, as virtually every household budget survey
shows, with a situation of permanent and often mounting

debt, the importance of an extra income — even the *chance* of an extra income — is far greater than the seemingly insubstantial sum involved. Even a family of subsistence farmers pays this opportunity cost. For the child supplies a significant input of labour even while still at school. Once he leaves school and decides to stay in the village rather than migrate to town, he plays a major role on the farm, at least releasing his elders to attend to village politics or the maintenance of social relationships — themselves important constituents of family welfare.

The significance of these costs is that children from poor families are less likely to attend primary school, are more likely to drop out, and are less likely to be found in the higher echelons of the educational system. The more regressive the system of educational financing (ie the higher the proportion of the cost borne directly by the parent) the greater the bias against the poor; and the lower the forms at which private finance is significant the earlier this economic selectivity begins to operate.

The social set of factors that bias the consumption of public goods against the very poor cover a wide range of psycho-sociological, relational and familial reasons that tend to ensure a lower take-up among the very poor of services that are in fact available. This is of course a problem familiar to social administrators in the rich countries and the parallels between inhibiting factors in rich and poor countries are, at least superficially, striking. The reluctance of immigrants to use health services for fear of being misunderstood, or being made to look foolish, is no less a problem in Kampala than in Birmingham (Bennett 1966). The fact that teachers' expectations of children from minority groups tend to be low is one explanation of the high drop-out among Indian children in West Malaysia as it is among Irish children in Liverpool (Educational Policy Research Division, Ministry of Education, Malaysia 1973). The reluctance to spend heavily on the education of girls is common to peasant families in Zambia and middle-class families in England.

If these parallels are clear — and those quoted are only a sample of the total — the differences in scale are no less significant. In societies sharply differentiated by race (as in

ex-colonial Africa, most countries of Latin America and a
few of South East Asia); by culture; by educational level
(even though much of the educational stock is of recent
origin); by income, expectation and aspiration; it is extra-
ordinarily difficult to design services that are comprehensive
in the sense of being equally available to all. Yet as soon as
they cease to be comprehensive, they become exclusive. And
given the political environment in which they exist it is
almost inevitable, even in a highly paternalistic situation, that
the structural biases are against the poorest and least
powerful.

A particularly good example of these structured biases is
afforded by health care. The great emphasis on curative
services and 'professional' (ie Western) standards has led to a
geographical, social and nosological bias against not only the
poor but even against the majority of the population (Bryant
1969; Sharpston 1972). Notorious examples of investments
abound that reflect this bias. In Lusaka the construction of a
new (and, on one view at least, wholly inappropriate)
teaching hospital was preferred to a system of rural health
centres that could have delivered basic health care to the
entire population. In Côte d'Ivoire, the university hospital
absorbs more than half the current budget of the Ministry of
Health, and in the Philippines, the First Lady's great interest
in cardiology combined with the political and economic
power of the medical profession (exerted through the system
of medical assurance) to divert huge resources from delivering
health care to the peasants to the construction of the most
sophisticated cardiac unit in South Asia.

These examples from health care are illustrative of a more
general socio-political bias against the poor. In housing, for
instance, successful attempts to provide genuinely low-cost
units for urban migrants are extremely rare. While by no
means all countries reflect the paralysis of policy in the
Philippines — where even site and service schemes are so
expensive that only the skilled employed can make use of
them — the usual situation is that public policy goes some
little way towards expanding the supply of housing to the
middle-income groups but leaves more fundamental needs
untouched. In some countries, of which Uganda, Zambia and

Ghana would be good African examples, the colonial tradition of providing housing to civil servants has been zealously upheld by independent governments with the result that housing subsidies are paid to one of the (perhaps the) most privileged groups in the country (Knight 1967; Tribe 1968).

By contrast public policy towards shanty towns, favellas, callumpas and squatter settlements has been almost universally bent on removing them by the dictate of the bulldozer — on the grounds that they imperil health standards in the town — or even that they embarrass tourists. Although social workers and local residents' organisations scored a notable victory over Nairobi City Council in getting this policy reversed for the notorious slums of Mathare Valley, the more usual experience is the Chinese opera in Manila where the government regularly flattens the shacks along the railway embankments and ignores their reassembly the following day.

The third set of factors that bias social consumption against the very poor is to do with spatial distribution. In most developing countries there are two associated features of economic geography. The first is the concentration of wealth and income, both absolutely and per head, in a small proportion of the total area; and the second is the relatively sparse settlement patterns in the poorest regions. To illustrate: Spain has one of the worst regional problems in Europe (Organisation for Economic Cooperation and Development (OECD)). There income per head in the richest province is now 2.8 times that of the poorest (it was 4.4 times in 1955). In Côte d'Ivoire the average yearly cash wage for those in employment differed by a factor of 3.4 between richest and poorest regions. If we take account of the distribution of unemployment the regional variation of income between richest and poorest rises to 8.7.

Secondly, the poorer districts tend to be less densely, indeed sparsely, populated, partly as a result of a more hostile natural environment with a lower carrying capacity of land. The Saharan perimeter of the coastal states of West and North Africa, the remote southern islands of the Philippines and the eastern territories of Malaysia and the inaccessible north-east of Brazil — these are all dramatic examples of poorly endowed regions that are characterised by widely scattered populations.

This combination of poverty and sparse population raises in particularly sharp form the familiar conflict between equity and efficiency in the distribution of social goods. For it means that the cost of providing in these regions an adequate 'cover' of services is a multiple of the cost of providing the same standard of service in the more developed areas. Indeed, it may well not prove possible to supply the same *standard* at any price. The best teachers and doctors will not go to the remote rural areas. The administrative task of delivering drugs and textbooks on time is beyond the capacity of any ministry. Inspection and quality control is nearly non-existent. Politicians and administrators are too remote to give consumers (patients or parents) a chance to complain.

These remote areas are not (usually) uniformly poor. In Northern Chile, high in the Andes, is one of the world's largest and most profitable copper mines. In the desert south of Tunisia is a whole complex of mines. On the island of Mindanao are some of the second eleven of the Filipino élite. In nearly all such remote areas there are clusters of civil servants, army officers, even a few prosperous farmers. But their very prosperity allows them to short-circuit the system by travelling to where the services are. They send their children away to school, their wives to distant hospitals, their sons to metropolitan universities. The local poor do not have that opportunity — though it is true that one of the lesser causes of rapid urban growth is the tendency of those who find themselves excluded from social services (supremely education) to send at least some member of the family to town, and especially to the capital.

Despite this influx, the metropolitan area is usually far better off than elsewhere. In Uganda, Kampala has 3.2 times as many hospital beds (per 1,000 population) as the next best-endowed district — and nine times as many as the worst. In Paraguay one estimate put the value of social capital in Concepcion at 80% of the national total. In Zambia up to 1966 all the tarred road in the country lay within the rich, well-developed (and predominantly European-settled) 'line of rail', connecting the administrative capital with the commercial and industrial centres of the Copperbelt.

In the present state of knowledge it is not possible to attach mathematical distributions to social consumption. We cannot therefore produce for social consumption the kind of table that we can, duly qualified, for income. But the foregoing has emphasised that the belief of governments and international agencies that programmes of public consumption automatically reach the poor is ill-founded. We need vastly more practical experiment and more determined political leadership to find ways in which the poor can obtain their fair share of this consumption.

Part II British policy and international poverty
What has been the stance of the British government in the light of the patterns of poverty revealed in Part I? Although less flamboyantly than its predecessor, the present government has recognised that world poverty poses a moral challenge which Britain as a relatively rich country must play its part in meeting. Thus the Minister for Overseas Development: 'Economic growth is not an end in itself but a means towards the development of more just societies. I believe that it is important for us always to keep this more fundamental objective very much in mind.' (Wood 1972). It is important to emphasise this for it is on this appeal to a moral rationale for an aid programme that the British government's record must be judged. There are, of course, other reasons for giving aid — maintaining friendly political relationships with developing countries, increasing exports of British industries, trying to establish a more secure local and ultimately global social and economic order, or as simply a response to political opinion at home and abroad. But if these were the sole reasons that a government gave for an aid programme there would be less reason to judge them by the criterion of their contribution to relieving world *poverty*. We should then judge them by their effect on British exports, their effect on British influence over given countries, and so on. But since one of the reasons officially advanced for giving aid is

precisely to relieve poverty it is fair to ask how far this aim
has been achieved.

Three ways of doing this suggest themselves. The first is to
look at the distribution of British aid by country: is British
aid going to the countries that need it most in terms of
poverty? Secondly, is British aid going into programmes and
projects that are likely to relieve poverty directly? Third, are
the quality and quantity of British aid consistent with
Britain's ability to respond or, if that is too demanding a
criterion, does it compare with the response of similar
countries?

The geographic distribution of British aid has been heavily
influenced by ex-colonial and Commonwealth links. Thus we
would not expect to find a large programme in Latin
America or in francophone Africa. That granted, is it the
case that large appropriations have been made to the British
Commonwealth — or ex-Commonwealth countries — that are
poorest? In general, this is not so. There is no statistical
correlation between British aid disbursements per head and
income per head: a statistical test revealed a correlation
coefficient of -0.001! The poorest countries such as India
and Pakistan receive on a per capita basis less assistance than
the relatively rich developing countries of Malaysia and
Jamaica. On this criterion, then, disbursements of British aid
cannot be regarded as a major contribution to helping solve
the problem of world poverty.

However, from what was said in Part I above it is clear that
a criterion couched in terms of average national income is
inadequate: it could be that although British aid has not been
going to the poorest countries, it has still been going to very
poor people. This raises the question of the second criterion
above. In the previous part of this essay we saw that two
features characterise the most vulnerable groups of the
poor — unemployment and landlessness. It is therefore
reasonable to ask what has been the effect of British aid in
increasing the employment of unskilled people in the urban
areas and what has been its effect in providing either direct
wage employment, the possibilities of acquiring land, or the
use of land in the rural areas.

It is exceedingly difficult to assess from published data the extent to which projects and programmes reach the poorest sections of the recipient countries. Some individual projects, often very small ones, are imaginative, bold, and designed precisely to reach the poorest and most vulnerable. But, bureaucratically, these are costly to administer and, almost by definition, are relatively risky. For that reason the ODA tends to prefer large, infrastructural projects — roads, dams, hydro-electricity. Less than 20% of project loans and grants in 1971—72 was devoted to social infrastructure: a further 10% went to projects concerned with 'renewable natural resources', presumably mostly agriculture and forestry. By itself this information is not very helpful, for the poor *may* benefit from aid to other sectors, especially transport and perhaps industry. But there is some evidence that the social infrastructure expenditures are not primarily concerned with reaching the very poor. This is well illustrated by medical aid. Very substantial sums of British aid have gone to large urban hospitals of the kind mentioned before: (Korle Bu in Ghana; Mulago in Uganda; University Hospital, Jamaica; Central Hospital, Zambia). Very much smaller sums have gone to preventive medicine programmes or the provision of rural health centres. Yet it is these that serve the poor (Bryant 1969).

There are a number of reasons for this. One is supreme — procurement policy. 47% of British bilateral aid in 1971 was contractually tied to the purchase of British goods and services: a further 17% was effectively tied (Foreign and Commonwealth Office, Overseas Development Administration 1972). It is hard to over-emphasise the extent to which this prejudices the effectiveness of British aid in general and in particular of projects that might have a direct effect on the poorest. To take medicine: the foreign exchange cost of rural health centres and preventive campaigns is nearly zero. The tying of aid therefore implies that the British contribution to this kind of activity — and the same is true *mutatis mutandis* of education, housing, nutrition, and water reticulation — is heavily constrained.

Precisely the same point applies to investment in the productive sectors. The effect of the tying of aid there is to prejudice investment decisions towards British technology,

British standards of specification, British machinery and even British manning structures – despite their patent unsuitability in developing countries. A recent graphic illustration of this showed the connection between tying, over-specification, and distributional bias against the poor in domestic water supply (Burton 1974).

The official position is that Britain cannot *unilaterally* make any major advance in untying. Progress must be coordinated with other major donors (Wood 1972). This argument is not wholly convincing, especially as it would be open to Britain to reduce the proportion of tied aid on an experimental basis as a test of the *bona fides* of other governments. The truth is that there are strong pressures from the Treasury, the Department of Trade and Industry and business lobbies, to maintain tying, especially while the British balance of payments is weak. The Minister evidently feels his position too insecure to expose these arguments for the meretricious (and perverse) nonsense they are. For with sterling now realistically valued, British exporters would gain from general untying rather than lose.

One other characteristic of the very poor is that they tend to be undereducated. Is there evidence that Britain is making a major contribution to the more equitable sharing of educational opportunity? Since the distribution of education is not easily divorced from its total supply, it could be argued that if Britain is increasing the size of the educational system, then she is contributing indirectly towards its democratisation. In aggregate terms 11% of British aid was devoted to education in 1971, (more than that in 1972 and 1973) the bulk of it in the form of technical assistance. There is also evidence of a structural change, away from 'grammarian' education towards technical and vocational training and, in a very preliminary way, informal rural education. But the geographical distribution of this effort is heavily skewed towards the richer Commonwealth countries. In Oceania there were 254 teachers on Technical Assistance terms in 1972. In Indonesia, perhaps the most educationally deprived country in the world, there were 3. In Malaysia and Singapore, both relatively rich countries with well developed educational systems and, in Asian terms, small populations (about 9 million), there were 67 British teachers: in India there were 15 (Foreign and Commonwealth Office, Overseas Development Administration 1973). The change in orientation in British educational aid might therefore profitably be followed by a change in distribution.

The third criterion referred to the quantity and quality of British aid in relation to the efforts being made by other countries. In this respect Britain compares poorly with her EEC partners. The UK is the only EEC country to have refused to accept the UN target of 0.7% of GNP to be given as official development assistance by the mid-1970s. In view of the fact that by 1975 the UK level may have reached 0.48% from its present lowly 0.41% this refusal has indeed a perverted logic. However, it has done much to cast doubts on the sincerity of the UK's efforts, which the substantial increase in aid volume between 1969 and 1972 has done little to allay. The absolute increase achieved in that period should not be minimised — a real term equivalent of £39 million in 1969 prices — but equally it should not obscure the fact that in 1972 UK was still only in the middle of the Development Assistance Committee (OECD) league table of *official* development assistance. It is regrettably true that major economic rivals came off even worse than the UK — Germany (0.34%), Japan (0.23%) and USA (0.32%) (Organisation for Economic Cooperation and Development, Development Assistance Committee 1972).

If the quality of the UK's aid was substantially better than that of other countries, shortcomings in quantity could be somewhat discounted. However, that is not so. In some respects the quality of UK aid is in fact the worst in the EEC, with the possible exception of Italy. Thus the UK gives a lower proportion of its aid in the form of grants than most EEC countries and the overall 'grant element' of total UK aid is worse than all EEC countries except Italy. This results from two conflicting features of recent British aid practice. While the terms of loans have improved — most are now interest free with sometimes fairly long grace periods — the proportion of total aid given as grants has fallen. Since Development Assistance Committee (DAC) members agreed on improving the terms of DAC aid in October 1972 to a total grant element of 84% it is likely that the quality of British aid will fractionally increase (Organisation for Economic Cooperation and Development, Development Assistance Committee 1972). While it is true that France and Germany are only just reaching the new DAC recommendation — and therefore only slightly better than Britain — some of the smaller donor countries such as Belgium and Denmark are approaching 100% of grant element. If the UK government was serious in its approach to world poverty that is the target towards which it would be striving.

On these criteria, British aid performance vis-à-vis the poorest of the poor is at best patchy. The probability is that it will not improve. For by joining the EEC Britain becomes a contributing member of the European Development Fund — of which the leading characteristics are failure to give aid to non-associated states (thus excluding most of the poorest countries) and a 'method of allocation [that] has in the past resulted in the poorest getting least' (Select Committee on Overseas Development 1973). While it is true that British contributions to the European Development Fund (EDF) will not match in volume Britain's bilateral aid programme, it is unlikely that the latter will be able fully to offset the biases in the former without a major shift in emphasis. Given the mixed motivation of British aid, such a shift seems improbable. It is less unlikely that Britain will be able to change the priorities and working style of the EDF: but that will depend on the terms of a settlement with France, the major supporter of the EDF's current policy, on a whole bag of other issues — such as the future of the Common Agricultural Policy, the Regional Fund, and international trade and money problems. The government will need more than the right-minded urging of the Select Committee on Overseas Development if it is to wring from the French a fundamental reorientation of the EDF — *and* major policy changes in these other areas.

It would be a mistake to judge the reaction of the UK government to world poverty purely in terms of its aid programme. Quantitatively, and many would argue qualitatively, its trade policy is much more important. If the British government were serious in its attack on world poverty we should expect to see a particularly liberal commercial policy extended towards those goods that are produced by the very poorest countries and those goods produced by unskilled labour or countries at the very early stages of industrialisation. We would thus look for generous treatment of tropical agricultural products (whether processed or not) and simple manufactures, particularly those, again, associated with agriculture (eg cotton textiles, leather goods, furniture, sawn woods).

The reality is complex. To take agriculture first: many major agricultural products that Britain imports from developing countries are not produced directly by peasants. They are produced on estates and plantations frequently owned by British interests, as in Sri Lanka and Malaysia. The wages paid on these estates are unrelated to profitability and indeed in many cases are appallingly low (Sundraman 1973; Amat 1973).

Further, some commodities that are imported by Britain and are produced directly by peasants are subject to international commodity agreements. The impact of British policy on the livelihood of the peasant producer is therefore at best indirect. But it is worth recording that the British government showed commendable resistance to a highly professional attack launched by trade interests in the summer of 1972 when the UK was playing a key (and perhaps decisive) role in negotiating a Cocoa Agreement. The purpose of this agreement is to limit the fluctuations in the price of cocoa and thus secure to the peasant producer in, for instance, Ghana, a more stable price for his crop. It is equally true that the British government fought hard for adequate protection of traditional British suppliers of cane sugar and bananas during the transitional period of British entry to the EEC. In this respect the proof of the pudding will be in the determination with which the government fights, particularly the French beet sugar producers, to secure a permanent share of the European market for cane producers.

This raises a wider issue which can only be touched on here. When Britain joined the EEC she adopted the Common Agricultural Policy (CAP) and thereby substituted European producers for traditional suppliers – principally Australia,

New Zealand and Canada. As the technical complexity and
political absurdity of the CAP became increasingly obvious it
was hoped that British influence would be able to modify it
in such a way that at least some of the total consumption
could be supplied by cheap producers. In this way it was
hoped that a share of the market could be opened for Latin
American and North African producers of temperate
products. Particularly for the latter this could have been an
important market for small peasant producers. However,
recent developments suggest that any frontal attack on the
CAP is likely to be rebuffed and that although a détente with
the United States may involve some slight modification,
particularly for US exports, there is little chance of securing
for peasant producers in the third world a substantial
proportion of the European market in agricultural products.

The position on manufactures is hardly more encouraging.
As a response to pressure from the United Nations Conference on Trade and Development (UNCTAD) the UK and
the EEC presented schemes for generalised preferences for
manufactures from the developing countries in 1972. The
British scheme was a great deal more liberal than that of the
EEC. In late 1972, however, Britain and the EEC agreed to
harmonise their Generalised Systems of Preferences (GSPs)
and it became clear during 1973 that this harmonisation
would imply only a very moderate liberalisation of the
European scheme and the preservation of some of the
features that the developing countries found most objectionable. These are the designation of a number of products of
particular interest to the developing countries as sensitive or
quasi-sensitive. Such a designation allows the importing
country to reimpose tariffs and/or quotas when the market
of a competitive domestic industry is threatened. These
products include leather, travel goods, sawn timber, textile
yarn, woven fabrics, porcelain, glassware, imitation jewellery
(United Nations Conference on Trade and Development
1973ab).

Now it is precisely in these industries that the developing
countries have a comparative advantage because they can use
labour intensive methods and unskilled labour — ie they can
offer employment to those most vulnerable to urban poverty.

By threatening to limit supplies of these goods to the European market (and in fact doing so since the common external tariff was reimposed nearly one hundred times by the EEC in 1972) the Community is directly threatening the livelihood of some of the poorer industrial workers in the developing countries. Much more important than the compromises that are eventually reached on the purposes and future of the European Development Fund is the renegotiation of the GSP. At the very least, Britain ought to be able to insist that the ceiling system of the EEC scheme is drastically revised and that the list of sensitive commodities is much reduced. The effect on poverty in this country of thus reducing the cost of some consumer imports would not be negligible.

One final point: a liberal trade policy on the so-called sensitive products is a policy that requires the poorer industrial workers in Britain to become unemployed for the sake of poor industrial workers (and less poor capitalists) in the third world. The import of textiles into this country represents a loss of employment to British textile workers. This cannot be denied. But there are two conclusions that can be drawn. One conclusion, much favoured by textile entrepreneurs and seemingly by textile unions, is that imports should be excluded. The other conclusion is that both capital and labour, but particularly labour, should be assisted to enter more productive employment in sectors of the economy in which Britain is relatively efficient.

From the point of view of long-term growth and welfare a radical policy of adjustment assistance is much to be preferred to the politically easier but more wasteful policy of subsidising the inefficient at the expense of the consumer. As in most other European countries British policy on adjustment assistance has been characterised chiefly by its lack of strategy and niggardliness. It is at least arguable that the diversion of a proportion of British aid funds from some of the more dubious projects abroad to a well-thought-out adjustment assistance strategy at home would represent better value for the developing countries at large and for their poor in particular. Better still, the implementation of a recent proposal for temporarily taxing cheap imports in order to bribe inefficient British producers to redeploy their resources, would be a major step forward in British policy on international poverty (Stewart 1973).

References

I. Adelman and C.T. Morris, (1971) *An anatomy of patterns of income distribution in developing nations*, Agency for International Development/Northwestern University.

Chaiku M. Amat, (1973) 'Socio-economic problems of the plantation workers', University of Malaya, unpublished thesis.

J. Bennett, (1966) 'The use of services by newcomers to the towns of East Africa', monograph no. 2, *Journal of Tropical Paediatrics & African Child Health*, vol. 12, no. 3.

J. Bryant, (1969) *Health and the developing world*, Cornell University Press.

I. Burton, (1974) 'Domestic water supplies for rural peoples in the developing countries' in K. Elliott and J. Knight (eds.), (1974) *Human rights in health*, Associated Scientific Publishers, Amsterdam.

C.M. Elliott, (1973) *Employment and income distribution in Uganda*, Development Studies Discussion Paper, University of East Anglia.

Educational Policy Research Division, Ministry of Education, Malaysia, (1973) Lapuran Jawatankuasa di atas kajian pendapat mengenai pelajaran dan masyarakat (Lapuran keciciran) — (Drop-out report), Chairman, Murad Bin Mohd. Noor.

K. Ewusi, (1971) *The distribution of monetary incomes in Ghana*, Institute of Statistical Social and Economic Research (ISSER), Technical Publication Series no. 14, Accra.

Foreign and Commonwealth Office, Overseas Development Administration (ODA), (1972) *An account of the British aid programme: text of UK memorandum to the Development Assistance Committee of the Organisation for Economic Co-operation and Development*, HMSO.

(1973) *British Aid Statistics*, Statistics Division, ODA.

J. Fry, (1971) *Prices, incomes, employment and labour productivity* (in Zambia), University of Zambia Economics Discussion Paper.

International Labour Office (ILO), (1970) *Towards full employment*, ILO, Geneva.

(1972) *Employment, incomes and equality: a strategy for increasing productive employment in Kenya*, ILO, Geneva.

J.B. Knight, (1967) 'The determination of wages and salaries in Uganda', *Bulletin of Oxford Institute of Statistics*, 29.

J. McFadzean, (1972) *Towards an open world economy*, Macmillan.

D. McGranahan, (1972) 'Development indicators and development models', in N. Baster (ed.) (1972) *Measuring development: the role and adequacy of development indicators*, Cass.

Organisation for Economic Co-operation and Development (OECD), Development Assistance Committee, (1972) 'Development co-operation: efforts and policies of the members of the Development Assistance Committee', *1972 Review OECD*.

(1973) 'Regional policy in Spain', *OECD Observer*, 64, OECD Information Service.

W. Rasaputram, (1972) 'Changes in the pattern of income inequality in Ceylon', *Marga*, vol. 1, no. 4, Hansa, Colombo.

Select Committee on Overseas Development, (1973) *The UK's entry into Europe and economic relations with developing countries*, Session 1972–3, HMSO.

M. Sharpston, (1972) 'The uneven geographical distribution of medical care in Ghana', *Journal of Development Studies*, vol. 8, no. 2.

F. Stewart, (1973) 'Adjustment assistance: a proposal', *World Development*, vol. 1, no. 6.

B. Sundraman, (1973) 'Indian squatter settlement in Shah Alam – a case study of redundant plantation workers', University of Malaya, unpublished thesis.

R.B. Tabarrah, (1972) 'The adequacy of income: a social dimension in economic development', in N. Baster (ed.), (1972) *Measuring development: the role and adequacy of development indicators*, Cass.

M. Tribe, (1968) 'The housing market in Uganda', unpublished MA thesis, University of East Africa.

United Nations Conference on Trade and Development (UNCTAD), (1973a) *The generalised system of preferences: effects of the enlargement of the EEC*, Trade and Development Board, Special Committee on Preferences, 5th Session, April, TD/B/C.5/8.

(1973b) *Review of the schemes of generalised preferences of developed market economy countries: operation and effects of generalised preferences granted by the EEC*, Special Committee on Preferences, 5th Session, April, TD/B/C.5/3.

United Nations Research Institute for Social Development (UNRISD), (1970) Contents and measurement of socio-economic development, *Report no. 70*, UNRISD, Geneva.

R. Wood, (1972) 'The place of British assistance in world development', *Journal of the Royal Society of Arts*, June 1972.

Index